MOLECULAR AND ANALYTICAL SPECTROSCOPY

MOLECULAR AND ANALYTICAL SPECTROSCOPY

Editor
N.P. SHARMA

KALPAZ PUBLICATIONS
DELHI-110052

MOLECULAR AND ANALYTICAL SPECTROSCOPY

(Chemistry)

ISBN: 81-7835-051-3

Published in 2001 in India by
Kalpaz Publications
C-30, Satyawati Nagar
Ashok Vihar Phase-III
Delhi-110052
E-Mail: kalpaz@hotmail.com

Laser Typesetting at : A.S. Printers
Printed at : Mehra Offset Printers, New Delhi

Preface

Spectroscopic technologies form the most important single group of techniques used in chemical analysis. This book provides an authoritative account of every aspect of molecular and analytical spectroscopy of current interest and demonstrates progress in this subject that has been made in the recent past. It takes a tutorial approach to the use of spectroscopic measurement techniques in analytical science, providing immediate guidance and advice to individuals in the course of their work.

The first section of this book gives a comprehensive description of molecular spectroscopy. Topics covered in this section are: techniques of molecular motion, cyclic molecules, molecular electronic structure, microwave spectroscopy etc. The second section covers technologies of analytical spectroscopy. It includes the topics of spectrochemical analysis, techniques of chemometrics, regression analysis, etc. Figures and explanations will help the students to digest the subject easily.

The book aims to provide students and practising spectroscopists with an introduction and guide to the application of analytical techniques. It also aims to provide the reader with sufficient detail of fundamental techniques to encourage further study and exploration in instrumental analysis. This book will highly informative to students in the field of chemistry and physics. The book also meets the needs of teachers who present this subject to students who do not have the time or perhaps the inclination to pursue it in depth, but who may also require explicit coverage of basic topics.

Editor

Contents

PART I

Molecular Spectroscopy

Chapter 1

Techniques of Molecular Motion

In this Chapter attention will be focused primarily on reorientational motions, such as rotational diffusion and-liberational motions. Vibrational motions will only be considered in the context of their interaction with reorientational motions and their contribution to the observed band profile. Lattice phonons in molecular crystals will not be considered here. Molecular motions in polymeric molecules will also be excluded.

Experimental techniques

To obtain meaningful information on molecular motion from spectral bandshapes; very accurate measurements of the spectral distribution $I(\omega)$) must be carried out. Particular care must be taken to eliminate instrumental effects and to perform the measurements sufficiently far into the wings of the band. Since the experimental requirements of i.r. absorption and Raman scattering are somewhat different they will be considered separately.

Infrared absorption—bandshape measurements.

The first and most important requirement for the suitability of an i.r. absorption band is especially in the wings, be free from extraneous absorptions arising from weak overtones and combination bands, hot bands, and overlapping fundamentals. These requirements are sometimes difficult to meet especially in fluids composed of fairly complex molecules, and artificial curve-resolving methods have to be resorted to. The effect of these techniques on the bandshape, however, is difficult to assess, especially in the wings of the band, and they should be avoided if possible. Bands of moderate intensity should be selected. If the band is very intense, the transmission must be measured through thin films, which results in distortion from interference effects within the films and from phase changes at the boundaries.

Conventional double-beam spectrometry is not applicable in this case and many investigators have turned to methods based on interferometry, simple reflection, or attenuated total reflection (ATR). In addition, changes in refractive index through an absorption band could lead to considerable inaccuracies with strong bands measured by conventional techniques. ATR measurements, however, overcome these problems, but the experiments are difficult to perform, requiring very accurate angular measurements and precise collimation if meaningful data are to be obtained. Detailed measurements on liquids using the ATR technique have been made by Irons and Thompson and by Crawford and co-workers.

The problems associated with thin-film measurements for strongly absorbing liquids have recently been considered by Young and Jones. These authors have also recently reviewed the characteristics and suitability of various spectroscopic techniques for recording accurate bandshapes.

Computation of dipole correlation functions.

The experimental dipole correlation function is computed from the observed spectral density $I(\omega)$ according to equation. Normally only the real part of $C(t)$ is calculated, the imaginary part contributing only a small quantum correction.

It is generally not necessary to use this expression, however, since the absorbance, $I(\omega) = \text{In}(I_0/I)$, is a sufficiently good approximation. The integration is performed over the whole band. Since it is not always obvious to what extent the measurements should be carried into the wings, Rothschild has developed a procedure for adjusting the integration limits to obtain the theoretical value of the second moment. This was accomplished by parallel shifting the zero-absorption line up or down so that its intersection with the absorption curve moved toward or away from the band centre.

The physical implications of this procedure are not clear at present since other factors such as shift fluctuations can also influence the second moment. The Fourier transformation of $I(\omega)$ is best carried out by numerical integration using a digital computer. It is advantageous if the intensity data can be produced in digital form, so allowing direct accurate processing to be performed. A large number of data points, $I(\omega)$, are to be processed it is sometimes an advantage to use a specially developed algorithm, the so-called Fast Fourier Transform.

This algorithm is particularly useful for deconvolution procedures and molecular dynamics calculations. Most calculations are carried out using time intervals of about 0.05-0.1 $\times 10^{-12}$ s. The extent to which the decay of $C(t)$ can be followed is limited by the resolution of the measurement. Thus the curves will become unreliable at times longer than about $1/\Delta\omega_r$, where $\Delta\omega_r$, is the experimental resolution. This corresponds to about 5 ps at 1 cm^{-1} resolution.

Raman scattering—bandshape measurements.

Most of the requirements for i.r. bandshape work also apply to Raman scattering. With modern double or triple Raman monochromators and high-intensity, stable laser sources, accurate band contours relatively free from instrumental distortion can be obtained. In addition, with photon-counting detection systems, the intensity data are already in digital form, greatly facilitating data processing. At the same time, increased accuracy can be obtained. Ideally, the intensity data $I(\omega)$, would be accumulated at predetermined frequency intervals across the band. The time interval over which the counts are accumulated would be determined by the accuracy required.

The statistics of the counting process are of course well known so that the data are well characterized statistically. A small dedicated computer is an advantage for this work. Unlike i.r. absorption, we have seen that the orientational and vibrational relaxation processes can be separated in the Raman case. To accomplish this, however, accurate measurements of the isotropic and anisotropic Raman scattering must be performed.

The theoretical arguments underlying the separation of vibrational relaxation and reorientation of anisotropy have already been discussed. The relevant expressions for the vibrational and reorientational correlation functions are given by equations (45) and (47). The study of strongly polarized lines requires an optical system capable of isolating the strong isotropic component from the depolarized spectrum.

A Glan-Thompson polarizing prism is useful to ensure that only light of the correct polarization enters the cell. A polarization rotator placed after the polarizer enables the plane of polarization to be rotated through 90°. An analyser is generally used to select the appropriate polarization of the scattered light. A quartz wedge polarization scrambler placed before the entrance slit is necessary if corrections for grating effects are to be avoided. Generally, the instrument functions are

Gaussian and both the intrinsic lineshape and orientational spectrum are Lorentzian, so that instrumental effects can readily be removed where necessary by the application of closed expressions. A second method useful for obtaining the orientational linewidths and associated correlation times for weakly polarized Raman bands has been described by Rakov and more recently revived by Bartoli and Litovitz.

The depolarized Raman linewidth $\omega(T)$ is measured over a wide temperature range so that at higher temperatures $\omega(T)$ has a large orientational contribution whereas at low temperatures $\omega(T)$ is approximately equal to the vibrational width. After removal of instrumental effects, the vibrational bandshapes of six liquids shown in Table 1 were approximately Lorentzian.

Table 1

Molecular reorientational times for some liquid systems from depolarized Raman linewidths $\omega(T)^a$

Liquid	Line	Point group	Assignment	τ_{vib}/cm^{-1}	τ_{or}/cm^{-1}
CCl_4	217	T_d	CCl_2deformation	2.3	3.0 $\pm$ 0.5
C_6H_{12}	1027	D_{3a}	CC stretch	3.0	3.1 + 0.5
C_6H_{12}	1266	D_{3a}	CH_2twist	3.0	3.1 + 0.5
Ch_3OH	1030	C_s	CO stretch	9.0	6.0 + 0.5
C_4H_9OH	1300	C	$_s$$CH_2$ twist	5.3	2.6 + 0.5
$C_8H_{17}OH$	1300	C_s	CH_2 twist	8.0	1.6 + 0.5

Assuming that the orientational spectrum is also Lorentzian, the observed spectrum will also be Lorentzian whose width will be the sum of the oriental width and the vibrational width. Thus we have

$$\omega(T) = \omega_{vib} + \omega' \exp(-A/T)$$

in which it is assumed that the reorientational linewidth has an Arrhenius temperature dependence, *i.e.*, $\omega_{or} = \omega'$ $\exp(-A/T)$, where ω' and A are arbitrary constants. The vibrational linewidth ω_{vib} was further assumed to be independent of temperature. ω_{vib}, ω', and A can be obtained by fitting the measured Raman linewidth to equation (100). This technique is particularly useful for liquids which form plastic crystals, *i.e.*, where rotational freedom persists in the solid phase. I.r. bandshapes can also be analysed by this method.

The use of linewidth instead of the complete correlation function is a useful technique, but it gives no information regarding the very short-time (the first fraction of a picosecond) behaviour of the system. This particular time interval is sacrificed in the interests of expediency. It should be remembered, however, that the data relating to this part of the rotational motion are contained in the far wings of the band contour, which is the part of the profile known with least accuracy.

Applications

Most of the bndshape work taht has been , considers rotational relaxation as the dominant broadening effect and competely neglects other energy relaxation proceeses which may be contributed to observed band profile. In some cases this procedure is justified but in others not depending on the nature of the particular system under consideration.

Care must be therefore be exercised where the quantitative interpretation of the orientational motion is being undertaken, particularly with larger, more complex system where the vibrational relaxation may be the dominant process.

Gaseous phase—One of the first quantitative studies by Armstrong, Blumenfeld, and Gray was aimed at an understanding of the intermolecular interactions in liquid methane. Extensive bandshape measurements on the v_3 and v_4 bands in CH_4-He, and on the v_3 band in CH_4-He, CH_4-N_2, and CD_4-He mixtures were carried out[15] pressures up to 3000 atm.

The distinction between the *P*-, *Q*-, and *R*-branches becomes less apparent and the total band narrows with increasing density. Rotational correlation functions, band moments, and intermolecular mean square torques were determined from the v_3 bandshapes.

The longtime behaviour is approximately exponential. Theoretical calculations of the mean square torque were in order-of-magnitude agreement with the observed values for the CH_4-N_2 and CH_4-CH_4 systems. Anisotropic multipolar, induction, and dispersion interactions were assumed in the calculations. For the CH_4-He, CD_4-He, and CH_4-Ar systems, however, the theoretical values were 2-3 orders of magnitude too small, indicating that in these cases the dominant contribution to the torques was derived from anisotropic overlap forces.

Correlation functions, correlation times, band moments, and intermolecular torques were computed from the v, rotation-vibration bandshapes in C_2H_2 and N_2O gas mixtures.

Pressures in the range 10-100 bar, C_2H_2 in mixtures with He, Ar, H_2, O_2, N_2, and CO_2 and N_2O in mixtures with He, Ar, N, H_2, O_2, and CH_4. The partial pressures of C_2H_2 and N_2O were held constant. It was found that the hindering of the rotation increased in the same order for C_2H_2 and N_2O mixtures, with the torque increasing in the order He $<$ H_2 $<$ Ar $<$ O_2 $<$ N_2 $\leq$ CO_2. Carbon dioxide was by far the most effective in this respect.

The perturbing influence of He on C_2H_2 is compared with that of CO_2. It seems likely that the interaction is associated primarily with the multipole moments of the molecular charge distributions. In this case, N_2, O_2, Ar, H_2, and He were the perturbing molecules. The transition dipole moment in vibrations of this type is perpendicular to the molecular axis and rotational transitions corresponding to $\Delta J = 0$ as well as $\Delta J = \pm 1$ are allowed, so that a strong Q-branch should be present.

These correlation functions, as well as those for N_2O, were quite different from those for the parallel band; they decay much more slowly and do not become negative. The curves are identical up to about 0.5-0.7 ps. The efficiency of the perturbing gases was found to be identical to that observed in the corresponding measurements for the parallel transitions.

The experimental second and fourth moments are presented in Table 2. The second moments are in good agreement with the calculated values in the classical limit. Approximate values of the mean square torque at a pressure of 100 bar are also given.

Table 2

Second and fourth moments and mean squaretorques for C_2H_2 and N_2O at 310 k

Quaninty	$v_3(C_2H_2)$	$v_5(C_2H_2)$	$v_3(N_2O)$	$v_2(N_2O)$
$M(2)_{exp}/cm^{-1}$	1100	550	400 200	100
$M(2)_{calc}/cm^{-1}$	1000	500	360 180	100
$M(4)/cm^{-4}$	290×10^4	114×10^4	42×10^4	17×10^4
$\langle(OV)2\rangle/cm^{-2}$	$\sim 8 \times 10_4$	—	$\sim 15 \times 10_4$	—

In the foregoing work, no attempt has been made to interpret the observed correlation functions in terms of physical models for the systems. Gordon has shown that his *M*- and *J*-diffusion models accurately reproduce the experimental correlation functions for CO both as pure gas and in mixtures with argon. The rotational correlation functions of CO and the parallel transition in N_2O have also been interpreted using the *M*-diffusion model.

Mixtures with N_2, O_2, H_2, and He at pressures of between 60 and 100 bar were used. Good agreement with the experimental data was obtained. Recently, Levi and Chalaye studied rotational diffusion in compressed CH_3D in mixtures with He, Ne, Ar, H_2, O_2, N_2 and CH_4 at pressures of up to 150 bar. The $v_2(A_1)$ parallel band at 2204 cm^{-1} was chosen and the computed rotational correlation function compared with the predictions of the *M*- and *J*-diffusion models.

Vibrational relaxation was neglected in this treatment since the half-width of the corresponding isotropic Raman band was only 2 cm^{-1} compared with the width of the i.r. band which was > 300 cm^{-1}. The *J*-diffusion model was found to give the best fit to the experimental data.

Condensed phase

Free rotational effects dominated the short-time dependence of the reorientational correlation functions whereas intermolecular effects became important at long times. Band moments and approximate intermolecular torques were also computed. In a later publication, McClung used the *M*- and *J*-diffusion model to calculate the reorientational correlation functions and spectral densities for CH, and CD_4 and compared them with the experimental values of Cabana *et al.*

The agreement was satisfactory for liquid CH_4 in the *J*-diffusion limit and for liquid Ar, Xe, and Kr solutions of CH_4 in the *M*-diffusion limit. Agreement was also good for CD_4 both as pure liquid and in mixtures with the noble gases. Attempts to fit liquid CH_4 and CD_4 to the *M*-diffusion model were unsuccessful, as were attempts to use the *J*-diffusion model for the noble-gas solutions. Rotational energy transfer is much more rapid in the neat liquid methanes than in the liquid noble-gas solutions, since in the J-diffusion model every 'collision' is effective in completely randomizing the angular momentum.

These results were confirmed in a later study of liquid CH_3D The dipole correlation function for the v_1 band at 2194 cm^{-1} was in good agreement with the predictions of the *J*-diffusion model, *i.e.*, the collisions were sufficiently energetic to change both the magnitude and direction of the angular momentum. This model also successfully reproduced the behaviour of the plastic solid at 41 K by changing the parameter τ_j from 0.9 to 0.6. When CH_3D was dispersed in a CH_4 matrix at 18 K considerable fine structure was observed in the v_1 absorption.

Different orientations of CH_3D on substitution sites in the CH_4 matrix. Some doubt concerning the validity of the classical *M*- and *J*-diffusion models was raised by McClung in his work on CH_4. To investigate this, Eagles and McClung applied the semi-classical diffusion model of rotational diffusion, developed by Gordon to interpret variations in the i.r. bandshape of CO, to calculate the v_3 band contour of methane.

This model, which is based on the transfer of intensity between vibration-rotation lines by collisions, was used to set up semi-classical analogues of the *M*- and *J*-diffusion models. The bandshapes predicted by these models were compared with the v_3 contours of CH_4 in liquid methane, in dilute solutions of liquid noble gases, and in high-pressure gas mixtures with He and N_2. The observed v_3 bandshapes of compressed CH_4 mixtures were compared with the spectral bandshapes computed with the semi-classical *J*-diffusion model. Equally satisfactory fits were obtained with both the *M*- an *J*-diffusion models. The best agreements were obtained with the *J*-diffusion model for pure liquid CH, and with the *M*-diffusion model for the liquid noble-gas solutions.

This was in accord with the earlier results of McClung using the classical diffusion models. Also, the bandshape computed from the classical model was compared with the symmetric part of the bandshape computed from the semi-classical model. The two models give similar results for Correlation times greater than 2×10^{-13} s but for shorter correlation times the semi-classical spectra begin to narrow much more rapidly than the classical spectra.

This implies that the asymmetry of a band is essentially quantum mechanical in origin, and a classical analysis of the symmetric part of the band led to the same dynamical results as the quantum models. Several i.r. studies of the molecular reorientation of small molecules in solution have been published recently.

Measurements have been made of the half-widths and band profiles of the three fundamentals and some harmonics of NO dissolved in a variety of solvents. In the case of non-polar solvents the widths of the bands were consistent with a rotational relaxational mechanism, but in other cases variations in the intermolecular potential were important. Spectral moments and dipole correlation functions were calculated and interpreted in terms of rotational diffusion.

Approximate values of the intermolecular torques were also calculated. Dipole correlation functions for the v_3 and v_5 bands of C_2H_2 dissolved in several polar solvents were also calculated. Again rotational relaxation was assumed to be the dominant broadening mechanism. The molecular motion of the condensed phases of the hydrogen halides have always held particular interest for the spectroscopist owing to the possibility of relatively unhindered molecular reorientation.

Much of the work on HCl has been carried out by the French group at Bordeaux. Huong, Couzi, and Perrot studied the vibration-rotation i.r. spectra of HF, DF, and HCl dissolved in liquid SF_6. The fine structure normally present only in the gas phase was found to persist in the SFO solutions. These spectral features were interpreted in terms of rotational motions in solution. Birnbaum and HO recently found rotational lines in the far-i.r. spectrum of HCl dissolved in liquid SF_6.

A theoretical interpretation of the spectrum was proposed by Galatry and Robert. Subsequently the work on SF_6 was extended by Perrot, Huong, and Lascombe to include other solvents. Absorption studies of HCl dissolved in a variety of solvents were carried out in the far-, mid-, and near-i.r. regions to observe pure rotation, rotation-vibration, and second and third overtones respectively.

The vibrational Raman bandshape of HCl in CCl_4 was also investigated. By hydrogen/deuterium substitution these workers were able to show that rotational relaxation accounted for most of the pure rotational band profile and was also the dominant mechanism in the pure and overtone vibrational absorptions. Nevertheless, a careful comparison of the profiles observed in the various spectral regions suggested that vibrational relaxation also contributed to the vibrational band contours.

This relaxation was interpreted as arising from fluctuations in the environment of HCl molecules and also from rotation-vibration interactions. The analysis of the Raman profile supported this conclusion. The influence of rotation-vibration interactions on the band profile was subsequently investigated by Perrot, Caloine, and Lascombe.

A technique for correcting the observed profile for these effects was developed and applied to the 0 $\rightarrow$ 2 absorption of HCl dissolved in liquid SF_6. Later i.r. studies on the HCl system by the same group have shown, in addition to fluctuations of orientational states, the presence of a distribution of vibrational frequencies.

The isotropic profiles of Raman bands were also found to originate essentially from the frequency distribution found in the i.r. The dipole correlation function approach has also been used to investigate rotational motion in the hydrogen halides. Rothschild used previously published extrapolated far-i.r. data to compute correlation functions for HCl, DCl, and HF dissolved in cyclohexane.

The results indicated that the dissolved halides undergo fast, large-angle rotational diffusion jumps. A quantitative estimate of collision-induced absorption between the HF and cyclohexane molecules indicated that dipole-induced dipole and quadrupole-induced dipole absorption was appreciable. The absorption band was corrected for quadrupole-induced dipole absorption in order to obtain the pure dipolar absorption bandshape.

The i.r. and Raman band profiles of HCl and CO dissolved in CCl_4 were recently analysed by Guissani and Leicknam using previously developed stochastic theories. The 0 $\rightarrow$ 1 absorption was studied for CO whereas for HCl the 0 $\rightarrow$ 1, 0 $\rightarrow$ 2, and 0 $\rightarrow$ 3 transitions were investigated. Both rotational and vibrational relaxation were found to be significant. Experimental dipole correlation functions were computed for CH_3Cl, HCl, and DCl dissolved in some Group IV tetrachlorides. By using these molecules as probes, the dynamics of the tetrahalides were investigated.

CH_3Cl has a shape and size similar to those of the host molecules, whereas the hydrogen chlorides can enter the interstices between the host molecules. Dipole-dipole interactions were negligible in the case of the HCl and DCl molecules but important for $CHCl_3$. Relatively simple cavity models were sufficient to explain the main features of the HCl and DCI absorptions. Considerable interest has recently been generated in the molecular dynamics of substituted methanes.

This is due in part to the suitability of these small and relatively simple molecules of differing molecular symmetries for testing theories of rotational and vibrational relaxation. Since the pioneering work of Favelukes, Clifford, and Crawford on CH_3I a number of studies on substituted methanes have appeared in the literature.

In Crawford's work, dipole correlation functions for the 885 cm^{-1} perpendicular band in CH_3I were computed from attenuated total reflectance measurements. The CH_3I molecules experience essentially free rotation over periods of about 0.2 ps, after which collisional effects begin to randomize the motion and rotational diffusion sets in. Substitution of D for H produced a slowing down of the diffusion rate. Essentially the same correlation function was obtained by Rothschild using conventional transmission measurements.

These data were consistent with a free rotational angle of 60° for the CH_3I molecule. Dipole correlation functions have also been computed from the v_1 bands of $CHCl_3$, $CHBr_3$, and CHI_3 dissolved in CCl_4 and CS_2, and for liquid and gaseous $CHCl_3$ and $CHBr_3$. CO dissolved in CCl_4 was also studied. The CO results were interpreted principally in terms of rotational fluctuations.

Vibrational relaxation was found to be important for some of the haloform systems. Spectral moments and intermolecular mean square torques were also tabulated.

The experimental moments *M*(2) and *M*(4) changed dramatically with different solvents for the CHX_3 molecules. The bandshapes of three fundamentals of methylene chloride of different symmetry were recorded by Rothschild. These were 283 (a_1), 895 (b_1), and 1266 cm^{-1} (b_2). Some overtone and combination bands were also investigated.

These are included in Table 3. A primary aim of this work was to determine if the correlation functions produced from different modes of the same symmetry in CH_2Cl_2 were identical within experimental error.

Table 3

Wavenembers and assignments of some vibrational transitions of CH_2Cl_2

Wavenember/cm^{-1}	*Mode*	*Species*	*Assignment*
283	v_4	$a1$	CCl_2 deformation
452	v_9-v_4	b_2	
895	v_7	b_1	CCl_2 rocking
1266	v_8	b_2	CH_2 rocking
2308	v_2-v_7	b_1	
2414	v_5+v_8	b_1	
2525	$2v_B$	a_1	
2688	v_2 +v_8	b_2	

The dipole correlation functions of all the absorption bands were computed using a technique which adjusted the integration limits of the Fourier transform to obtain the theoretical values of the second moment. Some correlation functions for modes of symmetry.

The effect of different integration limits on the

second moment and the correlation functions can be seen. Since the observed rate of decay of the correlation functions was faster when the smaller moments of inertia were involved, and the decay was non-exponential for a certain initial period, Rothschild concluded that the molecules did not obey Debye-type diffusion.

Indeed, the CH_2Cl_2 molecules were apparently able to turn through appreciable angles (27-38°) about their inertial axes. Agreement within experimental error was obtained between the correlation functions computed from different vibrational bands of the same species.

The anisotropy of the rotational motion in the liquid was found to resemble that of freely rotating CH_2Cl_2 molecules, indicating that the reorientational motion was not sensitive to intermolecular interactions. This behaviour is similar to that observed with CH_3I. Approximate values of the intermolecular torques were calculated from the observed $M(4)$, using the expression

$$\tfrac{1}{4}M(4)^{a} = (kT)^2[B^2(1 + C/A + A/C) + C^2(1 + B/A + A/B) \\ -A(B + C) + 6BC] + \langle (CV)^2_{b}\rangle B^2 + \langle (OV)^2_{c}\rangle C^2$$

which was derived from Gordon's general result. *A, B,* and C are rotational constants in this expression. Equation (101) describes the intermolecular effects influencing the motion of the inertial axis a (the relations for the other two axes are found by cyclic permutation of the symbols). *O* is an operator whose components O_a, O_b, and O_c along the axes, a, *b,* and *c* represent derivatives with respect tc angles of rotation about a, *b,* and *c;* the quantity *V* denotes the angle-dependent part of the intermolecular potential. The values obtained for the mean square torque were $\langle (OV)^2_{a}\rangle^{1/2} \sim 280$ cm^{-1} rad^{-1} and $\langle (OV)^2_{b}\rangle^{1/2} \sim \langle (OV)^2_{c}\rangle^{1/2} \sim 440 \pm 270$ cm^{-1} rad^{-1}, indicating that the torques in CH_2Cl_2 are not large and not very anisotropic.

The dynamical behaviour of acetonitrile CH_3CN is highly anisotropic owing to its molecular geometry. Because of the anisotropy of this elongated symmetric-top molecule, it pro-tides an interesting molecule for testing theories *of* rotational diffusion. Frenkel *et al.* have used CH_3CN as a test molecule for their variable-collision, rotational-diffusion model.

Using a Poisson collisional distribution, the simulated absorption spectrum peaked at 25 cm^{-1} compared with the observed absorption maximum of 60 cm^{-1}. The use of a modified distribution, however, enabled the observed absorption to be closely reproduced. The peak in the collision distribution that was used corresponded approximately to a frequency of 200 cm^{-1}, indicating that there was considerable coupling between the internal vibrations and the rotational motions.

The size of the rotational and translational diffusion steps in several simple liquids was the subject of an article by Rothschild. By using the dipole correlation function approach, he was able to show that the molecular reorientation in CH_2Cl_2, CH_3I, CH_3Cl, and C_6H_{12} consisted of angular jumps of the order of 20-60°.

During a jump, which takes place in about 0.4 ps, the molecules behave as free rotors, regardless of the size of the molecule or the intermolecular forces. Furthermore, it transpired that the translational diffusion occurred by a jump mechanism, with a molecular trapping time of the order of 10^{-11}-10^{-10} s and jumps of the order of a molecular diameter. Large rotational and translational jumps of CH_2Cl_2 were even observed in a very viscous solution of polystyrene. The macroscopic viscosity of the solutions appeared to have little effect on the rotational diffusion of the CH_2Cl_2 molecules.

This type of large-angle rotational diffusion seems to be quite general for fluids composed of fairly small molecules where there are no Specific strong interactions such as hydrogen-bond formation. The effect of weak complex formation on the reorientational motion of liquid $CHCl_3$ has also been discussed by Rothschild. The dipole correlation function and proton nuclear magnetic relaxation techniques were combined to obtain details of the rotational motion and of the translation motion in the $CHCl_3$-C_6H_6 system.

The contours of the 362 cm^{-1} parallel band in $CDCl_3$ and of the 1219 cm^{-1} perpendicular band in $CHCl_3$ were obtained in C_6H_6 solutions and Fourier-transformed. The resulting dipole correlation functions indicated that the two components forming the weak complex behaved essentially as random rotors, performing gas-like orientational jumps through average angles of 0.4-0.7 rad around their inertial axes. There was no evidence of any specific motion associated with the whole complex or of any directional intermolecular interaction. The translational motion appeared to be characterized mainly by large-distance jumps (*ca.* 5Å) of the individual moieties and not by jumps of the complex as a whole. It seems that the intermolecular interactions only exist during the lifetime of a molecular collision.

This aspect will be discussed more fully in the section on low-frequency studies. Similar results have been obtained for the C_6H_6-C_6F_6 and other weakly complexed systems. Both i.r. and Raman bands in water are unusually broad and asymmetric. The shapes of these bands are similar irrespective of their vibrational origin, indicating that their broadening and tailing is caused by similar perturbations. Time correlation functions were computed from Raman bands arising from both OH and OD stretching vibrations of HDO in liquid water. Both these functions rapidly decayed during the first fraction of a picosecond, faster in fact than the free-rotor correlation functions.

Klier observed similar behaviour for the dipole correlation functions of liquid water and of water adsorbed on a silica surface, which he interpreted as arising from strong vibrational perturbations of the rotational motion of the water molecules. This results in a periodic acceleration and slowing down (modulation) of the rotary motion. The application of first-order perturbation theory led to a correlation function which differed from the usual expression for uncoupled vibrations and rotations by the modulating factor $\exp[i(\Delta\omega_I - \Delta\omega_m)t]$ which gives rise to the observed modulation.

Thus the frequency of the modulation is determined by the difference between the average perturbation of the excited and ground-state vibrational levels. Expanding the modulating factor as a function of time gives

$$C(t) = \Sigma_\iota \rho_\iota \langle r_\iota | u(0) \,.\, u^*(t) | r_\iota \rangle$$
$$+ it\, \Sigma_\iota \rho_\iota (\Delta\omega_\iota - \Delta\omega_m) \langle r_\iota | u(0) \,.\, u^*(t) | r_\iota \rangle$$
$$- \tfrac{1}{2} t^2 \Sigma_\iota \rho_\iota (\Delta\omega_\iota - \Delta\omega_m)^2 \langle r_\iota | u(0) \,.\, u^*(t) | r_\iota \rangle$$

where the leading term in this expression is the uncoupled correlation function. This term is always positive at short times. The sum in the t^2 term must also be positive at short times so that the perturbed correlation function will decay faster than that for the unperturbed motion irrespective of the functional form of the angular perturbation.

This effect opposes that of the molecular torques which always produce a slower decay of $C(t)$ by a contribution in t^4. The observed correlation functions for bulk water obtained from the i.r. data of Luck 128 for the

($v_3 + v_2$) combination band. Apart from critical water, the correlation functions decay faster than the free-rotor $C(t)$, and then decay in an oscillatory fashion. No modulation of this kind was observed in the case of ice (at -9°C). Large, complicated molecules are generally not amenable to study by the dipole correlation function approach.

There are two main reasons for this: the generally complicated absorption spectrum leads to difficulties in finding a suitable isolated band and vibrational relaxation makes a significant and usually unknown contribution to the observed bandshape, especially at long times. One of the few such molecules to be studied is camphor.

The carbonyl stretching vibration at 1740 cm^{-1} was relatively free from overlapping features and was chosen for the computation of the correlation function. Solutions of camphor in various solvents ranging from cyclohexane to CS_2 were used. Analysis of the data was in terms of the quantity kT/I, which is the coefficient of t_2 in the series expansion of C(t) for a linear molecule [equation (58)]. Values of kT/I in the range 0.52-4.42 $\times$ 10^{24} s^{-2} were obtained, compared with the theoretical value of 0.60 $\times$ 10^{24} s^{-2} (using an averaged moment of inertia). This wide variation in kT/I was interpreted in terms of different contributions from vibrational relaxation processes. The rotational and vibrational contributions were then separated assuming the rotational contribution to be the experimental cyclohexane value.

The motion of the NH^+_4 ion in different environments has also been studied by means of the dipole correlation function approach. The analysis was performed on the 1400 cm^{-1} bending vibration of NH_4I in the NaCl-type lattice at room and liquid N_2 temperatures. The resulting correlation function was in fair agreement with a model consisting of a torsional oscillator, interrupted by collisions with phonons in the lattice.

Raman studies

Raman scattering has only emerged recently as a tool for elucidating the details of rotational dynamics in molecular systems.

Gaseous phase

Recent study of Raman scattering on gaseous systems investigated the self-broadening of HCl, DCI, HBr, and DBr and their broadening by gaseous SF_6 and C_2F_6. The total scattered intensity for HCl at pressures between 1 and 44 atom. The results were compared with calculations using van Kranendonck's theory of line broadening. It was shown that the self-broadening of the isotropic *Q*-branch does not follow the theory whereas broadening by a noble gas does.

Optical cross-sections for multipolar forces were derived by Gray from the general collision theory and applied to the special case of self-broadening of the rotational lines of HCl. The broadening was found to be strongly dependent on *J* and a maximum for the $J = 2 \rightarrow 4$ transition. These results were in good agreement with the HCl results obtained by Perchard *et al.*

Condensed phase

Main purpose of the correlation functions for liquid N_2, H_2, D_2, and CH_4 was to test the relationship between Raman and nuclear spin relaxation. The rotational correlational times derived from Raman and nuclear spin relaxation measurements were in reasonable agreement except in the case of CH_4. This discrepancy may arise from the presence of other relaxational processes in addition to molecular reorientation. Wang and Fleury used the Raman technique to obtain information on the molecular motion in HCl in its condensed phases. In the liquid and cubic phases, the depolarization ratio, the spectral shape, and the spectral width of the HCl stretching mode were studied as functions of temperature.

Since HCl has a dipole moment, in addition to the influence of the short-range intermolecular forces, the molecular dynamics are effected by the long-range electric dipole-dipole interaction. Moreover, the presence of hydrogen-bonding in liquid and solid HCl can modulate the polarizability and provides an additional mechanism for light scattering.

The polarized and depolarized spectra of HCl in condensed phases. Despite an appreciable narrowing, the depolarization ratio remains essentially unchanged on both sides of the liquid-solid transition temperature (158.9 K). In the temperature region 170-120 K, the depolarization ratio was about 0.06. This was taken to imply that the average value a and the anisotropy β of the polarizability tensor are approximately equal.

Thus, in the solid there must be considerable rotational freedom or else a disordered structure similar to that found in the ammonium halides. The lineshapes were not changed in any significant way in traversing the solid-liquid transition so the molecular motion must be rather similar in both phases. When the data were analysed, assuming only rotational relaxation, the barrier hindering rotational motion was found to be very small in both liquid and solid phases, indicating almost free reorientational motion. If this were the case, however, rotation-vibration and pure rotational structure should be observed. Fine structure was recently observed for quasi-free rotation of HCl dissolved in liquid SF_6 and C_2F_6. This would seem to indicate that other relaxation effects were contributing to the observed band profile in this case. In an attempt to resolve this problem, the combined techniques of Raman and Rayleigh scattering were used by Perchard, Murphy, and Bernstein to obtain information on molecular reorientation in liquid HCl, DCl, and HBr systems.

The results were discussed in terms of existing theories relating bandshapes and molecular motion. The comparison of the Rayleigh and Raman scattering results showed that the profile of the anisotropic Raman band could not be explained simply in terms of the molecular reorientational processes. Thus, the molecular motion was analysed in terms of both the rotational $G_r(t)$ and vibrational $G_v(t)$ correlation functions in the usual way. The results for HCl are presented. The resulting values of the rotational correlation time τ_r, shown in Table 4, were found to be in good agreement with the Rayleigh scattering results.

Table 4

Rotational vibrational correlation times for HCl, DCl, HBr, DBr($\tau \times 10^{13}$s)

Species	*From $G_v \times G_\tau$*	*From G_v*	*From G_τ*	*Rayleigh*
HCl	1.24	2.19	2.77	2.40
DCl	1.53	3.35	2.75	—
HBr	1.64	3.31	3.28	2.90
DBr	2.02	5.05	3.32	2.88

Three basic mechanisms for vibrational broadening were considered, *viz.*, translational motion, resonance broadening, and vibration-rotation coupling. Most of the broadening was found to be due to translational movement, but self-broadening could also contribute significantly. After rotation through angles of *ca.* 30—40°, the motion becomes Brownian with a correlation time of the order of 0.25—0.3 ps.

This correlation time was isotopically independent, in agreement with Debye's relaxation theory and the results of rotational Brownian motion theory. The second and fourth moments were calculated for the Raman and Rayleigh perpendicular components. Extensive measurements of vibratoinal and in some cases pure rotational Raman spectra of HCl, DCl, and DBr dissolve din SF_6 C_2F_6, CCl_4, and SO_2 were carried out at room temperature. band profiles of both the isotropic and anisotropic scattering were analysed and discussed in the light of existing theories of molecular motion in liquids.

The change in band profile with solvent was generally comparable for HCl and HBr; the bands became broader as the intermolecular interaction increased. For SF_6 and C_2F_6 solutions, the band profiles of the total intensity are similar to those observed with low pressure or gases pressured with noble gases. The perpendicualar components of HCl liquid and HCl dissolved in three solvents are compared. The *Q*-branch asymmetry due to the vibrartion-rotation interactions was clearly observed, but the individual lines could not resolved in the case of gases. In thecase of the inert solvent(SF_6, C_6F_6), the band contours were expalined by an extension of the collisional theory of Raman broadening.

The most dramatic result was the observation of rotational fine structure for the vibration-rotation bands of HCl and HBr dissolved in SF_6. These results can be compared with the pure rotational Raman spectra of the same solutions and with the corresponding vibration-rotation i.r spectra. From the frequencies of the vibration-rotation transitions J = 2 to J = 10, it was considered that the rotational constants for HCl and HBr are not appreciably different from their values in the low-pressure gas.

For the weakly perturbing solvent CCl_4, it was

shown that the isotropic scattering profile could be satisfactorily explained by vibration-rotation coupling as in the case of the inert solvents. This conclusion was demonstrated by fitting the band contour with broadened Lorentzian or Gaussian line profiles of each Q component. In the case of SO_2, an active polar solvent, vibrational relaxation was shown to contribute to the perpendicular band profile to an appreciable extent. Both the correlation functions $G_r(t)$ and $G_v(t)$ were therefore computed. Band moments and intermolecular torques were also computed; the values of the latter were in good agreement with the corresponding i.r. values. In similar work, the Raman spectrum of solutions of H_2 and D_2 in SF_6 and CCl_4 were investigated.

The observed spectra were discussed in terms of the contribution made by rotational and vibrational relaxation. Rotational fine structure was observed for H_2 in both solvents. The same group also analysed the half-widths of SO_2 in a variety of solvents. They found that the half-width of the v_1 symmetric stretch decreased with temperature whereas that of the v_3 asymmetric stretch increased.

The results were interpreted using a relationship developed by Rokov. Griffiths recently reported isotropic and anisotropic Raman bandshape analysis of the v_1 (a_1) fundamentals in liquid CH_3CN and CD_3CN. From the orientational width $\omega_{or}(T)$, a reorientational correlation time τ_{or} can be calculated from the relation,

$$\tau_{or} = [2\pi c\omega_{or}(T)],$$

and this can then be used to compute a value for the perpendicular component $D_\perp$ of the diffusion tensor by

$$D_\perp = (6\tau_{or})^{-1}$$

Values of $D_\perp$ determined by the Raman method can then

be used for comparison with values calculated from other techniques. Also, the experimental values of $D_{\perp}$ can be used to compare with theoretical values based on specific models. Acetonitrile was also included in an i.r. and Raman study of highly polar and strongly associated liquid systems.

In this work, the characteristics of the rotational-vibrational relaxation of acetonitrile, benzonitrile, propan-2-ol, and 1.4-dioxan were observed by determining the correlation functions of several i.r. and Raman bands. Benzonitrile and propan-2-ol were also investigated as dilute solutions in CCl_4 and in CS_2, whereas 1,4-dioxan was studied in a variety of polar and non-polar molecules.

The short-time behaviour of the correlation function is of primary interest in this study whereas in the previous work the method of analysis dictated that only information regarding the longer-time behaviour could be obtained. By concentrating on the short-time behaviour of the system, the effects of vibrational relaxation become less important.

The results show that the intermolecular forces need *ca.* 0.1-0.2 $\times$ 10^{-12} s to produce observable effect on the molecular motion and that regardless of the polarity or association of the liquids or solutions, rotational relaxation was the dominant mode of decay for times less than 0.5 $\times$ 10^{-12} s. Benzonitrile and 1,4-dioxan were exceptions, owing to fast vibrational decay. The rotation of CH_3CN was also shown to be strongly hindered in those motions which tend to tilt the permanent dipole moment axis, but it was also shown that the molecules undergo rotational jumps by ca. 0.5—1.2 rad about this axis.

The longtime decay (beyond 0.8 $\times$ 10^{-12} s), of the C—

C stretch in propan-2-ol was mainly governed by vibrational decay, whereas for shorter times rotational relaxation was dominant. Molecular relaxation in pure 1,4-dioxan and its solutions was apparently strongly influenced by vibrational relaxation effects. The rotational diffusion tensor of benzene was found to be approximately isotropic. This result was at variance with the data of Gillen and Griffith who found that reorientational motion in benzene was highly anisotropic.

Very little change in reorientational correlation times was found in transversing the liquid plastic crystal phase boundary. the temperature dependances of the i.r and Raman orientational times. This seems to rule out a reorintatonal mechanism in which reorientation can only occur during a translational jump of molecule. The recent work on benzene has shown the rotational diffusion tensor of benzene to be highly anistropic. By analysing Raman bandshapes and D n.m.r. relaxation times as a function of temperature, values for the diffusion constants $D_{\perp}$ and $D_{||}$ were obtained. Two models were used to interpret the data, the hydrodynamic and the slightly damped free rotor (SDFR).

These models represent opposite microdynamic extremes, and predict quite a different temperature dependence of τ, and so provide a rigorous test of theory. The hydrodynamic models assume small-angle rotational Brownian motion and specifically relate the rotational and translational motions, whereas in the SDFR model molecular reorientations approach those in the low-pressure gas phase with large-angle rotational jumps.

On comparison with the observed results, it was found that rotational motion about the symmetry axis of benzene was consistent with the SDFR model of diffusion whereas the rotational motion perpendicular to the C_6 axis was best interpreted in terms of small-angle rotational Brownian motion. A rotational correlation time for benzene has also been obtained from the 992 cm^{-1} band by Clark and Miller, assuming an exponential form for $C(t)$ at short times. They obtained a value of 1.3 ps, which is about a factor of two lower than the currently accepted value. Considerable interest has recently been generated in Raman studies of the orientational motion in substituted methanes.

The explanation for this, as in the i.r. case, is their suitability as model compounds with which to test the validity of current experimental techniques and to seek justification for the theory underlying the separation of the various relaxational processes. In one of the first such investigations, i.r. and Raman correlation times for the C—I vibration in CH_3I and C_2H_4I and the C—CI vibration in $(CH_3)_3CCl$ were obtained by Constant *et* al. Both pure liquids and solutions in a variety of solvents were investigated

The temperature dependence of τ was also obtained. Rayleigh scattering can also be used in principle to extract information concerning rotational behaviour. The expressions for G_v and $G_v \times G_r$ are analogous to the corresponding expressions for Raman scattering [equations (45) and (47)] except that the polarizability derivatives are replaced by the equilibrium polarizabilities. Vibrational relaxation does not contribute to these spectra, but other difficulties arise. The most important of these is the extent of the contribution of co-operative scattering between different molecules, but there are also experimental difficulties due to working very near the exciting line.

A comparison of both Raman and Rayleigh studies of rotational diffusion in the anisotropic molecule $CHCI_3$ has been reported. Correlation functions were computed from the v_6 Raman band and the depolarized Rayleigh scattering and compared with theoretical expressions. A comprehensive Raman study of the molecular interactions and motion in liquid CH_3I has recently appeared.

The temperature dependence of the 524 cm^{-1} (a_1) mode and the low-frequency Raman scattering (0—200 cm^{-1}) from room temperature down to its freezing point, and also in the supercooled liquid, were investigated. The reorientational line broadening was separated from contributions from vibrational and other line-broadening processes. Corrected correlation functions for isotropic and anisotropic scattering for the two temperature extremes.

The room-temperature reorientational correlation function G_r is seen to decay much more quickly than the non-reorientational (isotropic) function G_v; at the lowest temperature studied this situation is totally reversed. Thus at room temperature the dominant process is molecular reorientation, whereas as the temperature is decreased this mechanism becomes less important and other mechanisms become dominant. The approximate correlation function for short times.

$$G_{approx} = 1 - \tfrac{1}{2}(\partial^2 G/\partial\tau^2)|_0\, \tau^2 = 1 - [M(2)_{exp}/2]\tau^2$$

The free-rotor correlation function G_{fr} decays much more quickly than G_r, indicating that free rotation of CH_3I molecules is quite restricted, even at very short times. Finally, all three experimental correlation functions become exponential at long times, as predicted by the stochastic nature of the various contributing processes.

The reorientation correlation time τ_{or} = 1.6 ps was in good agreement with Bartoli and Litoviiz's room-temperature value of 1.5 ps. The temperature dependence of the correlation times associated with the 524 cm^{-1} band is shown in Table 5.

Table 5

Correlation times associated with the 524cm^{-1} CH_3I Raman band

T\K	*tiso/PS*	*taniso/Ps*	*tr/PS*
196	1.82	1.45	7.13
209	1.92	1.55	7.93
228	1.91	1.38	5.03
242	2.08	1.36	3.96
259	2.18	1.24	2.87
298	2.31	0.95	1.61

It can be seen that the τ_{iso} become larger with increasing temperature. All theories which describe the vibrational relaxation process predict a decrease in τ_{iso} with temperature, suggesting that vibrational relaxation does not contribute Significantly to the observed isotropic broadening. Another important mechanism, collision-induced broadening, often used to explain low-frequency rotational Raman lineshapes, again predicts the wrong temperature dependence. However, this model is based on isolated binary collisions, which is obviously a poor approximation for liquid systems. If the CH_3I is considered to 'bounce' around inside a cage of similar molecules the correct temperature dependence is obtained. Further Raman work on the substituted methanes CH_3I and $CHCl_3$ was recently reported by Johnson and Drago.

This paper also included a general discussion of the correlation function approach and considered in particular the problem of separating the Raman reorientational correlation from the contribution arising from other relaxational processes. Reorientational correlation functions were computed for the totally symmetric C—D stretching mode in $CDCl_3$ and the C—I stretch in CH_3I over a range of temperatures. Correlation times computed from the $\langle P_2[u(0) - u(t)]\rangle$ curves were used to evaluate an activation energy for the reorientational process according to

$$\tau = \tau_0 \exp(-E_a/kT)$$

The values of E_a obtained by this process agreed well with those obtained by n.m.r. relaxation, microviscosity, and dielectric relaxation. Virtually all treatments of i.r. and Raman bandshapes, both experimental and theoretical, have neglected any coupling between rotation and vibration. With this in mind, Goldberg and Pershan recently discussed the Raman bandshapes in CH_3I and CD_3I with particular emphasis on rotation-vibration coupling.

The rotational and vibrational correlation functions for the a1 bands were obtained in the usual way. On comparing the linewidths of the a, bands, it was found that, within experimental error, the v_2 width was equal to the v_3 width in each molecule, but the two v_1 widths were larger than the corresponding v_2 and v_3 widths. In the absence of rotation-vibration coupling the *a,* rotation-vibration lineshapes (both i.r. and Raman) must be identical. The experimental results therefore indicate the presence of such coupling. Significant A1-E-type Coriolis coupling was the proposed explanation for this rather unexpected result.

The v_2 and v_3 modes are unaffected by this type of coupling and therefore, provide more reliable information regarding molecular dynamics in the system. The diffusion coefficients $D_\perp$ derived from the v_2 and v_3 bands (1.5 and 1.2 × 10^{11} s^{-1} respectively) were in good agreement with $D_\perp$ values obtained from other techniques, but the $D_\perp$ value obtained from the v_1 band

(2.2×10^{11} s^{-1}), deviated significantly from other results. An interesting Raman study of reorientational motion in $CHCl_3$ as a function of pressure has been published by Campbell and Jonas.

The a_1 3019 cm^{-1} CH stretching band profile was analysed at pressures of 1, 1000, and 2000 bar at room temperature. The reorientational correlation function was separated from the effects of other relaxational processes in the manner discussed above. The predicted short-time behaviour of this function was obtained using the Gaussian function introduced by Bratos and Marechal. Deuterium spin-lattice relaxation times (T_1) were also obtained as a function of pressure and used to compute rotational correlation times.

Both n.m.r. and Raman experiments observe the same motion in $CHCl_3$, the reorientational motion about an axis perpendicular to the symmetry axis. The results from both sets of experiments are listed in Table 6.

Theoretical values of τ_{or} were also calculated using the multiviscosity approach of Gierer and Wirtz and Bridgeman's high-pressure viscosity results. These are also included in Table 6. Although the theoretical values of τ_{or} were about 1.3 times larger than the Raman results they both showed approximately the same temperature dependence.

Table 6

Reorientation correlation times for $CHCl_3$ as a function of pressure (τ_{or} $\times 10^{12}$ S)

Pressure/bar	T1/s	Theoretical	Raman(23°C)	N.m.r(25°)
1	1.39	2.60	1.97	1.74
1000	0.92	4.26	3.14	2.60
2000	0.77	6.36	5.42	3.10

This behaviour was not observed in the n.m.r. times. Mean square torques were also computed and found to be of the same order as those reported for CH_3CN in n-heptane. The librational motion of the NH^+_4 ion in NH_4Br below T_λ has been studied by Wang and Wright. The frequency, intensity, spectral bandwidth, and Raman polarizability correlation function associated with this motion were obtained as a function of temperature in the range 90—200 K. At temperatures above 170 K, all correlation functions appeared to decay rapidly in the 0.4-1.5 ps region, and then decay much more slowly at times greater than 1.5 ps. Below 150 K, the decay was slow with no change in the decay rate.

The two decay rates above 170 K indicated that two competitive intermolecular processes were probably present. Since the second moment of the band $M(2)$ is equal to the second derivative of the correlation function, the study of $M(2)$ as a function of temperature provides information regarding G_{lib} at short times and thus reveals the nature of the fast interaction process. The experimental second moments were found to increase exponentially with temperature, a result contrary to the behaviour expected if reorientational processes were dominant; $M(2)$ should increase linearly with temperature if this were the case. The magnitude of the observed $M(2)$ values was also inconsistent with a reorientational model.

Correlation times were computed from the area of the correlation function up to 10 ps. Both these and the spectral linewidths were found to exhibit an Arrhenius-type temperature dependence. These data were consistent with a thermally induced hydrogen-bond-breaking process as the dominant interaction in the modulation of the librational mode.

Low-frequency studies

Low-frequency Raman and far-i.r. studies of molecular motion have developed substantially in the past few years. Advances in experimental techniques have contributed in no small part to the increased exploitation of this important spectral region. It is now possible to investigate transitions down to a few wavenumbers both in absorption and light scattering. Molecular dynamics studies in the low-frequency region can be broadly classified under the headings of rotational and translational motions.

Since, however, in many systems the frequencies of the two motions are comparable it is difficult in some cases to make this distinction. No attempt will be made here to consider rotational and translational motions separately.

Far-infrared studies

There have been a number of recent studies of the far-i.r. rotational absorption of compressed non-polar and polar gases and of the effect of inert gases on pure rotational lines. Collision-induced spectra in the far-i.r. region yield valuable information on molecular motion and intermolecular forces. In the case of linear molecules, these spectra arise from a transient dipole moment induced in a pair of colliding molecules by the quadrupolar electric field. Tetrahedral molecules have no quadrupole moment but collision-induced spectra can arise from the transient dipole moment induced by the octupolar field and by molecular distortion due to overlap interaction.

Molecular quadrupole moments are sensitive to the outer electronic charge distribution in a molecule and so are useful as tests for electronic wavefunctions. Furthermore, the electric fields of quadrupole moments can make significant contributions to the orientation dependent part of the intermolecular potential. Theory of pressure-induced spectra of noble-gas atoms and of linear molecules is well established and has been recently extended to include tetrahedral molecules. In the case of tetrahedral molecules, the molecular octupole moment is related to the integrated intensity resulting from the modulation of the octupole-induced dipole moment by the rotational motion of the molecules.

Translational motion was not considered. It was shown that for the pure rotational spectrum the selection rules $\Delta J = \pm 1, \pm 2, \pm 3$, will hold (as well as $\Delta J = 0$). The $\Delta J = 3$ transitions contribute some I of the total intensity, thus dominating the shape of the spectrum. The analysis was applied to experimental far-i.r. spectra of CH_4, CD_4, and CF_4 and gave octupole moments in good agreement with those obtained by other techniques.

The general features of the spectra were also reproduced. As an extension of their work on tetrahedral molecules Rosenberg and Birnbaum measured the far-i.r. spectra (12-250 cm^{-1}) of SF_6 at pressures from 3 to 19 atm in the gas phase and at 0 and -40°C in the liquid phase. In view of the O_h molecular symmetry of SF, the lowest-order non-vanishing electric moment is the hexadecapole in the ground vibrational state. A number of absorption bands were found in the 12-250 cm^{-1} region. The intensity of one band at 50 cm^{-1} varied as the $(density)^2$ and so was attributed to collision-induced absorption. Other bands at 94 and 173 cm^{-1} were assigned to difference vibrations. The hexadecapole moment of SF_6 was estimated from the integrated intensity of the 50 cm^{-1} band. Despite the extensive interest in the collision-induced spectra of non-polar gases, very little work on polar gases has been reported.

This is due in the main to the complexity of these

systems. In one such investigation Weiss and Cole observed the collision-induced spectra of HCl and DCl in an attempt to separate the effects of dipolar and quadrupolar interactions. Quadrupole-induced dipole interactions lead to one member of a 'collision pair' being raised to a higher level whereas the other molecule remains in its original state.

The selection rules for rotational transitions of this kind are $\Delta J = 0, \pm 2$ rather than the usual dipolar ($\Delta J = \pm 1$). By making use of this difference in selection rules, together with the fact that different populations of the molecular rotational states are involved in the two cases, these workers were able to separate contributions arising from dipolar and quadrupole-induced dipole effects.

Molecular quadrupole moments calculated from the integrated intensities of the separated bands were $Q_{HCl} = 5.8 \times 10^{-26}$ esu cm^2 and $Q_{HBr} = 5.5 \times 10^{-26}$ esu cm^2. Pure rotational absorption in the far-i.r. region is proportional to the density of polar molecules whereas induced effects are proportional to the density squared. Baise used this effect to separate the quadrupole-induced dipole and dipole-induced dipole absorption from pure dipole-dipole rotational absorption in compressed N_2O.

Since the dipole moment of N_2O is small (0.17 D), the induced absorption becomes larger than the pure rotational absorption at high densities. The far-i.r. spectra (8-100 cm^{-1}) of gaseous N_2O in the range 34-64 bar were reported and an approximate value of the quadrupole moment was computed ($Q \sim 8 \times 10^{-26}$ esu cm^2). Measurements of line broadening in the pure rotational spectra of HCl in gaseous mixtures with inert gases have revealed that heavy atoms are more effective in broadening the rotational lines than are light atoms.

In this work, HCl was studied in the region 15-170 cm^{-1} at pressures of up to 100 atm in mixtures with He and Ar. The results were interpreted in terms of energy and momentum transfer in collisions of short duration. The effect of pressure perturbation on the pure rotational spectrum of HCl was also investigated by Fabre *et al.* Pure HCl at pressures of up to 35 bar and mixtures with argon in the pressure range 0—275 bar were the subjects of this Raman study.

A true linewidth was computed from the experimental spectra and was found to be proportional to the perturber pressure. The results were in good agreement with the predictions of Gray's theory which was based on the effects of anisotropic intermolecular forces. A number of far-i.r. studies of polar molecules dissolved in non-polar solvents have appeared in the literature. One point of particular interest in these studies involves the question of free rotation in these liquid systems. In most cases, no fine structure indicative of free rotation was found.

Only in the cases of HCl dissolved in liquid SF_6 and in liquid Ar and Kr have the remnants of fine structure been observed. The small perturbing effect of SF_6 in this case may be associated with the very high symmetry of this molecule.No fine structure was observed for DCl dissolved in liquid SF_6, which may be the result of the smaller spacing of the rotational transitions.

To obtain more information regarding the intermolecular origin of this fine structure, van Aalst and van der Elsken computed the pure rotational dipole correlation function for HCl dissolved in liquid argon and liquid krypton. Both absorption bands exhibit residual fine structure on the high-frequency side. The dipole correlation function for HCl dissolved in argon. A free-rotor correlation function for HCl is a periodic function with a period of 1.6 ps. At this time all freely rotating molecules should again have the same orientation as at $t = 0$.

The experimental $C(t)$ does indeed have a maximum at 1.6 ps, but it falls considerably below this correlation function near $t = 0$. Also, the experimental function oscillates much more rapidly around the secondary maximum. In the M- and J-diffusion limit, the ratio between the damping constants for HCl in argon and HCl in krypton should be 2: 7. In fact, this ratio was found to be <1.0. Thus the damping of the rotational motion in HCl must to a certain extent be determined by the specific properties of the host liquid.

Robert and Galatry have presented a detailed quantum mechanical calculation of the far-i.r. absorption spectrum of polar molecules dissolved in non-polar liquid solvents. They used a cell model to represent the solution and calculated the total interaction between the solute and solvent molecules. Using this interaction, they obtained the resulting average deformation of the rotational wavefunctions in lowest order. They compared their predictions with the spectrum of HCl dissolved in CCl_4.

In a subsequent report, these authors I'll examined theoretically the nature of the fine structure observed on the absorption bands of HCl and DCl dissolved in liquid SF_6. Two factors which govern the shape of an absorption band of a diatomic molecule dissolved in a polar solvent were discussed, the average value of the interaction energy between the dissolved molecule and its immediate environment, and the mean square of the fluctuations of that interaction. The periodic fine structure observed in the HCl solution in SF_6 was explained on this basis. Far-i.r. absorption of liquids has received increasing attention in recent years.

The absorption spectra of a number of polar and non-polar liquids have been reported. Low-frequency absorption in non-polar liquids has been interpreted in various ways, including librational motions in a cage and rotational-translational motions. In addition, since the absorption maxima in both liquid and solid phases appear in the same spectral region, these absorptions have also been termed 'liquid lattice' vibrations. It now seems established that the absorption in non-polar liquids arises from a bimolecular collision mechanism where the induced dipole moments do not cancel because of lack of long-range order.

Recently, Garg *et al.*, have accounted for the intensities of non-polar liquid absorption bands on the basis of multipole-induced dipole absorption and Davies *et al.*, have also considered this problem. More data on the far-i.r. absorption spectra of a number of simple polar and non-polar liquids were recently accumulated by Jain and Walker.

The absorption coefficient a_{max} for polar liquids was found to be directly proportional to the square of the electric dipole moment and inversely to the mean moment of inertia of the molecule. Furthermore, a_{max} was found to shift appreciably to higher frequencies with decrease in temperature in the case of polar liquids, whereas with the non-polar liquids there was no appreciable shift with temperature.

It was also found that, for polar liquids, the variation of an absorption band as a function of temperature could not be explained solely by a rotational mechanism. Pardoe has recently performed similar experiments on a number of non-polar liquids and some liquid mixtures. The non-polar absorption, although similar in contour and frequency to that of polar liquids, was about an order of magnitude less intense.

The temperature dependence of the non-polar liquid absorption was different from that observed by Jain and

Walker. A shift to lower frequencies with cooling as well as a narrowing of the band contour was observed. Which compares the variation in peak position for polar CH_2Cl_2 and non-polar CS_2. The concentration dependence and the observed intensity were both consistent with some form of collisional interaction between the molecules. In order to shed light on the nature of this collisional interaction, North and Parker carried out far-i.r. measurements on a number of non-polar liquid mixtures which were known to form weak charge-transfer complexes of differing strengths.

In these weak complexes, the charge-transferred state occurs only during the lifetime of a molecular collision. Rothschild's work on weak complexes in the mid-i.r. region supports this conclusion. The object of employing interacting molecules of this type was to enhance the collisional polarization and thus increase the absorption intensity. Carbon tetrachloride was used as the acceptor and benzene, toluene, *p*-xylene, and mesitylene were the donor molecules.

Chapter 2

Cyclic Molecules

Schwendeman has been investigating several carbonyl derivatives of cyclopropane. In studies concerned with cyclopropane-carbaldehyde and cyclopropanecarbonyl fluoride the torsional potential functions governing the twofold rotation of the planar carbon)] grouping with respect to the ring were derived and interpreted. Schwendeman and Lee have now extended these studies to cyclopropyl methyl ketone in an attempt to increase understanding of such potentials. Assignment difficulties in the very rich spectrum were overcome by the identification of characteristic E, A doublets arising from methyl-group internal rotation in the $J_{o,J}$ —$J_{1'J-1}$ series and by double-resonance experiments.

Effective rigid-rotor constants for the *A*-species transitions are interpreted as belonging to the cis-form (28) rather than the trans-form (rotation of the $COCH_3$ group by 1800 from cis) or an anti-gauche-form (rotation of the $COCH_3$ group by about 1500 from cis) according to a reasonable model structure calculation. Indeed, the last form is ruled out by establishing from $P_{cc} = (I_b + I_a - I_c)$ that the molecule has a symmetry plane. After subtracting out contributions from the two out of-plane hydrogens of the methyl group, P_{cc} becomes identical with those of the cis- and trans-forms of both cyclopropanecarbaldehyde and cyclopropanecarbonyl fluoride (P_{cc} = 19.75–19.80 a.m.u. Å^2).

The internal-rotation *E-A* splittings; in the vibrational ground-state transitions lead to a barrier to internal rotation of the methyl group of V_3 = 1180 ± 20 cal mol^{-1} when analysed according to the Herschbach formulation and the methyl-group moment of inertia is assumed as 3.12 a.m.u.$Å^2$. Such a barrier is characteristic of several CH_3COX compounds. Unfortunately no other rotamer of cyclopropyl methyl ketone could be detected and hence the barrier hindering internal rotation to a trans- or an anti-gauche-form was not determined.

However, rotational constants for the first three excited states of the CH_2CO-group torsional motion are a smoothly varying function of the torsional quantum number and hence indicate a fairly high barrier to the motion. The dipole moment components are μ_a = 0.47 ± 0.17, μ_b = 2.58 ± 0.26, and μ_{total} = 2.62 ± 0.26 D, with the vector associated with the latter value making an angle of ~1° with the CO axis.

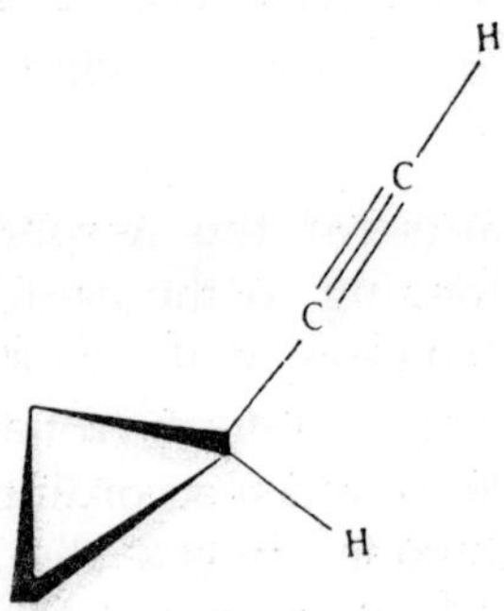

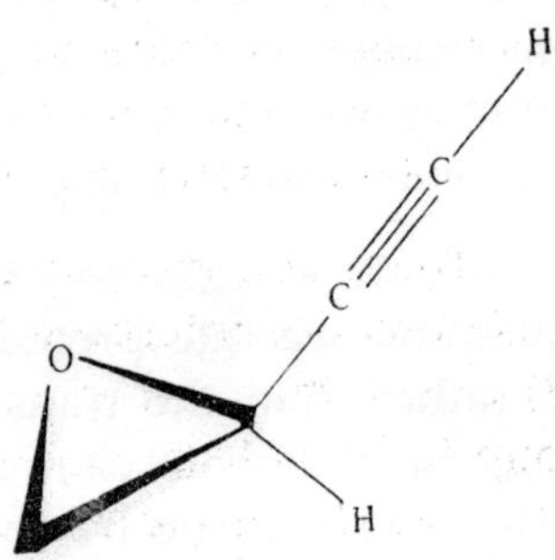

Structure determinations in the isoelectronic compounds cyclopropylacetylene (29) and epoxybutyne (30) pose interesting questions about conjugation of the cyclopropyl ring and attached groups. According to the Walsh model of cyclopropane each carbon atom is

sp^2-hybridized and the pure p-orbital on each carbon atom lies in the plane of the ring, able to overlap with similar p-orbitals on adjacent carbon atoms. Two of the three sp^2-hybridized orbitals on each carbon form bonds with hydrogen atoms above and below the plane of the ring whereas the third is directed toward the ring centre to form an intra-annular multicentre bond. Two types of conjugation of substituent groups with the ring are then postulated.

First, a pure p-orbital in the ring plane can conjugate with a properly oriented p-orbital in a substituent atom; hence the rationalization of the bisected forms (i.e. cis, trans, or both) in cyclopropyl methyl ketone, cyclopropanecarbaldehyde, cyclo-propanecarbonyl fluoride and others.

Secondly, conjugation between excess electron density on a substituent and the intra-annular multicentre bond is postulated. The observed conformations and the shortenings of C—X bonds in >—X, where X = Cl, Br, $N(H_2)$, or $P(H_2)$, relative to CH_3X compounds have been so rationalized. With the study of the microwave spectra of (29) ($C_3H_5C{\equiv}CH$ and $C_3H_5C{\equiv}CD$ species) by Collins. Britt, and Boggs and of ($C_2H_3OC{\equiv}CH$ and $C_2H_3OC{\equiv}CD$)species) by Collins and Boggs there is evidence that the above rationalisations are not without exception. In each compound the moments of inertia for both species have been combined with some reasonable structural assumptions to calculate the molecular parameters of most interest.

The main conclusion is that $r(\text{C-C}{\equiv}) = 1.466 \pm 0.018$ and 1.484 ± 0.02 A for cyclopropylacetylene and epoxybutyne respectively are longer than in the corresponding methyl analogue ($CH_3C{\equiv}CH$, 1.458 A), in contrast to the series >—X, where X = Cl, Br, $N(H_2)$, or $P(H_2)$, in which r(C—X) is 0.041, 0.04, 0.046 and shorter than in the corresponding CH_3X. It is interesting that cyclopropyl cyanide [isoelectronic with both (29) and (30)] also has r(C—CN) lengthened by 0.01 Å relative to methyl cyanide.

The dipole moment components are $\mu_a = 0.891 \pm 0.01$, $\mu_c = 0.048 \pm 0.01$, and $\mu_{total} = 0.892 \pm 0.01$D for cyclopropylacetatylene and $\mu_a = 0.316$, $\mu_b = 1.656$, $\mu_c = 0.618$, and $\mu_{total} = 1.795$ D for epoxybutyne.

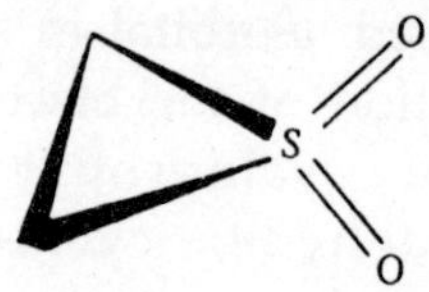

An r_0 structure has been determined for ethylene sulphone (31) from the observed ground-state moments of inertia of the $CH_2CH_2SO_2$ and $CH_2CH_2{}^{34}SO_2$ isotopic species. With the assumptions r(C—H) = 1.08 Å, HCH = 116° and H_2CC = 152° (from the microwave structure of ethylene sulphide), the structure so derived is that displayed in Table 1, wherein it is compared with those of sulphur dioxide, ethylene sulphide, and ethylene sulphoxide.

The errors quoted for the sulphone are generated from reasonable ranges of the assumed parameters. The striking feature of Table 1 is the progressive lengthening of the C—C bond from sulphide to sulphone.

Normally C—C bonds in three-membered rings are shorter than in ethane, the only other exception being the C—C bond opposite the carbonyl in cyclopropanone [r(C—C) = 1.575 Å]. The dipole moment of ethylene sulphone from the Stark effect is 4.47 ± 0.02 D.

Table 1

Structure of ethylene sulphone and related molecules

Species	*r(C—C)/Å*	*r(C—S)/Å*	*r(S—O)/Å*	*OSO°*
SO_2			1.408	119
$(CH_2)_2S$	1.492	1.819		
$(CH_2)_2SO$	1.504	1.822	1.483	
$(CH_2)_2SO_2$	1.586 ± 0.01	1.76 ± 0.02	1.42±0.02	124± 2

Much painstaking isotopic preparative and spectroscopic work has allowed Bak and Skaarup to derive very precise r_B structures for the closely related aziridine [32; X = H(I)] and 1-chloroaziridine (32; X = Cl).

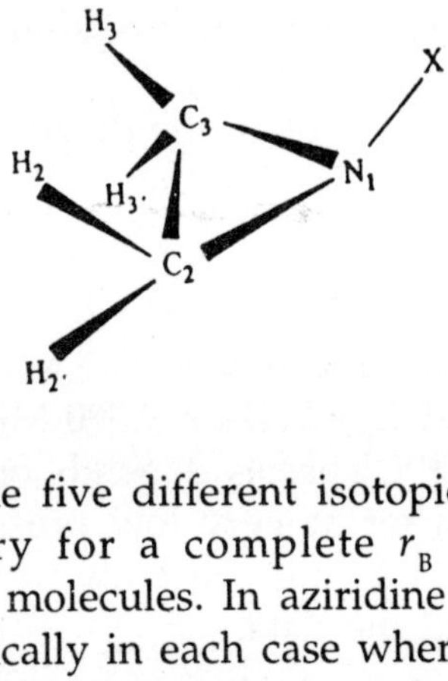

The spectra of the five different isotopically substituted species necessary for a complete r_B structure were observed in both molecules. In aziridine enrichment was carried out chemically in each case whereas the presence of chlorine made this necessary for only four isotopes in 1-chloroaziridine. Recourse to the pair of moment conditions $\Sigma m_i a_i = \Sigma m_i a_i c_i = 0$ (or their equivalent) was necessary in order to deal with problems of two small substitution coordinates occurring in both molecules.

The r_B structures of aziridine and 1-chloroaziridine are compared in Table 2 with an electron-diffraction structure of the former. The noteworthy points concerning the structures is the almost complete invariance of the ring structure to replacement of H(l) by Cl, except for a very small difference involving the C(2)—H(2) and C(2)—H(2') distances of the 1-chloro-compound. A slight structural distortion is also noted and is almost identical for both compounds.

The angle between the planes containing N(1)C(2)C(3) and H(2)C(2)H(2') is near to 87° in both molecules, so that the H(2) and H(3) protons are tilted together and H(2') and H(3') are tilted apart. Moreover, the plane through H(2)C(2)H(2') does not bisect the angle N(1)C(2)C(3) but divides it in the ratio 33.7° and 26.2° in aziridine and 37.6° and 22.5° in 1-chloroaziridine. Pochan and Flygare have recorded the $4_{22} \rightarrow 4_{23}$, $3_{22} \rightarrow 321$, $5_{33} \rightarrow 5_{32}$, and $7_{35} \rightarrow 7_{34}$ transitions of [$^{14}N_2$]diazirine (33) and the $0_{00} \rightarrow 1_{01}$ transition of the [^{13}C) species under high resolution in order to obtain the diagonal elements of the ^{14}N nuclear quadrupole coupling tensor in the principal inertial axis system.

They use the $I_1+I_2 = I$, $I+J= F$ coupling scheme to analyse their results and obtain Xaa = 0.196 ± 0.150, X_{bb} = –3.010 ± 0.150 and X_{cc}= 2.814 ± 0.300 MHz. The $0_{00} \rightarrow 1_{01}$ transition of the [^{13}C]species depends only on X_{aa} and its unresolved character at very low pressure was used to rule out a set of coupling constants with large X_{aa} which also initially fitted the data.

The coupling constants are in fair agreement with the results of an ab initio calculation: X_{aa} = –0.8, X_{bb} = –1.88, and X_{cc} = +2.69 MHz.

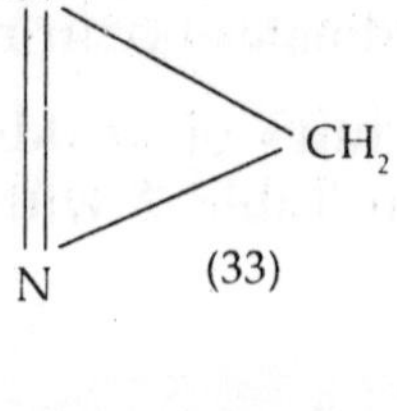

(33)

Of the bonding schemes considered the best appears to be the Walsh picture using the *sp*-hybrid orbitals on the nitrogen atoms in the plane of the ring (one pointing away from the other N and containing a lone pair, the other entering into a C—N σ–bond) with p_z and p_y unhybridized (z is perpendicular to the ring plane).

Table 2

Structures of aziridine and 1- chloroaziridine

	Aziridine [X= H(1)]	*1-chloroaziridine (X =Cl)*	
	Micromwave	*Electron diffraction*	*Microwave*
Distance/A			
N(1) —X	1.016	1.05 ± 0.07	1.738
N(1)-C(2)	1.475	1.49 ± 0.01	1.488
C(2)—H(2)	1.084	1.08 ± 0.03	1.079
C(2)— C(3)	1.481	1.48 ± 0.01	1.483
Angles/°			
C(2)N(1)C(3)	60.25	—	59.78
XN(1)C(2)	109.31	—	111.70
H(2)C(20H(2')	115.72	117	117.11
H(2)C(2)N(1)	118.26	—	115.18
H(2)C(2)N(1)	114.27	—	113.66

Four-membered rings

The three experimental papers in this area published during the past year all have four-membered rings containing a carbonyl group and an oxygen atom as their subject.

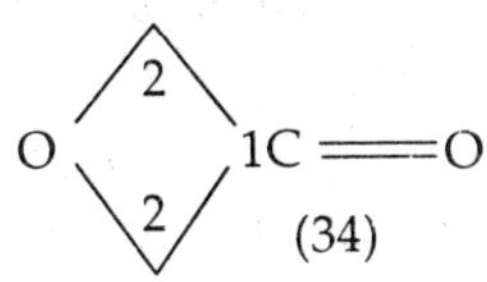

(34)

Oxetan-3-one (34) is the latest in a series of four-membered rings studied by Harris and his co-workers. Although Gibson and Harris have analysed the rotational spectrum of this molecule in the ground state and in the first five vibrationally excited states of the ring-bending mode to give rotational constants, they do not derive a potential function for the bending mode by the method of fitting the observed rotational constant variation by the familiar expansion in expectation values $<z^n>_{vv}$ of the reduced vibrational co-ordinate *z*. Rather, they present arguments why the coefficient *b* of the quartic term in a potential function of the type $V(z) = hv_0(z^2 + bz^4)$should not be well determined by such a procedure when, as in the present case, the dependence of the rotational constants on the ring-bending quantum number is only very slightly non-linear. Instead, they fit the constants and obtain the coefficients β_0, β_2 and β_4 in $B_v = \beta_0 + \beta_2 <z^2>_{vv}$ by calculating the values using the potential function derived from the far-i.r. spectrum.

Observation of the [^{13}Cl] and [$^{13}C_2$] isotopically substituted species in natural abundance allows the r_B co-ordinates of these atoms, and therefore the r_B parameters r[C(1)—C(2)]= 1.522± 0.002Å and C(2)C(1)C(2')= 88.06° means of the moment equations, after the data have been extrapolated and to be determined. The oxygen atom positions are calculated by means of the moment equations, after the data have been extrapolated to the hypothetical planar state, using the diagnostic least-squares procedure introduced by Curl. The final structure so obtained is:

r[C(1)—C(2)] = 1.524 ± 0.001Å C(2)C(1)C(2) = 88.23 ± 0.11°

r[C(20 —O = 1.441 ± 0.013Å C(2)OC(2) = 94.82°

r[C(1) = O] = 1.222 ± 0.015Å

if the values r[C(2)—H] = 1.09 Å and H—C(2)H = 110°

are assumed. The dipole moment measured is $\mu = 0.887 \pm 0.005$ D. An approximate model for the ring-bending vibration is discussed and the potential function for the vibration is interpreted in terms of contributions from the ring angle deformations and torsional interactions.

In a study of the related β-propiolactone (35), Boggia, Favero, and Sorarrain measure rotational constants for the first four excited states of the ring-bending vibration. Using the relative intensity measuring facility of the Hewlett Packard 8400C spectrometer, they carefully derive the vibrational separations/cm^{-1} for the first four levels as:

V =	1← 0	2←1	3←2	4←3
	158 ± 2	188 ± 5	167± 8	185 ± 13

They attribute the irregular level spacing to the existence of a double-minimum function for the vibration. A slight zig-zag behaviour of the rotational constants is also consistent with this conclusion. A function $V(z) = hv_0[z^2/2 + \lambda \exp(—\beta z^2)$ as final parameters is obtained by fitting the vibrational data and the rotational constants.

The barrier height for this double-minimum function is 19 cm^{-1}, with the ground vibrational state 105 cm^{-1} above the maximum: hence the mild zig-zag in the rotational constants. Tigelaar, Gierke, and Flygare deduce from the molecular Zeeman effect the *g*-values, molecular magnetic susceptibility anisotropies ($2X_{cc}—X_{bb}—X_{cc}$ and $2X_{bb}—X_{aa}— X_{cc}$) the diagonal elements of the molecular quadrupole tensor(Q_{aa}, Q_{bb}, Q_{cc}) and the diagonal elements of the diamagnetic susceptibility tensor(X_{aa}, X_{bb}, X_{cc}) for β-propiolactone (35) and diketen (36).

A method whereby molecular electric dipole and

quadrupole moments and X_{aa}, X_{bb} and X_{cc} values can be calculated by summing empirically derived atom dipole moments has been developed.

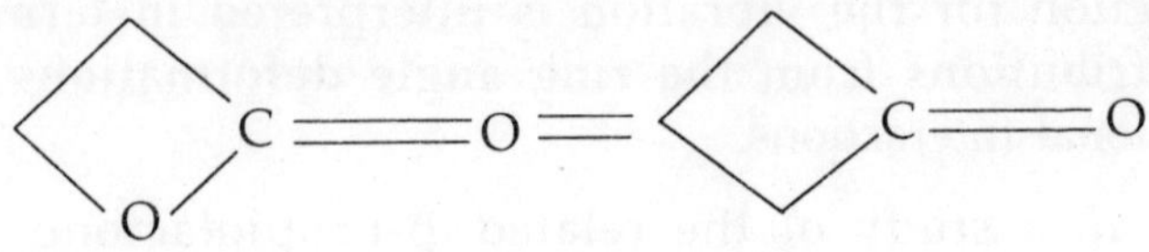

(35) (36)

Using an established set of reduced atom dipoles, deduced originally on the basis of the successful prediction of the properties of many molecules, good agreement is achieved between observed and calculated values of the above molecular properties. Also of interest is a comparison of observed and calculated values of the out-of-plane minus average in-plane magnetic susceptibilities $\Delta_X = X_{cc} - (X_{aa} + X_{bb})/2$.

Flygare and his co-workers have already shown that for unstrained, acyclic compounds it is possible to reproduce a large number Δ_{Xobs} values simply by the summation of the local group Δ_X values which compose the molecule. For β-propiolactone and diketen the ring strain apparently gives rise to a positive contribution to Δ_X since Δ_{Xobs} is larger (more positive) than Δ_{Xcalc} from local group values. This is interpreted in terms of an increased paramagnetic susceptibility anisotropy arising from the raising of the ground-state energy because of the ring strain. Although not strictly related to microwave spectroscopy, there are some papers dealing with the theory of ring-puckering vibrations which should be mentioned.

Gunthard and his co-workers discuss a new set of puckering co-ordinates for four-membered-ring molecules and also describe the exact solution of the rotation-ring-puckering problem for a cyclobutane-type four-membered ring by infinite matrix diagonalisation while Malloy proposes a semi-rigid model for the ring-puckering vibration in some pseudo-four-membered-ring molecules such as cyclopentene.

Five-membered rings

Fulvene (37), the non-alternant isomer of benzene, is of some theoretical interest and a detailed molecular geometry is therefore important as a basis for calculations. A complete and precise geometry is reported by Baron, Brown, Burden, Domaille, and Kent from the microwave spectra of seven different isotopic species, viz. the normal species and the[1-^{13}C], [2-^{13}C] and [6-^{13}C]-, [2-^{2}H]-, and [3-^{2}H] species. The [^{13}C] species were detected in natural abundance whereas the deuterio-species were synthesized. Rotational constants were derived from a rigid-rotor analysis with some attention given to ensure satisfactory determination of *A*.

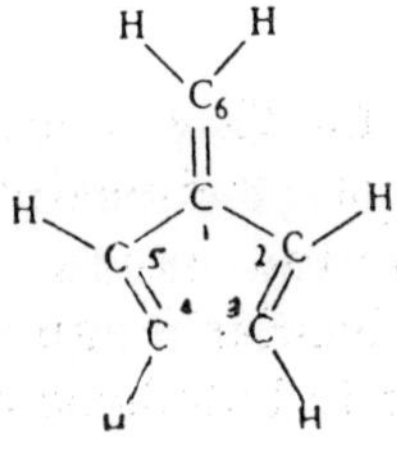

As required, the [1-^{13}C]- and [6-^{13}C]-species leave *A* essentially invariant and all species exhibit a small positive inertia defect (in the range 0.005—0.01 a.m.u. Å^2). $r_{B,}$ Co-ordinates have been determined for all atoms with the exception of the small a co-ordinate of C(2) and C(5) and the co-ordinates of H(6), which are derived from simultaneous solution of the moment of inertia and first-moment conditions using all other r_B co-ordinates.

The essentially r_B structure reported is in Table 3.

Table 3

Bond length/Å and bond angles/°of fulvene

r[C(1)—C(6)	1.3485 ± 0.0005
r[C(1)—C(2) = r[C(1)—C(5)	1.470 ± 0.0001
r[C(2)—C(3) = r[C(1)—C(5)	1.355± 0.001
r[C(3)—C(4)	1.476 ± 0.002
r[C(2)—H(2) = r[C(1)—C(5)	1.078 ± 0.001
r[C(3)—H(3) = r[C(1)—C(4)	1.080 ± 0.001
r[C(6)—H(6)	1.13 ± 0.02
r[C(2)C(1) C(5)	106.62 ± 0.12
C(1)C(2)C(3) = C(1)C(5)C(4)	107.71 ± 0.13
C(1)C(2)H(2) = C(1)C(5)H(5)	124.66 ± 0.15
C(2)C(3)H(3) = C(5)C(4)H(4)	126.39 ± 0.18
H(6)C(6)H(6)	

It is interesting that the C—C bond lengths are g almost identical with those of 6,6'-dimethylfulvene derived from an electron-diffraction study and also that the C(2)C(3)H(4)C(5) molecular fragment bond lengths are very similar to those in butadiene and cyclopentadiene.

The very precisely measured dipole moment of fulvene is 0.4236 ± 0.0013 D. Methylenecyclopentane (38) is conformationally very similar to cyclopentanone and not, as reported in an i.r. study, significantly more rigid.

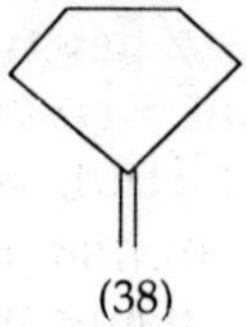

(38)

The microwave spectrum of (38) is of the effective rigid-rotor type exhibiting one strong satellite progression, assigned to successive excited states of the ring-bending mode (v_B), and another weaker satellite, assigned to the first excited state of the ring-twisting mode (v_T).

The two modes appear to be quite independent, with an essentially harmonic v_B indicated by almost linear dependence of the rotational constants of the associated satellite series on the corresponding quantum number. The previous i.r. study was unable to decide between the possibilities of 68 cm^{-1} and 158 cm^{-1} for the $1 \leftarrow 0$ energy separation in the bending mode, but microwave relative-intensity measurements give 63 ± 10 cm-1 and 270 cm^{-1} respectively for the bending and twisting modes, so that the first of the i.r. values must be chosen.

The measured dipole moment components $\mu_a = 0.60 \pm 0.01$ and $\mu_c = 0.0 \pm 0.06$ D, and the fact that the rotational constants of methylenecyclopentane are closely reproduced when the twisted ring atom structure from cyclopentanone and the methylene structure from 2-methyl-propene are assumed point to a permanently twisted ring, as does the closely similar behaviour of v_B and v_T in methylenecyclopentane and cyclopentanone. Some conclusions from microwave spectroscopy about the electronic properties of furan (39), thiophen (40), and selenophen (41) are of interest.

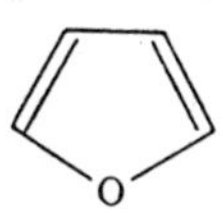

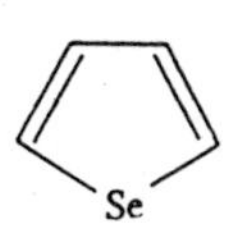

Rotational Zeeman studies of [2,5-^{2}]H_2]furan and selenophen give rise to molecular *g*-values, molecular magnetic susceptibility anisotropies ($2X_{aa}—X_{bb}—X_{cc}$ and $2X_{bb}—X_{cc}—X_{aa}$), diagonal elements of the electric quadrupole moment tensor(Q_{aa}, Q_{bb}, Q_{cc}) and several other valuable molecular properties. The change of *g*-values and rotational constants of furan on deuteriation can be used to determine the sign of the dipole moment and, although there is an unhappy near-compensation in the two changes, it is tentatively concluded that the negative end of the dipole points at the oxygen atom.

The out-of-plane minus the average in-plane magnetic susceptibility, $\Delta_X = X_{cc}—½(X_{aa}—X_{bb})$as a criterion of aromaticity has been reviewed previously. Exhaltation of the experimentally determined Δ_X over the sums of assigned group or atom Δ_X values is taken as evidence of a ring current. Since local atomic Δ_X values for S, Se, and O are not very different, the change in observed Δ_X from +38.7 through —50.1 to —51.0 for furan, thiophen, and selenophen points to aromaticities of the order furan < thiophen selenophen.

3-Methylthiophen exhibits a fairly low barrier to internal rotation of the methyl group (V_3 = 740 cal mol^{-1}), as calculated from appreciable *A-E* splittings of transitions in the vibrational ground state using Herschbach's theory and the methyl-group moment of inertia 1, = 3.19 a.m.u. A^2. This barrier is to be compared with 1088 cal mol^{-1} in 3-methylfuran. There is possibly a connection between the increased aromaticity and the decrease of V_3 for the 3-methyl compound in passing from furan to thiophen.

The same authors also report the dipole moments p = 0.55 0.01 D for thiophen and μ_a = 0.92 ± 0.03, μ_b = 0.12 and μ_{total} 0.95 ± 0.06 D for 3-methylthiophen, which are to be compared with μ_{total} = 0.55 ± 0.04 and 0.82 D respectively from dielectric constant measurements.

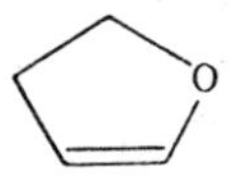

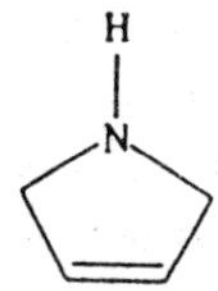

Conflicting interpretations of the ring-puckering mode of 2,3-dihydrofuran (42) have been neatly adjudicated by Durig, Li and Tong from the microwave spectrum. According to their interpretation of difference bands in the mid-i.r. spectrum, Ueda and Shimanouchi report 16.58, 65.33, and 44.52 cm^{-1} for the fundamental and first two hot bands of the ring-puckering mode whereas Green *39 assigns the frequencies 19.1, 88.5, and 84.2 cm^{-1} to these bands in the far-i.r. spectrum, although both groups evolve the same barrier height for the ring inversion.

Durig et. al. observe a satellite series in the microwave spectrum which they attribute to the first five excited states of the ring-puckering mode. The spacing of the v = 2 state satellite (assigned via its relative intensity) is obviously irregular. The effect is reflected in the distinct kink at the $v = 2$ state shown in the variation of the rotational constants with v, which indicates this state to be near the top of a barrier to ring inversion and $v = 3$, 4, and 5 to be above it. Relative-intensity measurements give 20, 85, and 86 cm^{-1} for the first three vibrational separations of the mode, amply confirming the far-i.r. assignment.

The potential function $V/cm^{-1} = 28.3(x^4 - 3.44x^2)$ (x is a reduced co-ordinate) determined from the vibrational separations gives a barrier to the planar ring of 83 cm-1. Evidently, the replacement of CH_2 by O in going from cyclopentene to 2,3-dihydrofuran reduces the unfavourable eclipsed methylene hydrogen interactions in the planar ring and reduces the barrier from 232 cm^{-1} in the former molecule. The electric dipole moment varies little with V and all values are close to those of the ground state: The microwave spectrum of another molecule isoelectronic with cyclopentene, 2,5-dihydropyrrole (43),241 has also been assigned in the vibrational ground state and the first excited state of the ring-inversion vibration. A large value of $\Delta = I^0_c —I^0_b —I^0_a$ indicates the ring to be permanently bent. Additional assignments of the rotational spectra of the ^{15}N, ^{13}C, and ^{2}H singly substituted species (the first two in natural abundance) of 1, 3, 4-oxadiazole (44) now published allow a detailed and precise molecular structure to be determined.

An analysis under high resolution of quadrupole hyperfine structure arising from the two equivalent ^{14}N nuclei leads to X_{aa} = —3.80 ± 0.01, X_{bb} = 2.02 ± 0.02 and X_{cc} = 1.78 ± 0.02 unperturbed frequencies for transitions. Moreover, ^{13}C and ^{2}H substitution allows a knowledge of the off-diagonal element, X_{ab} = 2.65 ± 0.05MHz so that necessary corrections for unresolved hyperfine structure in the [^{15N}]-species can be made through coupling constants obtained by applying the appropriate rotation to the coupling tensor of the parent. Thus a centrifugal distortion analysis of unperturbed transition frequencies of all isotopic species is possible to give precise rotational constants leading to the following structure: r(C—O) = 1.348, r(C—N) = 1.297, r(N—N) = 1.399, and r(C—H= 1.075 Å, COC = 102.0, OCN = 113. CNN= 105.6, OCH = 118. 1, NCH = 128.5°.Uncertainties are less than 0.001 A and 0.1.

Although the absence of substitution at 0 requires that its co-ordinate be determined using r_B. co-ordinates of all other atoms in $\Sigma_i m_i a_i$, the reported structure is effectively of the r_e type. Through a comparison of ring bond lengths with those in similar positions in furan (I), 1, 2, 5-oxadiazole (II), 1, 3, 4-thiadiazole (III), thiophen (IV), and 1,2,5-thiadiazole (V), the authors suggest orders of electron delocalisation in these molecules relative to cyclopentadiene and benzene as: cyclopentadiene < (I) < 1, 3, 4-oxadiazole (II) for oxygen compounds and (III) <(IV) < (V) <benzene for sulphur rings.

A microwave study of ethylene ozonide (45) (1, 2, 4-trioxacyclopentane) has been undertaken to elucidate the mechanism of ozonolysis of ethylene from isotopic labelling. As part of the study, Gillies and Kuczkowski report a detailed structure from isotopic substitution. The μ_b spectrum of the parent molecule exhibits statistical-weight effects consistent with the 5:3 ratio of intensities expected for transitions originating in symmetric states to those from antisymmetrical states (all other intensity factors having been accounted for) if the molecule has a C_2 axis.

Moreover, the increase in $P_{cc} = ½(I_a + I_b — I_c)$ on ^{13}C substitution shows that the carbon atoms do not lie in a symmetry plane and, taken together with the above-mentioned nuclear spin statistics, establishes a C_2 point group for the molecule. Such symmetry is consistent with the observed two conformers of the monodeuteriated species HD_BCOOCH_2O and HD_ACOOCH_2O and of the trans dideuteriated species ($HD_AOOCHDAO$ and $HD_BCOOCHD_BO$). The ring is bent in a half-chair configuration with the peroxy-oxygen atoms (O_p) twisted considerably from the CO_eC plane.

The observation of three successive, well-behaved satellites associated with v = 0-3 of the ring-bending vibration (confirmed by the correct nuclear spin statistics) sets a lower limit of 500-600 cm $^{-1}$ on the barrier to pseudorotation in this ring. A value of 1.09 0.01 D is reported for the dipole moment ($\mu_b = \mu_{total}$).

Table 4

Structural parameters of ethylene ozonide

Bond lengths/Å	*Bond angles/°*	*Dihedral angles/°*
C—H_A 1.096± 0.005	COC 102.83 ± 0.44	$C_1O_eC_2O_p$ = −16.60 ± 0.40
C—H_B 1.094 ± 0.00	COO 99.23 ± 0.38	$C_1O_pO_pC_2$ = −50.24 ± 1.26
C—Op 1.395 ± 0.006	OCO 106.25 ± 0.64	OeCOpOp =41.27 ± 0.96
C—O_e 1.436 ± 0.006	HCH 112.93 ± 0.48	$C_1O_eC_2H_A$=−132.09 ± 0.50
O_p—O_p 1.470 ± 0.015	O_eCH_A 109.43 ± 0.34	$C_1O_eC_2H_B$= 103.90 ± 0.98
O_p—O_p 1.470± 0.015	O_eCH_A 109.43 ± 0.34	$C_1O_eC_2H_B$ = 103.90 ± 0.98
	O_eCH_B 109.08 ± 0.64	

Six-membered rings

Several papers have appeared dealing with mono-and di-substituted benzenes. Mirri and Caminati complete their investigation of the percentage double-bond character in the C—X bonds of the halogenobenzenes with the publication of accurate diagonal elements of the principal-axis quadrupole coupling tensor for the chlorine and bromine nuclei in chloro- and bromo-benzene. In order to obtain very precise values of X_{aa}, X_{bb} and X_{cc}, a small second-order correction is necessary in bromobenzene but such effects are negligible in chlorobenzene.

The asymmetry parameter $\eta = (X_{bb} = X_{cc})/X_{aa}$,

recorded with the X's for the whole family X = Cl, Br or I in Table 5, shows each C—X bond to possess cylindrical symmetry in the bond (a = z) direction while the difference in the number of electrons in the np_x and np_y orbitals ($x \perp$ plane of ring) given by $2/3\ (X_{cc}\text{-}X_{bb})/eq_{n10}Q$ indicates a small but decreasing percentage of double-bond character $2/3\ (X_{cc}—X_{bb})eq_{n10}Q$ for np_x assuming np_y in the ring plane cannot be involved in π-bonding. In the course of an analysis of the dependence of the observed rotational constants on the vibrational quantum number associated with the NO_2 torsional mode (v_{36}) of nitrobenzene using their rotation-internal-rotation theory, Ribeaud, Bauder, and Gunthard encounter an interesting difficulty.

They find that the exact solution of the rotation-internal-rotation problem consisting of a C_{2v} frame (phenyl group and nitrogen atom) and a C_{2v} rotor (two oxygen atoms) cannot explain the observed variation of the rotational constants, particularly A, with the torsional state.

However, when the rotation-internal-rotation approach is extended so that the angle ONO may vary synchronously with the torsional angle, a very satisfactory quantitative agreement for the variation of A (and B and C) is obtained. It is found that the angle ONO widens by 1.3° in going from the coplanar to the perpendicular configuration.

Such a striking improvement in the analysis makes it tempting to consider the relaxation of the ONO angle as a significant phenomenon associated with large-amplitude internal motion. The torsional motion of the CFO group against the benzene ring in benzoyl fluoride (46) is considered in a detailed study of that molecule by Kakar. Seven torsionally excited states (vibrational quantum number τ = 1–7) in a vibrational satellite series as well as the ground-state spectrum are assigned. The vibrational satellites tentatively assigned to the out-of-plane wag (168 ± 10 cm^{-1}) and the in-plane bend (215 ± 10 cm^{-1}) of the CFO group are also observed.

A planar molecular equilibrium structure is established from the inertia defect, $\Delta_0 = -0.325$ a.m.u. Å^2, which although negative becomes equal to +0.286 a.m.u. Å^2 on extrapolation to the hypothetical torsionless state, a behaviour pattern also exhibited in benzaldehyde and nitrobenzene. By use of the expression of Oka and Morino for $\Delta\tau$ the change of inertia defect with torsional state is shown simply to be $\Delta_{\tau+1} - \Delta\tau$ which for $\tau = 1$ gives the torsional separation $\omega_\tau = 55.2$ cm^{-1}.

Moreover, careful relative-intensity measurements among torsional satellites using a Hewlett Packard 8460 spectrometer give $\omega_\tau = 59.5 \pm 3$, 117 ± 7, 177 ± 10, 236 15, 295 ± 15, 354 ± 17, and 411 ± 20 cm^{-1} for the separations of the τ = 1, 2, 3, 4, 5, 6, and 7 states respectively from the ground state. This almost harmonic behaviour is consistent with the near-linear variation of the rotational constants with τ and a considered with the $\tau = 1 \leftarrow 0$ separation of 59.5 cm^{-1}, to the twofold barrier $V_2 \sim 1560 \pm 160$ cm^{-1} for the torsional motion, which value should be compared with 1175 cm^{-1} in phenol, 1350 cm^{-1} in nitrosobenzene, and 1000 ± 500 cm^{-1} in nitrobenzene.

Partial structures of some interest are reported for two disubstituted benzenes. The microwave spectrum of four isotopic species of m-fluoroaniline (47) containing the groups NH_2, *cis*-NHD, *trans*-NHD, and ND_2, are assigned by Cazzoli, Diamani, and Lister in order to characterize the amino-group structure.

The r_B co-ordinates of the amino hydrogen atoms referred to the principal axis system of both the NH_2 and the ND_2 species are calculated. The amino-group geometry is determined by assuming r(N—H) = 1.00Å as in aniline and by choosing the FC_6H_6N fragment geometry from aniline and fluorobenzene so that the moments of inertia of all isotopic species are reproduced to within 1%. The parameter of most interest is ϕ the angle between the bisector of the HNH angle and the extension of the CN bond.

The value 36.2°(based on the NH_2 species as the parent molecule) compares with 37.6° in aniline and 46.4° in p-fluoroaniline, which confirms a steeper R—NH_2 pyramid in the latter molecule and is consistent with the extra possibility of a mesomeric interaction of the nitrogen atom and the fluorine atom through the ring therein. It is of interest to compare here a closely related investigation of 2-aminopyridine (48) by Kydd and Mills. Again, four isotopic species are analysed, R-NH_2, the two R-NH_2 species, and the R—ND_2 species, to obtain r, co-ordinates of the amino-group hydrogen atoms.

The striking result is that one hydrogen atom is consistently 0.08 Å closer to the *ab* inertial plane (and therefore to the ring plane since the two planes nearly coincide) than the other, whether the NH_2 or ND_2 species is used as the parent molecule. Moreover, the same atom is closer to the *bc* plane and, although it is not known which of the two hydrogen atoms this is, it seems likely the NH_2 group is distorted so that the hydrogen nearer to the ring nitrogen lies closer to the plane.

The angle θ (defined above) is estimated to be 31.60 on the basis of some structural assumptions and the observed inertial constants, and so 2-aminopyridine has a more planar NH_2 group than has aniline, as might be expected from increased conjugation of the ring and amino-group owing to the greater electronegativity of the ring nitrogen.

The transitions in the rotational spectrum of (48) also

exhibit a strong satellite, assigned to be the 0^- component of the inversion doublet (the ground state is assigned as 01). Relative intensity measurements give 135 ± 25 and 95 ± 30 cm-1 for the separation of the 0^+—0^- inversion levels in the NH_2 and ND_2 species respectively, compared with 40 cm^{-1} in (NH_2) aniline.

From an analysis of the microwave spectra of the normal, –OD, and -$CH^{18}O$ species of salicylaldehyde (49), Jones and Curl first established coplanarity of all the atoms from the small negative inertia defects in the three species which, as discussed above, is a characteristic observation for a benzene ring in conjunction with a coplanar group capable of large torsional motions about the planar equilibrium structure. The data also allow the Kraitchman co-ordinates of the carbonyl oxygen and the phenolic proton to be located.

The distance between these atoms, which follows immediately' is 1.76 Å and is less than the sum of their van der Waals' radii. Further calculations illustrate an interesting point. A molecular model based on an X-ray diffraction structure of salicylic acid and the formaldehyde structure for the aldehyde group can only reproduce the observed moments of inertia and the Kraitchman co-ordinates of the two atoms simultaneously if the C—O bond is tilted away by 6° from the line bisecting the ring angle, as indicated in (49). Microwave spectra of *m*-chlorofluorobenzene have also been reported. The energy difference W_e between the vibrational ground states of the axial and equatorial conformers of cyclohexyl fluoride (50) as isolated molecules in the gas phase is now available.

Scharpen has measured very carefully the relative intensities of rotational transitions of the axial and equatorial forms using the partial power saturation technique described by Harrington. The precision of the measured intensity ratios was good and the error estimated from reproducibility was 1-2 %. Instrumental uncertainties and reported errors in the measured dipole moment values contribute more heavily so that the result is quoted as W_c= 259 ± 28 cal mol^{-1}. This is in excellent agreement with free-energy differences measured from ^{1}H and ^{19}F n.m.r. studies in solution as 276 ± 15 and 248 ± 12 cal mol^{-1} respectively. (The differences in rotational and vibrational partition functions between the conformers necessary to convert W_c to a free-energy difference are estimated to have little net effect on the numerical value.) Four papers concerning halogenopyridines are published. Sharma and Doraiswamy discuss the detailed determination of rotational and centrifugal distortion constants for 2-fluoropyridine Scappini and Guarnieri report rotational constants and X_{aa} X_{bb} and X_{cc} values for the ^{35}Cl nucleus in 2–[^{35}Cl] chloropyridine (51).

Some assignment difficulties are solved using the RFMDR technique in which radiofrequency transitions such as $2_{20} \leftarrow 2_{21} 3_{30} \leftarrow 2_{21}$ are strongly pumped and μ_a microwave transitions such as $3_{31} \leftarrow 2_{20}$ and $3_{30} \leftarrow 2_{21}$ are observed. A planar structure is dictated by the inertia defect Δ = 0.0385 a.m.u. Å^2 and the values r(C-C) = 1.72 ± 0.01 A and NCCl = 116°25' ± 10' are derived by fitting the rotational constants after the pyridine structure is assumed. The near coincidence of the a-axis and the C—Cl bond axis allows the X_{aa} X_{bb} and X_{cc}. values for the ^{35}C1 nucleus to be used in the usual way to determine the asymmetry parameter η and the degree of double-bond character δ for the carbon-chlorine bond (in the manner and with the definitions of η and δ given in connection with 1-halogenobenzenes earlier in this section).

The results are compared in Table 5 with those from a similar study of 2-bromopyridine and 4-bromopyridine

(52) by Caminati and Forti. The C—X bond characteristics appear to be very similar in this family of molecules.

Table 5

Coupling constants/MHz and C-X double bond character halogenopyridines

	2-[^{35}Cl]Chloro pyridine	2-[^{79}Br]Bromo pyridine	4- [^{79}Br]Bromo pyridine
X_{aa}	−70.79 ± 0.17	552.2 ± 1.2	557.5 ± 1.3
X_{bb}	39.01 ± 0.45	−304.4 ± 0.004	−0.078± 0.005
η	−0.10 ± 0.01	−0.102 ± 0.004	− 0.078 ± 0.005
δ	4%	4.77%	3.58%

Phosphabenzene (53), the phosphorus analogue of pyridine, exhibits only a μ_a rotational spectrum. The derived inertial constants lead to the inertia defect $\Delta = 0.0522$ a.m.u. Å^2 , a value consistent with the expected molecular planarity. Moreover, a planar molecule with a C_2 axis about which rotation exchanges two pairs of equivalent protons is indicated by an observed 10:6 intensity alternation between contiguous transition pairs such as 6_{06}—7_{17} and 6_{16}—7_{07} in the vibrational ground state.

Although a complete structure determination is not currently possible, the ranges for the parameters of interest [r(C—P) = 1.70—1.73 Å and C(5)PC(1) = 101—104°] have been established from the inertial data with the following assumptions guided by X-ray studies of substituted phosphabenzenes: r(C—H) = 1.08 Å,C(2)PC(3) C(4) = 122°, C(1)PC(2)C(3) the C—H bond bisects the corresponding ring angle, and the C—C bonds are restricted to the range 1.40—1.44Å (cf. 1.397 Å in benzene). Thus, the P—C bond length is intermediate between the single-bond length (1.843 Å) in trimethylphosphine) and the double-bond length (1.66 Å in $Ph_3P{=}CH_2$) as might be expected.

The two most intense vibrational satellites in phosphabenzene correspond to vibration modes of 290 ± 40 and 325 ± 40 cm^{-1} according to relative intensity measurements and have been assigned to v_{16b} (B_2) and v_{16a}(A_2) respectively by analogy with the lowest two modes of pyridine, correct behaviour of the inertia defect, and correct nuclear statistical weight patterns. The dipole moment of phosphabenzene is 1.54 ± 0.02 D. The microwave spectrum of a single conformer of 1,3-dioxan is assigned by Kewley.

The observation from Stark-effect measurements of a value of μ_a very close to zero(μ_a <0.06 ± 0.1, μ_b = 1.61 ± 0.02, μ_c = 1.29 ± 0.01. and μ_{total} = 2.06 ± 0.03 D)rules out the boat form (55) or any twisted form since these require non-zero values of all three components. Further arguments based on reasonable models, the observed moments of inertia, and the dipole moment components militate in favour of the chair form (54) and against the other boat form (56) or a half-chair or a flattenea chair form.

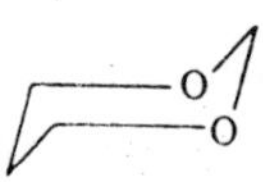
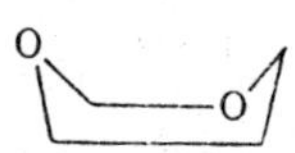
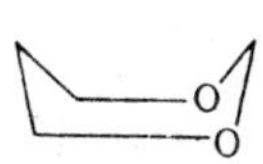

Several vibrational satellites are identified and their intensities relative to the ground-state transitions measured to give values 257 ± 25, 290 ± 25, 432 ± 50,439 ± 50, and 472 ± 50 cml for the five lowest modes of vibration in the molecule.

Fused rings

The rotational spectra of bicyclic and tricyclic systems have recently evoked an increased interest. The small bicyclic hydrocarbon bicyclo[2, 1, 0]pentane (57) is investigated thoroughly by Suenram and Harmony.

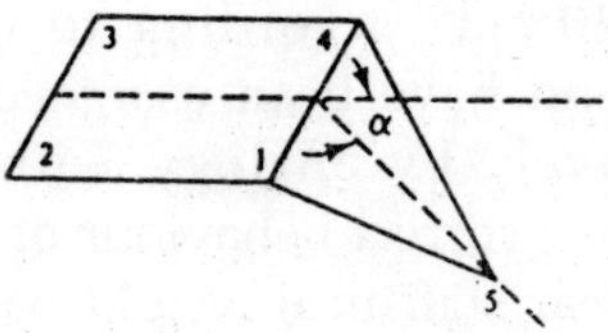

A noteworthy feature of this work is that it has been possible, through a long and skilful synthesis, to produce an isotopic mixture of composition 10% [1-^{13}C]-, 10% [2-$^{13}{}_{C}$]-, 5% [5-1^{3C}]-, and 75 %P_2C1-bicyclo[2, 1, 0]pentane starting only with barium carbonate of 60 % ^{13}C enrichment. Another feature is the use of a computer-controlled spectrometer with signal averaging and storage as an aid in the search and measurement of some of the weaker ^{13}C transitions.

The two cbservations of significance are that only c-type transitions can be observed and that substitution in the 5-position leaves $I_a + I_c - I_b$ invariant. Thus the molecule has a plane of symmetry (*ac* plane) with the *a*-component of the dipole moment presumably too small to allow observable μ_a-transitions. The isotopic distribution in the synthesis product is in accord with a plane of symmetry. The r_B structure of the carbon skeleton reported is:

r[C(l)-C(4)] = 1.536 ± 0.001Å, r[C2)-C(3)j = 1.565 ± 0.001Å

r[C(l)-C(2)] = r[C(3)--Q4)3 = 1.528 ± 0.002Å, r[C(1—C(5) =

r[C(4)-C(5)] = 1.507 ± 0.002Å, and a = 67.26 ± 0.180

The planar cyclobutane ring entity thus has three C—C bonds shorter than 1.548 A in cyclobutane and one longer. It is pointed out that Σr(C—C) for cyclobutane rings in several bicyclic compounds is sensibly constant so that in a given environment any necessary bond shortening (or lengthening) must apparently be accompanied by a corresponding lengthening (or shortening) elsewhere in the ring.

The skeletal structure of bicyclo[2,1,0]pentane is in fact in serious disagreement with a recent electron-diffraction study but an analysis of the radial distribution function by Suenram and Harmony leads them to propose that a false local minimum has been found in the original least-squares fit. The dipole moment components are μ_a = 0.00 ± 0.01 D, μ_b and μ_c = 0.26 ± 0.01D. Some information about the electronic charge distribution in bicyclobutane (58) is obtained from a high-field molecular Zeeman study of rotational transitions in this molecule by Gierke, Benson, and Flygare.

They derive molecular g-values (g_{aa} = 0.0593 ± 0.0002, g_{bb} = 0.0025 ± 0.0002 and g_{cc} = 0.0412± 0.0002), the molecular magnetic susceptibility anisotropies ($2X_{aa}$ — X_{bb}—X_{cc} = —5.9 ± 0.3 and $2X_{bb}$— X_{aa} —X_{cc} = 21.1 ± 0.3 in units of 10–13 J G^{-2} mol^{-1})and molecular electric quadrupole moments (Q_{aa} = 1.3 ± 0.2, Q_{bb} = –2.6 ± ± 0.3, and Q_{cc} = 1.3 ± 0.4 in units of 10-26 e.s.u. cm^2). Arguing from the various contributions to the g-values, these authors interpret the positive g-values as indicating the electrons in bicyclobutane to be nearer the centre of mass than the nuclei, i.e. there exists a concentration of electronic charge beneath the bridgehead. Such a charge distribution is consistent with both the enhanced reactivity of the bridgehead bond and the observation that electrophilic attack occurs from beneath the bridgehead.

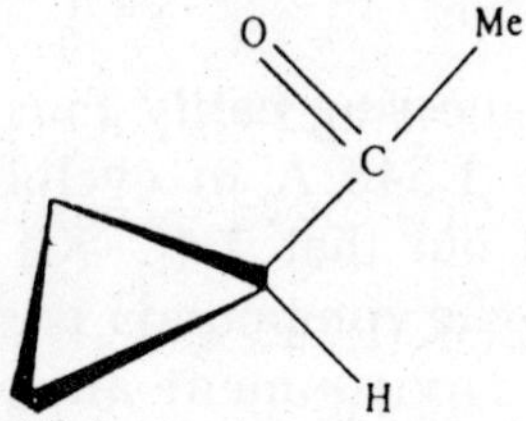

Following his work with bicyclo [2,1,1] hexan-2-one, Coffey now reports the rotational constants and dipole moment of the isomeric bicylo [2, 1, 1] - hexan-5-one (59). The interesting conclusion is that the dipole moment μ_{total} = 3.18 ± 0.02 D, which is estimated to make an angle of only 1.7 ± 1.70 with the C=O bond direction, is anomalously high and similar in this respect to those of cyclopentanone and bicyclo[2,1,1] hexan-2-one. This confirms the author in his opinion that such molecules containing a cyclopentanone entity have anomalously high dipole moments compared with most carbonyl compounds.

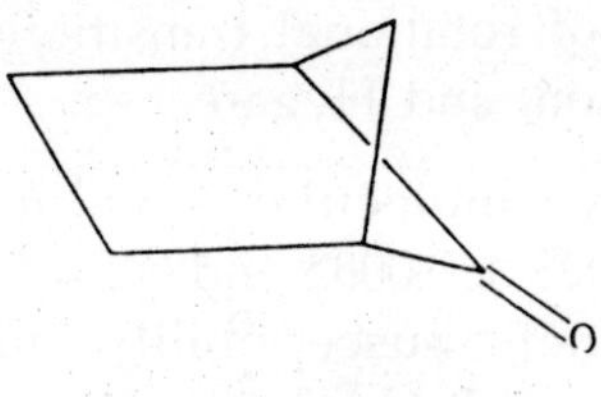

(59)

The large number of independent structural Parameters of cyclohexene oxide make a detailed deter-mination from microwave spectroscopy a formidable task. However, Ikeda, Kewley, and Curl are able to use the ground-state rotational constants of the common isotopic species to establish a twisted carbon atom skeleton for the molecule. Their assumptions, based on previous studies of cyclohexene oxide and related molecules, are as follows:

(a) r[C(1) —C(4)] = 1.536 ± 0.001Å, r[C(2)—C(3) = 1.565 ± 0.001Å

r[C(1) —C(6)] = 1.48 and r[C(1) — O] = 1.42Å

(b) atoms C(5) C(6) C(1) C(2) are coplanar:

(c) C(5)C(6)C(1) = C(6)C(1)C(2), C(4)C(5)C(6) = C(1)C(2)C(3)

C(5)C(4)C(3) = C(2)C(3)C(4);

(d) C(6)C(1)C(2) = 122°

(e) standard hydrogen parameters, to which the reported conclusions are insensitive.

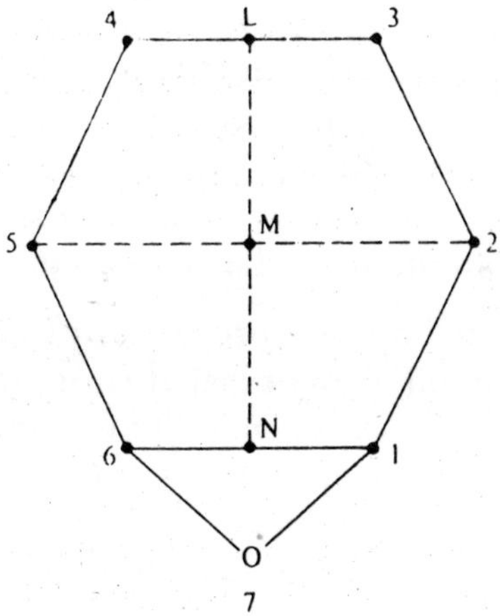

Fig. 1.

The remaining skeletal parameters are the angle β = 180°— LMN, the twist angle τ between C(2)—C(5) and C(3)—C(4), and the, dihedral angle θ between the epoxy-ring and the C(5)C(6)C(1)C(2) plane. In view of a probable C_2 symmetry for the carbon ring (β = 0), the rotational constants are fitted to τ and θ for several β values near to zero. The fit is best with β so near to zero that it is assumed to be identically so, in which case τ = 34°26' and θ = 68°23'.

The results of an electron-diffraction study are close [β = 0 (assumed), τ = 33°26', and θ = 75°34') while θ is similar to the values near to 75° reported for cis-2,3-epoxybutane and propene oxide. The twisted ring is consistent with indications of a high barrier to inversion of the ring by twisting, as inferred from the twisting-mode frequency of 280 cm^{-1} from satellite relative intensities and the liquid-phase i.r. spectrum.

The dipole moment components are μ_a = 0.18± 0.08 , μ_c = 1.52 ± 0.01 and μ_{total} = 1.91± 0.02D. Christen, Bauder, and Gunthard have returned to the study of azulene (60). They analyse exhaustively and with high sensitivity the rotational spectrum in the ground state and six vibrationally excited states (v_{23} = 1, v_{23} = 2, v_{48} = 1, v_{48} =2, v_{23} + v_{48}, and v_{47} = 1) and with a centrifugal distortion treatment appropriate to a planar molecule.

In addition, by a careful application of the Harrington partial power saturation technique for relative-intensity measurements, these authors determine the 1←0 vibrational separations for the three lowest vibrational modes of azulene, v_{48} (B_2), v_{23} (A_2), and v_{47} (B_2), to be 180.3 ± 1.9, 188.0 ± 2.4, and 272.7 ± 5.0 cm-1 respectively. Their measurements exhibit an excellent internal consistency.

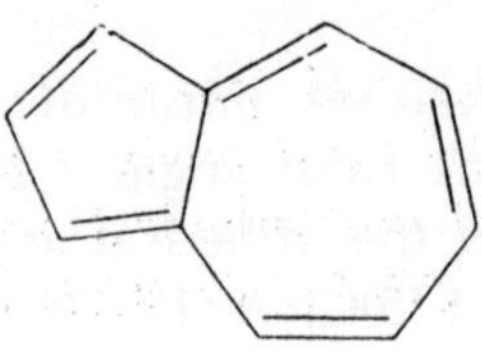

Assignment of the satellites to a particular mode is aided by nuclear-spin statistical-weight considerations, for the weight ratio between the ground and first excited states of B_1 or B_2 species modes for the planar molecule in which three pairs of equivalent hydrogen nuclei are exchanged by a C_2 rotation is 9/7 for rotational transitions originating in states with K_{-1} even and 7/9 for those with K_{-1} odd.

On the other hand, no change is expected between the ground state and excited states of A_1 or A_2 modes. This work settles the assignment problem in the far-i.r. spectrum of a single crystal of the compound, wherein four absorption bands at 275 (vw), 189, 180, and 170 cm^{-1} respectively were observed but the assignment of the v_{48}, v_{23} and v_{47} modes could not be made.

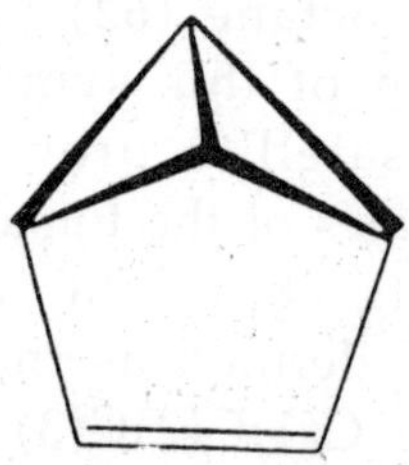

A preliminary analysis of benzvalene (61) (tricyclo[3,1,0,02,6]hex-3-ene), has also appeared. Suenram and Harmony report rotational constants and the dipole moment $\mu = \mu_a = 0.883$ D, which are consistent with a molecular model formed by combination of bicyclobutane (58) and cyclobutene fragments. In particular, the sum of the dipole moments of bicyclobutane (0.68 D) and cyclobutene (0.139 D) gives a value in good agreement with that observed for (61). If the unsaturated end of the cyclobutene fragment defines the negative end of the dipole, the negative end of the bicyclobutane fragment lies beneath the bridgehead bonds, in agreement with conclusions from the Zeeman work on bicyclobutane already mentioned.

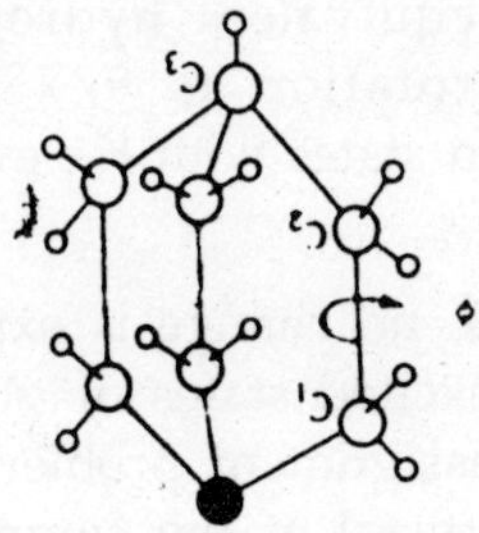

Hirota and Suenaga have extended their treatment of the 1-halogenobicyclo [2,2,2] octanes to include 1-azabicyclo[2,2,2] octane (62) (quinuclidine). Each rotational transition of this symmetric-top molecule exhibits a strong satellite progression assigned to successive excited states of the torsional motion in which the molecule twists about the symmetry axis [the torsional angle ϕ is defined as the angle between the NC(1)C(2) and the C(1)C(2)C(3) planes]. Irregular spacing between the v = 0, 1, and 2 members of the progression is attributed to the existence of a shallow double-minimum potential function governing the torsional motion and therefore indicates an equilibrium structure of C_3 symmetry in which the C(l) and C(2) methylene groups are twisted away from the energetically unfavourable eclipsed configuration appropriate to the C_{3v} structure.

The satellite irregularity is attenuated relative to that of the 1-halogenobicyclo [2,2,2]octanes, suggesting a lower barrier at the C_{3v} structure in the present case. The quantitative variation of rotational constants with the torsional quantum number can be fitted by a potential function of the form

$$V(\phi) = -V^2\phi^2 + V_4\phi^4 + V_6\phi^6$$

to give the height of the barrier to the C_3, molecule $V_0 = 39 \pm 15$ cal mol^{-1} and the equilibrium torsional angle $\phi_0 = 10.7 \pm 1.7°$. The corresponding values for 1-fluorobicyclo[2,2,2]octane, 191 ± 52 cal mol^{-1} and 16.4 ± 1.6°, indicate that the equilibrium structure is nearer to C3 symmetry in 1-azabicyclo[2,2,2]octane. Evidence of a differential distortion of the cage structure in 1-fluoroadamantane relative to other 1-substituted adamantanes (63; X= Cl Br, I, or CN) is suggested in a recent publication. From the symmetric-top rotational spectra of the $[^{12}C^{14}N]^-$,$[^{13}C^{14}N]^-$, and $[^{12}C^{15}N]$– isotopic species of 1-cyanoadamantane (63; X=CN) it is straightforward to derive r_B co-ordinates of the C and N atoms and therefore to subtract the contribution of these atoms from the parent-molecule moment of inertia, I_b, to give the moment of inertia of the adamantyl radical referred to the molecular principal axis system.

Further, the application of the parallel axis theorem generates I^*_{rad}, the moment of inertia of the radical referred to its own principal axis system. Such a procedure when also applied in the cases X = Cl or Br leads to I^*_{rad} values invariant for X = Cl, Br, or CN, suggesting an adamantyl cage structure sensibly independent of the nature of the 1-substituent.

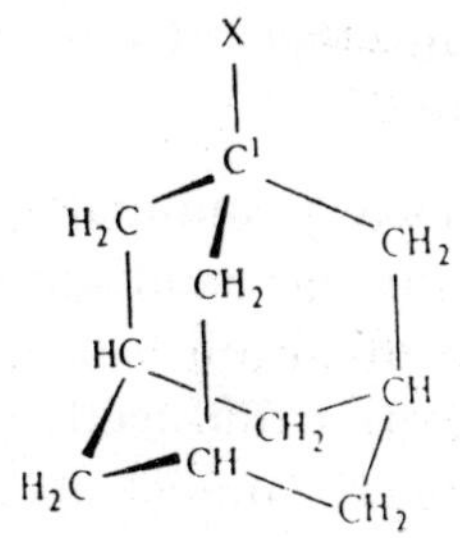

Accordingly, to proceed further it seems reasonable to assume a cage with all C—C bond distances equal, all angles 109Å^{2} and all C—H distances at 1.09Å, as in adamantane itself. Then, the experimental I_{rad} values lead to 1.541 ± 0.001, 1.542 ± 0.002, and 1.543 + 0.002 Å for the C—C distance in the cases X = Cl, Br, and CN respectively. The C—X distances simultaneously generated are shown in Table 6 compared with those of the corresponding methyl, ethyl, and t-butyl compounds .

Table 6

Comparison of r(C—X)/Å in adamantyl, methyl, ethyl, and t-butyl compounds

	Methyl	*Ethyl*	*t-Butyl*	*Adamantyl*
F	1.385 ± 0.001	1.398 ± 0.005	1.43 ± 0.02	1.370± 0.004
Cl	1,781 ± 0.002	1.788± 0.002	1.803 ± 0.002	1.790 ± 0.002
Br	1.939± 0.001	1.950 ± 0.004	1.98	1.947± 0.006
I	2.39	2.139 ± 0.005	2.19	2.160 ± 0.002
CN	1.458± 0.001	1.473± 0.002	1.496 ± 0.015	1.466 ± 0.003

Unfortunately, the absence of stable isotopes other than ^{19}F and ^{127}I precludes extension of the procedure to X = F or I. However, assuming the cage structure as in the 1-chloro-compound the *r*(C-F) and *r*(C-I) values shown in Table 6 are obtained. We note that, for all cases but X = F, the adamantyl *r*(C—X) values agree closely with the ethyl values.

The C—F distance is anomalously short, suggesting that in the case of the electronegative fluorine atom the assumption of cage invariance is invalid. As a simple model for the distortion induced by the fluorine atom, the bridgehead CC(1)C angles are allowed to vary by moving the C(l) atom along the molecular symmetry axis while the positions of all other atoms are unchanged. A value of *r*(C—F) in 1-fluoroadamantane equal to that in ethyl fluoride can then be obtained if the bridgehead CC(1)C angles are increased by relative to those in the chloride.(64) shows the structure of beryllium chloride molecule. The symmetric-top nature of the rotational spectrum of the parent and ^{37}Cl species is consistent with a structure of C_5, symmetry.

Moreover, the regular variation of a vibrational satellite series associated with successive quanta of the clopentadienyl-ring-beryllium-chlorine bend indicates that the vibration is quite harmonic with no potential barrier at the fivefold symmetry axis.

The structural parameters recorded in Table 7 are of the r_0 variety and reproduce all observed rotational constants better than 0. 1%. Table 7 shows the result of an electron-diffraction investigation of the cyclopentadienylberyllium chloride structure.

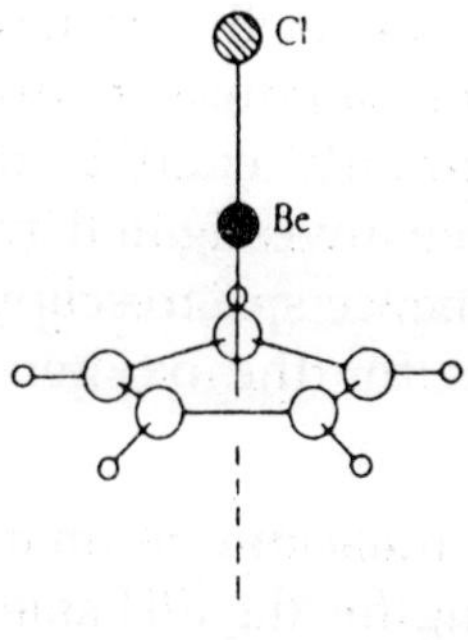

The agreement between the two techniques is excellent. The Be-Cl bond is longer than in $BeCl_2$. Moreover, the dipole moment, 4.25 ± 0.16 D, is high and the ^{35}Cl nuclear quadrupole coupling constant, eqQ = 22 ± 2 MHz, is low. All this is evidence for an ionic Be-Cl bond. The spectra of a number of diatomic molecules have been studied by one or more of various techniques, viz. microwave spectroscopy, gasphase electron paramagnetic resonance, molecular-beam electric resonance spectroscopy, laser magnetic resonance, and the use of pure rotational lasers.

Table 7

Structural parameters of cyclopentadienylberyllium chloride/Å

	Microwave r_0	Electron diffraction r_g
C—H	1.090	1.097
C—C	1.424	1.424
Be—Cl	1.839	1.837
Be-ring(h)	1.485	1.484
Cl...C	3.538	3.535

The microwave spectrum of the BrO radical has been further examined and transitions have been measured for the first excited vibrational state of the III, ground electronic state. The results have been combined with results of a re-analysis of the ground vibrational state to give the equilibrium internuclear distance r_e = 1.717(l) ± 0.0013 Å. Vibrationally excited states of the oxygen molecule have been investigated by gas-phase electron paramagnetic resonance spectroscopy Is and an improved set of parameters for the oxygen molecule has been obtained.

Molecular-beam electric resonance studies have been made of Λ-doubling for the $a^3\Pi$ state for CO and the $2\Pi_{1/2}$ and $2\Pi_{1/2}$ states of NO. Hyperfine structure has been measured for NO and it is shown how it may be accounted for theoretically. For CO, Λ-doubling has been observed for a number of transitions with v = 0—5.

The vibrational dependence of the Λ-doubling is accounted for and it is shown that the v = 4 and v = 5 states are perturbed by the v = 0 and v = 1 states of the

$a'\Sigma^+$ electronic state. The analysis leads to a number of molecular parameters, including information about dipole moments. The dipole moment of the $a^3\Pi$ state is obtained as function of v and J. For the $a'\Sigma^+$ state it is found that $\mu = 1.06 \pm 0.2$ D and that the sign is —CO+ whereas for the $^3\Pi$ state $\mu = 1.37$ D and the sign is +CO—.

The NF species in the $^1\Delta$ state has been studied by electron paramagnetic resonance spectroscopy. Hyperfine coupling constants of the ^{14}N and ^{19}F nuclei have been determined and the dipole moment is found to be 0.37 ± 0.06 D. A further study of SH by the paramagnetic resonance technique has led to information about the second rotational state, $J = 5/2$, and molecular parameters have been obtained from the analysis of the spectrum. For OH and OD pure rotational laser oscillations have been observed. A total of 44 lines have been measured for OH and 17 for OD in the region 500-800 cm^{-1}.

Accurate values of rotational and centrifugal distortion constants have been obtained. A Stark-modulated spectrometer for the study of free radicals has been described. The cell consists of a Pyrex tube containing plane-parallel Stark electrodes which are covered with Teflon to reduce recombination. Transitions with the spectrometer have been observed for NS, SO, and OH.

Chapter 3

Molecular Electronic Structure

Quantum mechanics has made it possible to understand the nature of chemical bonding and to predict the structures and properties of simple molecules. Our ideas about covalent bonds go back to 1916, when Lewis described the sharing of electron pairs between atoms. The pairs of electrons held jointly by two atoms were considered to be effective in completing a stable electronic con figuration for each atom, This approach provided only a qualitative picture of chemical bonding.

The first successful quantum mechanical explanation of a chemical bond, specifically that in molecular hydrogen, was made in 1927 by Heitler and London using the valence bond method. Since then the molecular orbital method has become the method of choice, and so it is emphasized in this chapter, Today the electronic structure, energy levels, bond angles, bond distances, dipole moments, and spectra of simple molecules may be calculated with a high degree of accuracy. For molecules with more than one electron, approximations have to be introduced. However, even approximate calculations are very helpful in understanding molecular structure, chemical properties, and molecular spectra.

Born-Oppenheimer approximation

The Schrodinger equation for a molecule is

$$H\psi(r, R) = E\psi(r, R) \qquad (1)$$

where the wavefunction depends on the coordinates of' all the electrons (represented by *r*) and the coordinates of all the nuclei (represented by R), The Solution of this equation is not known even for the simplest molecules: however, there is an approximation, introduced by Born and Oppenheimer, which gives a very good description of the solutions.

The approximation is based on the fact that the nuclei are thousands of times more massive than the electrons, but the forces on each are equal. Thus, to a very good approximation, the nuclei can be treated as stationary when considering the electronic motion, and the nuclei can be considered to move in the average electronic configuration. To implement the approximation for the electronic motion, we simply neglect the nuclear kinetic energy. To simply the discussion, we consider the hydrogen molecule ion, H_2^+, which has two protons at a separation R and one electron.

Notice that the latter term is a constant since the inter nuclear distance R is fixed. We can solve this equation for all R, giving us the electronic energy $E(R)$ as a function of R. Actually there will be many solutions of this equation at each value of R, corresponding to different electronic states. The lowest energy electronic state is called the ground state and the higher energy states are called excited states.

For other diatomic molecules with more electrons, the electronic Hamiltonian will contain terms similar to those in equation 2, but will include, in addition, electron-electron electrostatic repulsion. At large R, the molecule dissociates into atoms. For bound electronic states the electronic energy is lowered as R decreases until it reaches R_e, the equilibrium inter nuclear distance. As R gets still smaller, the inter-nuclear repulsions and electron-electron repulsions become very large and the energy rises rapidly.

The other aspect of the Born-Oppenheimer approximation is the approximate Schrodinger equation for the nuclear motion. Since the nuclei feel the average electronic configuration at each R the electronic energy $E(R)$ becomes the potential energy for the nuclear motion and the Schrodinger. Since the electronic energy as a function of R, $E(R)$, is the potential energy for nuclear motion, we often call $E(R)$ simply the potential energy curve or potential energy for short, But we should remember that it is the total electronic energy at that inter-nuclear separation.

Dissociation energies of diatomic molecules

As the atoms of a stable diatomic molecule are slowly brought toward each other from an infinite distance, there is a mutual attraction and a reduction in the electronic energy of the molecule. Then the energy goes through a minimum and rises rather steeply. The equilibrium inter-nuclear distance R, corresponds with the minimum in the energy curve. At this distance attraction and repulsion are balanced.

The depth of the energy minimum with respect to the energy at infinite separation is referred to as the equilibrium dissociation energy D_e, or the well depth. This is the dissociation energy that is obtained most directly from the solutions of the Schrodinger equation for a diatomic molecule, but we must be careful to distinguish it from the spectroscopic dissociation energy D_0.

The spectroscopic dissociation energy D_0 is the energy required to dissociate a molecule in its ground vibrational state into two atoms. A diatomic molecule can exist in one of a series of vibrational energy levels, of which only the ground state. In accordance with the Heisenberg uncertainty principle, a vibrating diatomic molecule has this zero-point energy, even in the lowest state. If the vibrational motion were that of a harmonic oscillator, the energy would be $\omega_e/2$, the energy of the lowest state of the harmonic oscillator above the potential minimum. Real molecules are not harmonic oscillators, so a correction to this has to be made. We will see that the equilibrium dissociation energy D_e for a diatomic molecule may be calculated from the spectroscopic dissociation energy using

$$D_e = D_0 + \frac{\omega_e}{2} - \frac{\omega_e x_e}{4} + \frac{\omega_e}{8} \tag{2}$$

where ω_e is the harmonic vibration wavenumber, and $\omega_e x_e$ and $\omega_e y_e$ are an harmonicity constants. The constants ω_e, $\omega_e x_e$ and $\omega_e y_e$ are determined from vibrational spectra and are usually expressed in wavenumbers, so one must be careful to express D_e, D_o, and ω_e in wavenumbers when using this equation. The two types of dissociation energies D_o and D_e for H_2^+ and H_2. The values of dissociation energies are given in eV, cm^{-1}, and kJ mol^{-1} because each of these units has certain advantages.

Spectroscopic measurements in the ultraviolet, visible, and infrared regions are usually ex pressed in terms of wavelengths or wavenumbers. Thus, experimental results are usually expressed in cm^{-1} because conversion to other units involves the use of physical constants whose values may change. The results of theoretical calculations are frequently expressed in electronvolts. Before discussing the quantum mechanical calculation of the potential energy curves of H_2^+ and H_2, we must discuss the relations between these two molecules and certain aspects of their potential energy curves.

The potential energy curves for the ground states of H_2^+ and H_2 are shown in Fig. 1. In this figure energies are measured with respect to the ground state of the hydrogen molecule. The energy of two protons and two electrons, infinitely far from each other, is shown. The ionization energy $E_i(H_2)$ for hydrogen is the energy required to remove an electron to an infinite distance from H_2^+, and has been measured accurately:

$$H_2(g) = H_2(g) + e^- \quad E_i(H_2) = 15.4259 \text{ eV} \tag{3}$$

Thus, the zero-point levels of H_2 and H_2^+ are separated by 15.4259 eV. The potential energy curves for H_2 and H_2^+ at infinite inter-nuclear distance are separated by the ionization potential of a hydrogen atom in its ground state.

$$H(g) = H^+(g) + e \quad E_i(H) = 13.598\ 396 \text{ eV} \tag{4}$$

$$E_i(H_2) + D_o(H_2^+) = D_o(H_2) + E_i(H) \tag{7}$$

Since it is difficult to measure $D_o(H_2^+)$, this relation has been used to obtain the most accurate value for this quantity. Now that we have placed these potential energy curves in a context, we want to talk about their calculation from quantum mechanics. We want to understand why a stable molecule H_2^+ is formed when two protons and an electron are brought together, and why at) even more stable molecule H_2 is formed when two protons and two electrons are brought together.

Hydrogen molecule ion

The electronic Schrodinger equation for this simplest molecule, which is given by equation 3, can be solved exactly. The details of this calculation are not given here, but the results are. At each internuclear distance a series of values of $E_{el}(R)$, and therefore of $E(R)$, are obtained. For the ground electronic state, H_2^+ is dissociated into a proton and a ground-state hydrogen atom at $R = \infty$.

It is useful to think about the electronic energy $E(R)$ without the internuclear repulsion energy, equal to I/ $(4\pi\varepsilon_o E(R)$. We define

$$E_{et}(R) = E(R) \quad \frac{e^2 r}{4\pi\varepsilon_o R}$$

It is also convenient to discuss these energies in units of Eh 27.211 396 1 eV. We know the value of E_{el}(R) at two values of R. At R = ∞ the energy is equal to that of a hydrogen atom and a proton infinitely far from each other, $-E_h/2$. At R 0, $E_{el}(R = 0)$ must equal to the energy of a helium ion (since at R =0, the two protons have the same attraction to the electron as a helium nucleus), so $E_{el}(0) = 2E_h$. $E_{el}(R)$ is a smooth function of R.

The balance between $E_{el}(R)$ and the internuclear repulsion leads to an equilibrium distance R_e of 106 put and a dissociation energy D_e of 2.793 eV (269.483 U mol$_{-1}$). The electronic Schrodinger equation can be solved exactly for H_2^+ and yields a set of orbitals that are molecular in the sense that they extend over the entire molecule. We could use these as a basis to discuss homonuclear diatomic molecules, just as we used the H atom orbitals to discuss the electronic states of many electron atoms.

The exact molecular orbitals for H_2^+ are not simple to write down, but we have a very good approximate form for them based on the atomic orbitals of the H atoms. This approach is called the linear combination of atomic orbitals (or LCAO) method. In this approach, we begin by noting that if the two protons are far apart, either one could have an electron in the Is hydrogen atom orbital.

The electron probability densities along the line of the two nuclei are given for ψ_g and ψ_u in Fig. 3.The squares of the wavefunctions

$$\psi_\gamma^2 = \frac{1}{2(1 + s)} \quad [(1s_A)^2 + 2(1s_A)^((1s_B) + (1s_B)^2]$$

$$\psi^2_\upsilon = \frac{1}{2(1 - s)} [(1s_A)^2 + 2(1s_A)(1s_B) + (1s_B)^2]$$

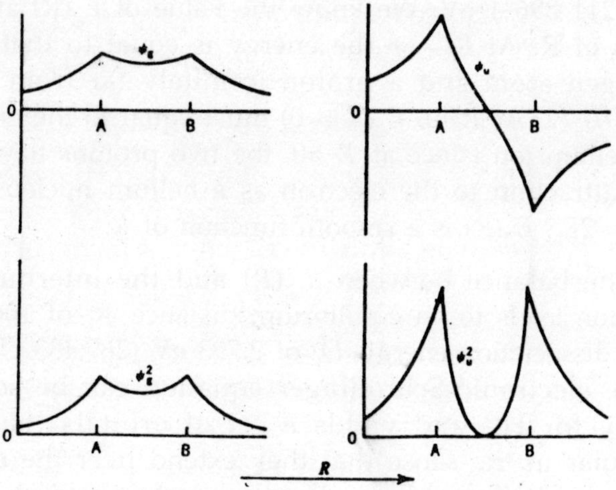

Fig. 1. Molecular orbitals ψ_g and ψ_u for the hydrogen molecular ion and probability densities ψ_g^2 and ψ_u^2 along the internuclear axis.

show that the electron density is increased between the nuclei with ψ^2_υ and decreased with ψ^2_υ. In fact, in ψ^2_υ the electron density is zero in a plane bisecting the line between the protons; that is, there is a node midway between the protons. In ψ_υ there is constructive interference between $1S_A$ and IS_B and in ψ_υ there is destructive interference.

The ground-state wavefunction for H_2^+ is ψ_g. Since this orbital is symmetrical around the internuclear axis, it is referred to as a sigma (σ) orbital, and since it is even (gerade) and is made up of two Is orbitals, it is designated σ_gIs. If the electron is placed in the state with the wavefunction ψ_υ the energy of the molecule is more than that of the dissociated molecule ($H + H^+$), and so this molecular orbital is referred to as an antibonding orbital. The antibonding orbital is symmetrical about the internuclear axis and is referred to as a uu Is orbital. The energy for ψ_υ is higher than that for ψ_g for all R. The value of E_g calculated from equation 20 by carrying out the indicated integrations for different values of R does show minimum, and so this very simple molecular orbital theory does account for the bonding in $h2^+$.

However, it yields R_e = 123 pm (experiment 106 pm) and D_e = 1.77 eV (experiment 2.793). The calculations can be improved by adding further terms to the wavefunctions and using the variation method to evaluate further adjustable parameters. However, this sample calculation shows that molecular bonding occurs when electron density accumulates in the region between the nuclei as in the $\sigma_u$ls orbital. We can use the same LCAO procedure to form other molecular orbitals from the atomic orbitals on the two protons. This is useful only if the molecular orbitals that are found have the bonding characteristics of the σ_glS or σ_uIs orbitals we have discussed.

Two conditions must be met for (his to be true: The two atomic orbitals must have about the same energy and they must have the same symmetry properties with respect to rotations about the internuclear axis. If the latter condition is not satisfied then the integrals corresponding to H_{AB} and to S_{AB} are zero for all R; if the former condition is not satisfied then the integrals corresponding to H_{AA} and H_{BB} will be very different. In either case the coefficients c_1 and c_2 will be very different (one approximately 0 and one approximately 1) so that little or no bonding takes place. It is quite easy to determine whether the overlap integral S_{AB} is zero by examining the positive and negative parts of the orbitals.

The situation when two Is orbitals (or two *ns*

orbitals) are brought together: The orbitals overlap and bonding can occur. Here the overlap is zero since the overlap of the positive lobe of the p orbital with the s orbital is exactly cancelled by the overlap of the negative lobe of the p orbital and thus no binding can occur. If two parallel p orbitals are brought together, bonding can occur. The orbital the internuclear axis is called a p orbital.

The bonding orbital changes sign on inversion and ungerade ($\pi_u 2p$). while the antibonding orbital is gerade ($\pi_g 2p$). Note that there is another pair of orbitals exactly like these, formed from the 2p orbitals perpendicular to the page. Therefore, the π orbitals are doubly degenerate.

Molecular orbital description of the Hydrogen molecule

Using the Born-Oppenheimer approximation, the electronic Hamiltonian for the hydrogen molecule. When the electronic Hamiltonian for the hydrogen molecule is used in equation 2 an exact solution cannot be obtained because of the $1/r_{12}$ term, just as in the atomic case. This is the reason that the LCAO-MO method is used to obtain an approximate solution.

According to the LCAO-MO approach molecular hydrogen is formed by putting two electrons with opposite spin in the σgls orbitals. That is, we assume that each electron can be assigned to an orbital and that the electronic wavefunction for the molecule is the product of the two wavefunctions for the two electrons:

$$\psi_{MO} = \psi_i(1)\psi_j(2)$$

where *i* and *j* designate the different orbitals and 1 and 2 designate the two electrons. According to the Pauli principle, two electrons with opposite spin can be assigned to a given spatial orbital, and so as a first approximation we will assume that in the ground state of the hydrogen molecule the two electrons are placed in the lug orbital developed for F_2^+. Thus, the electronic configuration of H_2 will be described as $(I\ \sigma_g)2$, just as we described the electronic configuration of He as $(Is)^2$. Although simple molecular orbital theory does account for a large proportion of the binding energy of the hydrogen molecule, it has to be extended to yield accurate results.

A detailed description of the improvements that are possible is beyond the scope of this book, but the general directions can be indicated. We can see one deficiency in the approximate wavefunction

$$I_{SA}(2) + I_{SB}{}^{(1)}I_{SA}(2) + I_{SB}(I)I_{SA}(2) + I_{SB}{}^{(1)}I_{SA}(2)$$

The first term and last term correspond to forms of the hydrogen molecule with ionic bonding, namely $H_A^-\ H_B^+$ and $H_A^+\ H_B^-$, so that this molecular orbital wave function describes a state at $R = \infty$ that is 50% H^+ and H^- and 50% H + H, which is clearly not correct. This problem can be reduced by introducing variable coefficients c_1 and c_2 in

$$\psi = c_1(R)\psi_{covalent} + C_2(R)\psi_{ionic}$$

where

$$\psi_{covalent} = I_{SA}(I)1S_B(2) + I_{SA}(2)I_{SA}(1)$$

$$\psi_{ionic} = I_{SA}(I)S_A(2) + I_{SB}(1)\ I_{SA}(I)1S_B(2)$$

Using the variation method the values of c_1 and c_2 can be determined at each value of R. Since equation 14 yields R_e= 74.9 pm (experimental 74.1 pm) and D_e = 386 kJ mol^{-1} (experimental 458 kJ mol^{-1}), the inclusion of one variational parameter leads to considerable improvement. Further improvements can be obtained by increasing the number of atomic orbitals used, that is, enlarging the basis set, as, for example, by adding 2s and $2p_z$ orbitals, and thereby introducing more variational parameters. The evaluation of parameters can be done in a systematic way by using the Hartree-Fock self-consistent field method that is used to obtain atomic orbitals. Equations of the form

$$H_{ef\phi}\psi_i = E_i\psi_i$$

where H_{eff} is the effective one-electron Hamiltonian, ψ_i, is the molecular orbital for the ith electron, and E_i is the orbital energy for the ith electron, are solved by the iterative methods for atoms to obtain self consistent molecular orbitals.

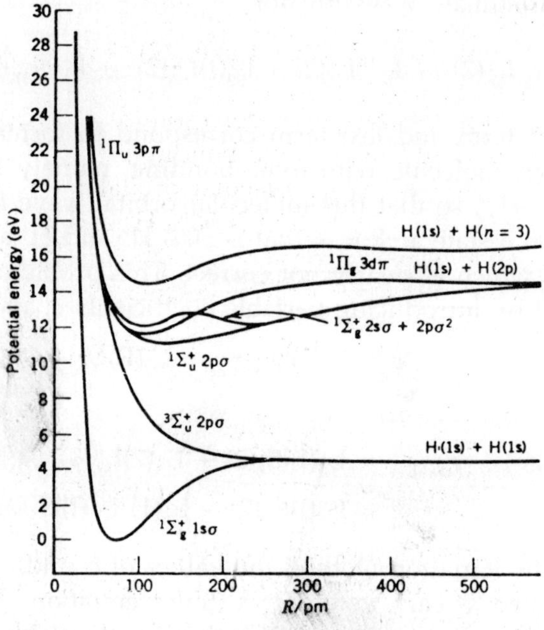

Fig. 2. Potential energy curves for ground and excited states of H_2.

These Hartree-Fock wavefunctions do not ad equality correlate the motion of electrons with unlike spins, and further improvements can be obtained by using a wavefunction that is a linear combination of functions representing different electronic configurations of the molecule. For example, the doubly excited configuration $(I\sigma_u)^2$ may be added to the molecular orbital because it has the same symmetry. By using 100-term, wavefunctions Kolos and Wolniewicz have obtained D_0 = 36 117.8 cm^{-1} in comparison with the observed value of 36 117.3 ± 1,0 cm^{-1}. Their theoretical value of the internuclear distance R_e of H_2 is 74.140 pm, Compared with the experimental value from spectroscopic measurements of 74.1.39 pm. The hydrogen molecule has a large number of excited electronic states. In diatomic molecules the orbital angular momenta of the electrons couple to give a resultant orbital angular momentum *L*, and the electron spin momenta combine to give a resultant spin angular momentum *S*. The component of the orbital angular momentum along the axis of the molecule is given by

$$M_L = m_1 + m_2 + ...$$

where m_i = 0 for a a orbital, m_i = ± 1 for a π orbital, and so on. The quantum number Δ is defined as the absolute value of M_L and is represented by the code letters

Λ	=	0	1	2	3
Symbol	=	Σ	Π	Δ	Φ

in analogy to atomic term symbols. The multiplicity of a state of a diatomic molecule is given by 2*S* + 1, where *S* is the sum of the spins of the electrons in the molecule. The term symbol of a molecule is represented by

$$2^{s+1}\Lambda$$

For the hydrogen molecule in the ground state, there are two electrons in (T orbitals and so m_1 = 0, m_2 = 0, and M_L = 0. Since Λ = 0, the molecule is in a I state. Since the spins of the electrons are opposed, S 0, and the molecular term symbol is $^1\Sigma$ (a singlet sigma state).

For Σ terms a superscript of plus or minus is added

according to the behaviour of the wavefunction upon reflection in the plane containing the internuclear axis. A plus sign indicates that the wavefunction is invariant under this operation, and a negative sign indicates the wavefunction changes sign on reflection in this plane. If a diatomic molecule has a center of symmetry a right subscript of g or u is attached to the term symbol to denote the parity of the orbital.

The parity of an orbital is determined by observing the inversion symmetry. When a point on an orbital is inverted an equal distance through the center of the molecule, the orbital is gerade if it has the same sign at the two points. The parity of a multielectron molecule is obtained by noting g or u for every orbital and forming products using g × g = g, g × u = u, and u × u = g.

Electron configurations of homonuclear diatomic molecules

The order in which molecular orbitals of homonuclear diatomic molecules are filled depends upon the nuclear charge and the internuclear distance. The variation in the sequence in energies is similar to that encountered with the relative energies of atomic orbitals of the elements which depend on atomic number. To derive the possible sequences from the lowest energy up, it is useful to introduce a second way of bridging the gap between atomic and molecular systems.

In addition to the separated atoms approach, there is the united atom approach. In this approach, the molecule is thought of first as the atom obtained from coalescing all the nuclei in the molecule. The united atom for H_2 is ^2H_e, and the united atom for N_2 is ^{28}Si. The electronic structure of the molecule is obtained by thinking about the changes in orbitals that occur when the nucleus of the united atom is pulled apart to form the nuclei of the molecule at their equilibrium distances.

It is useful to define a bond order that is roughly proportional to the strength of bonding. The bond order is equal to the number of bonding pairs of electrons minus number of antibonding pairs. Bond orders of 1. 2, and 3 correspond with what are usually called single, double, and triple bonds.

We now discuss, one by one the homonuclear diatomic molecules of the first row elements.

He_2^+

The third electron ion is in art antibonding orbital, but there is net bonding because there are two electrons in bonding orbitals. This ion is observed in electronic arcs.

He_2

According to simple molecular orbital theory, a pair of electrons would occupy the lor, orbital and a pair would occupy the lu, orbital. Since both the bonding and antibonding orbitals are filled, there is no decrease in energy as compared to two isolated helium atoms, and a stable He_2 molecule is not formed.

Li_2

The additional pair of electrons beyond those for He, go into the 20r, orbital. Thus, there is a single bond between the two nuclei. The vapour of lithium metal is primarily monatomic because the Li_2 bond is quite weak and a high temperature is needed to vaporize the metal.

Be_2

The additional pair of electrons beyond Li_2 goes into the $2\sigma_u$ antibonding orbital. Thus, as in the case of He_2, there is no net stabilization as compared with isolated Be atoms.

C_2

The additional two electrons beyond B_2 fill the two half-vacant 1pu bonding orbitals. Thus, C_2 has four electrons in bonding orbitals that are not compensated by electrons in corresponding antibonding orbitals. Since C_2 has a bond order of 2, compared with I for B_2, we would expect C_2 to have tighter binding and a smaller internuclear distance than B. Although C_2 exists in high-temperature gases rich in carbon, other species (C_3, C_4,.....) also exist, and carbon forms networks in the solid state (diamond and graphite) rather than condensing as C_2.

Both of these phenomena are due to the fact that the energies of the $1\pi_u$ and 3σ are so close that the molecule C_2 is easily raised into the excited configuration $(1\pi_u)3(3\sigma_g)$. The unpaired electrons in this molecule can form bonds with further carbon atoms and thereby compensate for the energy of excitation.

N_2

The additional pair of electrons beyond C_2 fills the $3\sigma_g$ bonding orbital. Thus, N_2 has a singlet ground state and a triple bond. Because of this strong bonding to form diatomic molecules, N_2 is a very stable molecule with a short inter nuclear distance. The first excited state of N_2 is 6.2 eV above the ground state.

O_2

According to simple molecular orbital theory, the additional pair of electrons beyond N_2 go into the 17r., orbitals. Since there are two degenerate liT. orbitals, the two electrons can go into either the same or different orbitals, If they go into the same orbital a singlet state is formed, and if they go into different orbitals a triplet state is formed. As in the case of atoms where Hund's rule predicts that the triplet state has the lower energy, in O_2 the electrons go into different orbitals and have parallel spins. Therefore, in the ground state O_2 has a spin of one and is paramagnetic. This prediction was one of the early triumphs of MO theory.

F_2

The additional two electrons beyond O_2 fill the $1\pi_g$ orbitals so that the ground state is a singlet. Since the electron pairs in two $1\pi_g$ antibonding orbitals approximately cancel the bonding due to two electron pairs in the bonding orbitals, the bonding is weaker than O_2, and the internuclear distance is greater.

Ne_2

The $3\sigma_u$ orbital would be filled, and so the antibonding effects cancel the bonding effects, and no stable molecule is formed. For atomic orbitals in two atoms to be involved in bonding, they must have the same $\sigma,\pi,$.... properties and energies that are not too different. The electrons in heteronuclear diatomic molecules tend to localize more around one nucleus than the other, so that the molecule tends to have a dipole moment. In the extreme case, ionic molecules are formed. The difference in affinity of different atoms in a molecule for electrons is discussed in terms of electronegativity.

Electronic structure of polyatomic molecules

The electronic structure of polyatomic molecules can also be described by the LCAO molecular orbital method, but now the electronic energy will depend on many internuclear distances and angles. Therefore, finding the equilibrium geometry by minimizing the energy (calculated with the variational method) with respect to all these coordinates is a difficult and time-consuming process. Such calculations are becoming more routine as more powerful computers be come available.

The accuracy of the calculation depends on the number of atomic orbitals used. When a very large number of atomic orbitals or basis set is used, the internuclear distances and bond angles of small molecules (less than 6 atoms) can be calculated as accurately as they can be measured (distances to a few pin and bond angles to a degree or two). However, the energies are usually not calculated accurately enough to be used in thermodynamic calculations. Since chemical bond energies are the difference between large numbers (of the order of the energy of a Is orbital in the hydrogen atom or 1300 U mol^{-1}), one must calculate these large numbers to very high accuracy to obtain chemical accuracy in the difference. It is therefore important to have simple ways of thinking about chemical bonding and molecular structure which, although not accurate, give a qualitative picture with little numerical work.

One such method, introduced by Heitler and London for H_2 just after the advent of quantum mechanics, is called the valence bond method. The valence bond method is based on the idea that a chemical bond is formed when there is good overlap between the atomic orbitals of the participating atoms. When the idea (if hybrid orbitals is added to this, an explanation of the bond angles in simple molecules is found.

Hybrid orbitals are linear combinations of atomic orbitals on a single atom with definite angular relationships among them. We will illustrate these ideas by examining the molecules BeH_2, BH_3, CH_4, NH_3 and H_2O. The H–Be–H bond angle is 180°. The ground-state electron configuration of the beryllium atom is $ls^2 2s^2$. To represent the direclionalnv of the BeH_2 bonds and the fact that they are equivalent, two hybrid orbitals of beryllium are formed by taking a linear combination of the 2s orbital and one of the 2p orbitals.

Energy is required to excite a 2s electron to a 2p orbital but more than enough energy for this is obtained when a stable chemical compound with two bonds is formed. The two sp orbitals formed in this way are

$$\psi_{sp(i)} = 2^{-1/2}(2s + 2p_x)$$

$$\psi_{sp(i)} = 2^{-1/2}(2s - 2p_x)$$

where these orbitals have been normalized in the usual way. There are two of these hybrid orbitals because two beryllium orbitals have been used. When an s orbital is hyrbridized with a p, orbital it must be remembered that the p, orbital is positive on one side of the nucleus and negative on the other.

The node in the radial function for the 2s orbital, inside of which the orbital is negative and outside of which it is positive, may be neglected since the nodal surface is quite close to the nucleus and the contribution of this region to bonding is small. In $\psi_{sp(i)}$ the amplitudes tend to cancel on one side of the nucleus and add on the other.

The $\psi_{sp(i)}$ orbital is equivalent but points in the opposite direction. The lobes of these orbitals extend much further along the x axis than the 2s and $2p_x$, orbital, and so they provide more overlap with the Is orbitals of the two hydrogen atoms in BeH_2. The two Be–H bonds are described by combining the Is_A and Is_B orbitals for the two protons with these hybrid orbitals to obtain the following two bond orbitals:

$$\psi = c_1 ls_A + c_2\psi_{sp(i)}$$

$$\psi' = c'_1 ls_B + c'_2\psi_{sp(i)}$$

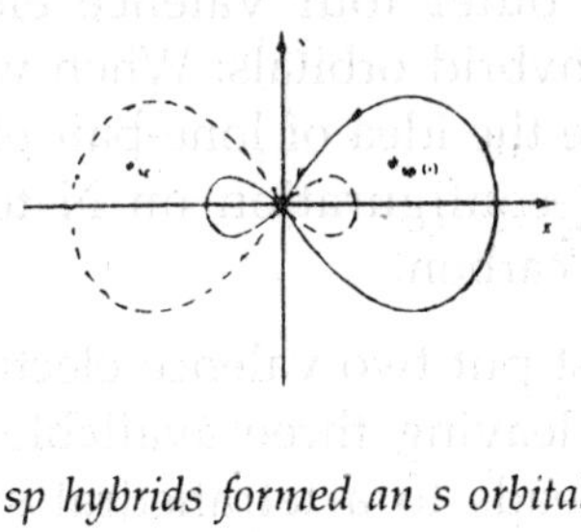

Fig 3. The two sp hybrids formed an s orbital and a p orbital.

According to valence bond theory BeH_2 is stabilized by the overlap of the two beryllium sp orbitals and the two hydrogen Is orbitals The Is^2 electrons of beryllium are not involved.

The three B–H bonds in BH_3 lie in a plane with H-B-H angles of 120°. The boron atom has the configuration Is^22s^22p. The following three hybrid orbitals of boron are constructed to account for three equivalent bonds in $BH_{3:}$

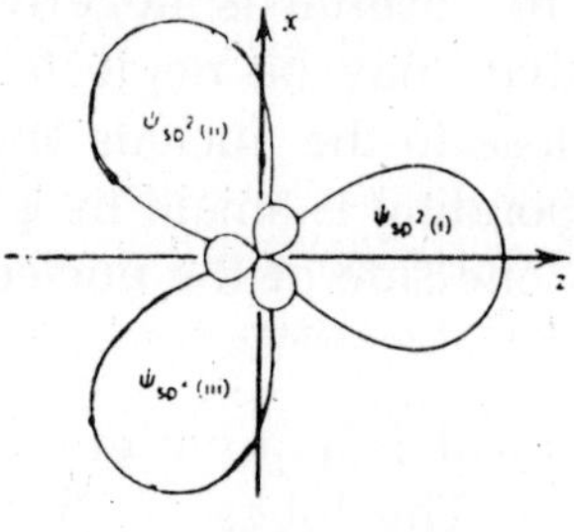

Fig. 4. The three sp^2 hybrids orbitals formed an s orbital and two p orbitals.

These wavefunctions have been normalized and are orthogonal. By substituting the expressions for the angular parts of the p, and p, orbitals, it is readily shown that the sp^2 orbitals lie in a plane with lobes pointed in directions separated by 120°, as shown in Fig 6.

Carbon atoms have the electron configuration $Is^22s^22p^2$ and the outer four valence electrons may be used to form sp^3 hybrid orbitals: When we come to NH_3, we must introduce the idea of lone-pair electrons. We use the $2s^22p'^x2p'^y2p^{1z}$ configuration on N to form four sp' hybrids just as in carbon.

Now we must put two valence electrons of N in one of these orbitals, leaving three available to bond to the hydrogens. This leads to a tetrahedral structure of NH_3

(bond angle 109°) with one apex of the tetrahedron containing a lone electron pair. These lone pair electrons are available for binding to, for example, a proton, H^+, to form NH^+_4. The water molecule can he treated in much the game manner, except that we now have two lone pairs. This predicts that the bond angle in H_2O is the tetrahedral angle 109° instead of the experimentally observed 104°.

The small difference can he accounted for by adding more terms to the wavefunction. The lone pairs of H_2O are available to bond to other atoms. In particular, the interaction between hydrogen atoms on other water molecules and the lone pairs gives rise to the hydrogen bond and the unusual properties of H_2O.

Huckel molecular orbital theory

Molecules with extensive π bonding systems, like benzene, are not described very well by valence bond theory. Their electronic structure can be described in a simple, but approximate molecular orbital method developed by Huckel in 1930.

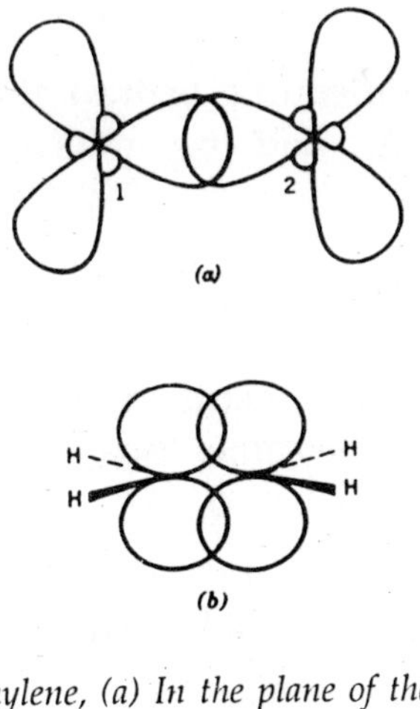

Fig. 5. Bonding in ethylene, (a) In the plane of the nuclei: formation of a bonds between carbon atoms 1 and 2 using sp^2 orbitals, (b) Perpendicular to the plane of the nuclei: formation of π bonds between p orbitals.

Ethylene is a planar molecule, and the bonds between the carbon and hydrogen atoms in the plane are sp^2 hybrid orbitals of carbon and Is orbitals of hydrogen. This forms the σ-bond framework shown in Fig 7a. The 2p, orbitals of the carbon atoms that are not involved in the or framework overlap sideways forming the p system, as shown in Fig 7b. This simple picture explains the bond angles in ethylene and its planar structure.

Huckel molecular orbital theory is concerned with the p electron system which is responsible for the special properties of conjugated and aromatic hydrocarbons. The wavefunction of the delocalized p orbital of ethylene is represented by

$$\psi = c_1\phi_1 + c_2\phi_2$$

where ϕ_1 and ϕ_2 are the $2p_z$ orbitals of the two carbon atoms. The corresponding secular determinant is

$$\begin{vmatrix} H_{11} - ES_{11} & H_{12} - ES_{12} \\ H_{21} - ES_{21} & H_{22} - ES_{22} \end{vmatrix} = 0$$

where H_{ij} = f ϕ_1 Hϕ_1 dv and $s_{ij = f}$ $\phi_i\phi_{jdv}$

In Huckel molecular orbital theory, the secular equation is simplified by making the following assumptions:

1. Overlap integrals S_{ij} are set equal to zero unless i = j, when S_{ij} = 1.
2. All the diagonal elements in the secular equation are assumed to be the same; thus, the Coulomb integrals H_{ij} are all set equal to α.
3. The resonance integrals H_{ij} are set equal to zero, except for those on neighbouring atoms which are set equal to β.

With these assumptions the secular equation for the p electrons in ethylene becomes

$$\frac{\alpha - E}{\beta} \quad \frac{\beta}{\alpha - E} = 0$$

In Huckel theory, the Coulomb integral a and the resonance integral 0 are regarded as empirical parameters to be evaluated from experimental data on the molecule. Thus, in Huckel theory it is unnecessary to specify the Hamiltonian operator. Readily solved for $\alpha \pm \beta$. Thus, there are bonding and antibonding orbitals, as shown in Fig.

The resonance integral is negative, and so the energy of the lowest level is u + 0. The bonding orbital is occupied by an electron pair, and so the p electronic energy of ethylene is $2\alpha + 2\beta$. The wavefunctions for the bonding and antibonding orbitals are obtained by going back to the pair of linear algebraic equations that gave rise to the secular equation:

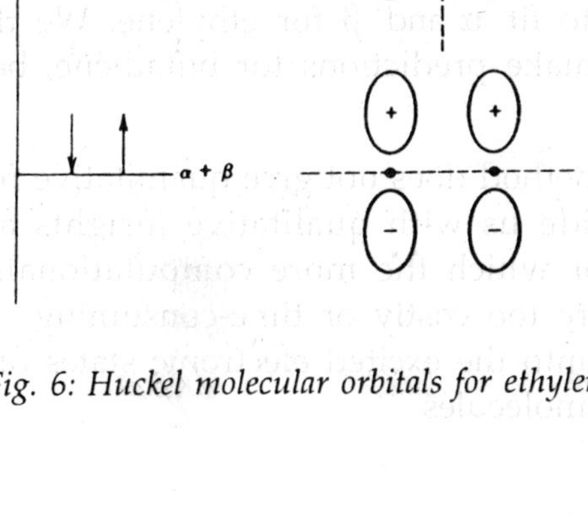

Fig. 6: Huckel molecular orbitals for ethylene

$$c_1(\alpha - E) + c_2\beta = 0$$
$$c_1\beta + c_2(\alpha - E) = 0$$

Substituting $E = \alpha + \beta$ in either equation yields $c_1 = c_2$ so that the wave function for the bonding orbital is

$$\psi_1 = 2^{-1/2} (\phi_1 + \phi_2)$$

The bonding orbital is shown in Fig. alongside the energy level. Substituting $E = \alpha - \beta$ into equation 31 or 32 yields $c_1 = -C_2$, so that the wavefunction for the antibonding orbital is

$$\psi_2 = 2^{-1/2} (\phi_1 - \phi_2)$$

The antibonding orbital is also shown in Fig. Notice the resemblance to the LCAO orbitals of H_2^+. The equations for the six Huckel molecular orbitals for benzene are not given here, but the corresponding electron densities are shown in Fig 9. Note that the P electronic energy in C_6H_6 is more negative than three times the value in C_2H_4, indicating that C_6H_6 is not three double bonds.

The difference is called the conjugation energy. The Huckel theory is an example of a semiempirical molecular orbital method. We have used a simple Hamiltonian (neglecting many terms) to find the orbitals and their energies. We now can use experimental quantities to fit α and β for ethylene. We then use the values to make predictions for butadiene, benzene, and so on.

This method does not give quantitative results, but it does provide us with qualitative insights about larger systems for which the more computationally intensive methods are too costly or time-consuming, and it gives us insight into the excited electronic states of conjugated P electron molecules.

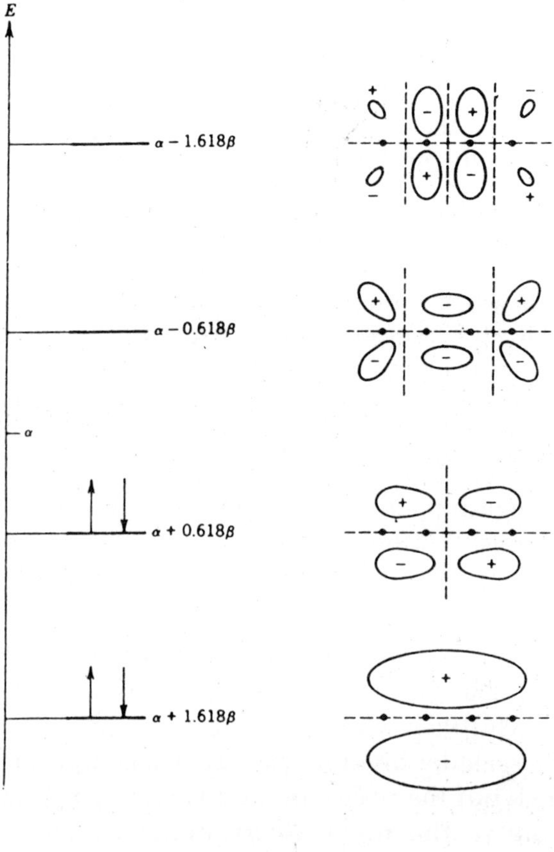

Fig. 7: Huckel molecular orbitals for 1, 3-butadiene.

Electronegativity

There are several ways of measuring electronegativity, which is a quantitative measure of attraction of an atom in a molecule to electrons. For example, in a molecule AB it is measured by the relative stabilities of A^+B^- and A^-B^+ The energy difference between these Structures is given by

$$E(A^+B^-) - E(A^-B^+) = (E_{i,A} - (E_{ea.B}) - (E_{i,B} - E_{ea,A})$$
$$= (E_{i,A} + (E_{ea.B}) - (E_{i,B} + E_{ea,A})$$

where Ej is the ionization energy and E_{ea} is electron affinity. Mulliken defined the electronegativity difference between atoms A and B as $\frac{1}{2}[E(A^+B^-)$ $E(A^-B^+)]$. Thus, he defined the electronegativity of an atom as $\frac{1}{2}(E_i + E_{ea})$. The electronegativity of an atom depends on its Valence state, and so the ionization potential and electron affinity used are not those of the ground state of the atom. The Pauling electronegativity scale is based on his observation that the AB bond energy exceeds the mean of the A-A and B-B bond energies if the A-B bond is polar. Pauling defined the electronegativity difference between A and B as 0.050 $(\Delta_{AB}/\text{kJ mol}^{-1})^{1/2}$, where

$$\Delta_{AB} = E(A\text{–}B) \quad \tfrac{1}{2}[E(A\text{–}A) + E(B\text{-}B)]$$

The E's are the dissociation energies for the bonds in question. The electronegativity of H was set at 2.1. Values on the Mulliken scale in eV can be converted to the Pauling scale by dividing by 3.17. Exact agreement is not obtained, but the scales are in relatively good agreement. Fluorine is the most electronegative atom (4.0 on Pauling's scale), and cesium is the least electronegative atom (0.7 on Pauling's scale). As we go down a column of the periodic table, the atoms become less electronegative because of the increasingly effective screening of the charge on the nucleus by inner electrons

The alkali-metal atoms have a great tendency to lose their outer electrons and therefore have a low electronegativity. By use of electronegativities it is possible to predict which bonds will be ionic and which bonds will be covalent. Two elements of very different electronegativity, like a halogen and an alkali metal, form air ionic bond because an electron is almost completely transferred to the atom of higher electronegativity. Two elements with nearly equal electronegativities form covalent bonds. For instance, carbon, which occupies an intermediate position in the electronegativity scale, forms covalent bonds with elements near it in the periodic table. If there is a considerable difference between the electro-negativities of the two elements, the bond is polar (i.e.. possessed if a high degree of ionic character), as in the case of sodium chloride.

In the majority of chemical bonds the sharing of the electron pair is not exactly equal, o that the bond has Some ionic character that results in a dipole moment for the bond.

Ionic bonding

When atoms with nearly the same electronegativity form bonds, the molecular orbitals are spread more or less evenly over the two atoms, and covalent bonds, are formed. When atoms have somewhat different electronegativities, the bonding electrons are not evenly shared, but are drawn toward the more electronegative atom. When the electronegativities are quite different an electron moves completely to the more electronegative atom and an ionic bond is formed. The interaction energy $E(R)$ of an ionic bond can he calculated using Coulomb's law. As two ions approach each other closely because of Coulomb attraction an equilibrium position is reached at some point because of repulsive forces which balance the attraction.

The short-range repulsion energy increases very rapidly when the charge clouds of the two ions begin to overlap. The repulsion energy may be represented by an empirical expression such as $b\ \exp(-aR)$. Thus, the potential energy $E(R)$ of a diatomic molecule is approximately.

$$E(R) = \frac{Q_1 Q_2}{4\pi\varepsilon_0 R} + be^{-aR}$$

where the energy is measured with respect to the separated ions. Further effects may be taken into account; for example, the electric field of each ion polarizes the electron cloud of the other ion and produces a further energy of attraction. However, the short-range repulsion energy and polarization energy are small close to R_e that the Coulomb, attractive term alone gives a good approximation to the energy of an ionic molecule.

Dissociation into separate ions. Further effects may be taken into account; for example, the electric field of each ion polarizes the electron cloud of the other ion and produces a further energy of attraction. However, the short-range repulsion energy and polarization energy are so small close to R_e that the Coulomb attractive term along gives a good approximation to the dissociation energy of an ionic molecule.

Hydrogen bonds

A number of unusual structures such as HF^-_2 and formic acid dimer in the gas phase are evidence for the formation of hydrogen bonds. The unusually high acid dissociation constant of salicylic acid, as compared with the meta and para isomers, is also evidence for a hydrogen bond. A hydrogen bond results when a proton may be shared between two electronegative atoms, such as F, O, or N, that are the right distance apart.

The proton of the hydrogen bond is attracted by the high concentration of negative charge in the vicinity of these electronegative atoms. Fluorine forms very strong hydrogen bonds; oxygen, weaker ones; and nitrogen still weaker ones. The unusual properties of water are due to a large extent to the formation of hydrogen bonds involving the four lone-pair electrons on oxygen. In ice there is a tetrahedral arrangement with each oxygen, atom bonded to four hydrogen atoms. Hydrogen bonds are formed along the axis of each lone pair in ice, and their existence in liquid water is responsible for the high boiling point of water is compared with the boiling points of hydrides of other elements in the same column of the periodic table (H_2S, –62°C; H_2Se, –42°C; H_2Te, –4°C) .

When water is vaporized, these hydrogen bonds are broken, but in formic and acetic the hydrogen bonds are strong enough for dimmers of the type to exist in the vapour. Hydrogen bonds between N and O are responsible for the stability of the a helix formed by polypeptides and found in protein molecules.

Intermolecular forces

When two neutral molecules come close to one another, the various interactions between the electrons and nuclei of one molecule and the electrons and nuclei of the other produce a potential energy of interaction. At very small distances, the molecules repel each other strongly. At certain intermediate distances, the potential energy of interaction is negative the molecules attract each other, but usually weakly. At very large distances, the potential energy approaches zero.

Attractive forces

The long-range attractive interactions between neutral molecules are called van der Waals forces and include a number of terms, all arising from the electrostatic interactions. For example, if the two molecules have permanent dipole moments, then at fixed angles with respect to one another the interaction between molecules varies as R^{-3}, where R is the intermolecular distance. In the gas or liquid phase, molecules will have random orientations, so the thermal average over the angular part of the interaction causes the first nonzero term in the interaction to be

$$(V(R))_{dd} = -\frac{2}{3kT}\frac{\mu_A\mu_B}{4\pi\varepsilon_0}\frac{1}{R^6}$$

where μ_A and μ_B are the permanent dipole moments of the two molecules, T is the temperature and dd means dipole-dipole. Notice that the interaction is negative (attractive) since there is a preference in the thermal (statistical mechanical) averaging for the molecules to orient in such a way as to attract each other and lower their mutual energy. As the temperature increases, this tendency is less important, so the attraction decreases.

Another term in the attractive potential energy arises from the dipole-induced dipole interaction between molecules. If molecule A has a dipole moment α_A, this creates an electric field which polarizes the charges on molecule B, creating an induced dipole moment of magnitude $\alpha_B J \mu_A$, where α_B is called the polarizability of molecule B. The dipole-induced dipole attractive energy is given by

$$(V(R))_{ind} = -\frac{\alpha_A {\mu^2}_A + \alpha_A {\mu^2}_B}{(4\pi\varepsilon_0)^2 R^6}$$

Notice that it also varies as R^{-6}

There is a third term varying as R^{-6} which was explained by London in 1930 and is sometimes called the London force or dispersion force. It occurs even when the molecules have no permanent dipole moment and can be visualized as the interaction between the fluctuating charge distribution on molecule A with that of molecule B.

The rules of quantum mechanics say that even though molecule A has no permanent dipole moment, the average value of the square of the dipole moment operator is not zero. Therefore, we can say that at any instant, the molecule has a dipole moment that polarizes molecule B (and vice versa), leading to a potential varying as R^{-6} The exact form is complicated, but a good approximation is

$$(V(R))_{disp} = -\frac{2}{3}\frac{E_A E_B}{E_A + E_B}\frac{\alpha_A \alpha_B}{(4\pi\varepsilon_0)^2}\frac{1}{R^6}$$

where E_A and E_B are approximately equal to the energies of the first electronic transitions of these molecules, aA and an are their polarizabilities, and disp means dispersion. These three terms add to give the total attractive energy between molecules A and B. In most cases, this energy is on the order of 2×10^{-3} eV at a distance of 0.5 nm. Of course, the larger the dipole moments or the polarizabilities, the stronger is the attraction.

Intermolecular potential energy

At small distances, the molecules repel strongly, so when this force is added to the attractive forces we have discussed, we obtain the total intermolecular potential energy. To represent this as a simple function of R, we can take the repulsion to be proportional to R^{-n} or $e^{-\alpha R}$. where n and a have to be fit empirically. One very useful empirical function is named for J. E. Lennard-Jones and is given by

$$V = 4\varepsilon \quad \frac{\sigma^{12}}{r} - \frac{\sigma^6}{r}$$

In this "6–12" , the twelfth power dependence for the repulsive energy is chosen for convenience and because it is a reasonable fit to the data. The minimum in this potential is at $r = (2)^{1/6}\sigma$ where V = -ε. Note that V 0 at r

= σ, so the energy rises very steeply for small *r*. The values of σ and o can be found by fitting experimental data on the second virial coefficient, gas viscosity, and molecular beam scattering cross sections. Typical values for the parameters ε and σ for interactions between like atoms or molecules.

Dipole moments of molecules dipole moments

Other important properties of a molecule that may be understood using quantum mechanics arc its dipole moment and its polarizability These microscopic properties of individual molecules can be obtained from macroscopic measurements of dielectric constants and from spectra. The dipole moment of a molecule is a measure of the separation of the centers of positive and negative charge within the molecule. If a positive charge $+Q$ is separated from a negative charge $-Q$ by distance r, the dipole moment has the magnitude $\mu = Qr$. The dipole moment μ is a vector pointing from the negative charge to the positive charge with a magnitude of $|\mu|$. The SI unit for dipole moment is Cm.

The dipole moment for a group of point charges Q_i is

$$\mu = \sum_i r_i Q_i$$

where r_i is the vector from the origin to charge Q_i For a charge density p(x, y, z) the dipole moment is defined by

$$\mu = \iiint r\,(x,y,z)\; p(x,y,z)\; dx\; dy\; dz$$

For a distribution of zero total charge the dipole moment is equal to the product of the absolute charge of either the positive or negative distribution times the vector distance *r* between the centers of the two distributions:

$$\mu = Q^{+}r = |Q^{-}|\,r$$

Dipole moments may be calculated from measurements of the capacitance of an electric capacitor containing the substance.

The capacitance C of a parallel plate capacitor is defined as the ratio of the charge on one of the plates to the potential difference between the conductors. Thus, the capacitance has the units coulombs per volt; this unit is referred to as the farad F, that is, F = 1 C/V. The capacitance C of a parallel plate capacitor depends on the properties of the insulating material between the plates, A capacitor has the smallest possible capacitance when there is a vacuum between the plates. When an insulating material (dielectric) is placed between the plates of a capacitor, the capacitance increases. To see why the dielectric increases the capacitance, consider that a parallel plate capacitor is charged tip and then any electrical conductor between the two plates is disconnected.

When a dielectric is inserted between the plates of the capacitor, the potential difference between the plates is reduced, because the electric field polarizes the dielectric. The dielectric remains electrically neutral inside, but a net surface charge density arises on its surface. Since the sign of the surface charge is opposite to the sign of the charge on the plates, the electric field within the dielectric is reduced below that which would have existed in the capacitor with the same charge on the plates in the absence of the dielectric.

Since the potential difference between the plates is reduced by the dielectric and the capacitance is equal to the ratio of the charge on one of the plates to the potential difference between the plates, the capacitance increases. The relative permittivity (dielectric constant) ε_r of a dielectric is defined as the ratio of the capacitance $_{Cd}$ of the capacitor filled with dielectric to the capacitance C when the capacitor is evacuated:

$$\varepsilon_r = \frac{C_d}{C}$$

Thus, the relative permittivity of a vacuum is unity. The magnitude of the relative permittivity of a substance depends on the temperature and, if an alternating electric field is used, the frequency. The relative permittivities of a few gases and liquids. These values of the relative permittivity apply at frequencies sufficiently low that equilibrium is maintained as the electric field varies.

The electrical permittivity ε of a dielectric is given by $\varepsilon = \varepsilon_r\varepsilon_0$, where ε_0 is the permittivity of vacuum. The surface charge density of the polarization charges is referred to as the electric polarization. The polarization vector P is perpendicular to the Sol face and points from the negative surface charges on the dielectric to the positive surface charges.

The magnitude of the polarization vector has the units C m^{-2} or C mm^{-3}, that is, electric dipole moment per unit volume. The magnitude of the polarization is proportional to the applied electric field. Now, we want to obtain the relation between the polarization V the relative permittivity ε_r, and the electric field E. To do that we need to Introduce the electric displacement vector D, which is defined by

$$D = \varepsilon_0 E + P$$

The electric displacement has the units Cm^{-2}. The electric displacement has the units Cm^{-2}. The electric displacement vector is useful because it does not change when a dielectric is introduced into a capacitor and the same free charges remain on the plates of the capacitor.. When there is no dielectric in the capacitor, then

$$D = \varepsilon_o E_0$$

where E_0 is the electric field between the plates in this case. When a dielectric is inserted between the plates. D does not change and so

$$D = \varepsilon_o E_0 = \varepsilon_o E_0 + P$$

Since the polarization of the medium opposes the charge on the capacitor plates, it is responsible for lowering the electric field by a factor equal to the relative permittivity. Thus, $E = E_{0/}\varepsilon_r$ and

$$P = E_0 (\varepsilon_r - 1)$$

When an electric field is applied to a sample, time is required for the establishment of the equilibrium polarization. Thus, the relative permittivity is a frequency-dependent quantity. We will first consider a static field, or one that is changing so slowly that the polarization has its equilibrium value at all times.

Chapter 4

Microwave Spectroscopy

Microwave spectra are reported for the first time for AlBr and AlI, and improved measurements have been obtained for AlCl[1]. Dunham coefficients have been evaluated and r_e/Å values obtained as follows:

AlCl	AlBr	AlI
2.13011(3)	2.29480(3)	2.53709(3)

Nuclear quadrupole coupling coefficient is also reported for the iodine nucleus in AlI. Measurements have been made of the $J = 0 \rightarrow 1$ transitions of four isotopic species of GaCl, including the hyperfine structure. Transitions for vibrational states up to $v = 3$ have been measured and Dunham coefficients as well as rotational constants have been obtained.

A value of 2.201681(3) Å has been obtained for r_e. The dependence of nuclear quadrupole coupling coefficients on vibrational state is given in Table 1. Hyperfine structure for InF has been measured,with a high-resolution-beam electric reso-nance spectrometer, for

Table 1

Vibrational dependence of nuclear quadrupole coupling coefficients for GCl

$$^{35}Cl\text{: } eq_aQ = [\,-13.20 - 0.20(v + ½) \pm 0.15]\text{ MHz}$$

$$^{69}Ca\text{: } eq_1\,Q = [\,-92.40 + 0.68(v + ½) \pm 0.14]\text{ MHz}$$

the J =1 and J = 2 rotational states of several vibrational levels, and eqQ values are reported. Thallium halides have been the subject if a number of studies. The Stark effect for TIF has been studied with a molecular-beam electric resonance spectrometer and the dipole moment has been obtained, among other parameters. Deviations from the Stark effect for a rigid-rotor model are discussed and additional terms arising from anharmonicity, centrifugal distortion, vibration-rotation interaction, and electronic polarizability are examined. The dipole moments/D of TlBr and TlI have also been determined giving:

TIF	TlBr	TlI
4.2282(8)	4.493 ± 0.050	4.607 ± 0.070

Molecular-beam studies on TlCl include an examination of the Stark effect of different isotopic species in various vibrational states. The microwave spectrum of CS has been used via the Zeeman effect to determine the sign of the electric dipole moment as —CS+, in the same direction as found for CO.

Table 2

Vibrational dependence of halogen nuclear quadrupole coupling co-efficients on vibrational states for caesium halides

$$_{eqv}Q_{cl} = +\,1.830 - 0.118(v + ½) \pm 0.150 \text{ MHz}$$

$$_{eqv}Q_{Br} = -\,6.79 + 0.73\,(v + ½) \pm 0.15 \text{ MHz}$$

$$_{eqv}Q_{I} = -\,14.28 - 2.10(v + ½) \pm 0.35 \text{ MHz}$$

The microwave spectrum of CSe has been reported for the first time and molecular g-values and the electric quadrupole moment have been evaluated from the observed Zeeman effect. For silicon monosulphide the sign of the dipole moment has also been shown to be +SiS.

The equilibrium intermolecular separation is found to be r_e = 1.929 254(3)Å. A further study has been made of GeTe and hyperfine structures have been measured for the J = 2→ 3 transition, leading to eqQ = 153.1 MHz. Two independent studies have been made for phosphorus mononitride, PN. The J = 0 → 1 transition has been measured for a number of vibrational states and Dunham coefficients have been evaluated, giving r_e = 1.490 85Å. In another study, rotational transitions from J = 1→2 to J = 7 → 8 have been observed in the millimetre and submillimetre regions.

The analysis of the results leads to r_e= 1.490 80(2)Å, in close agreement with value from the study of the J = 0→1 transitions. A new analysis has been made of all frequency data at present available for the oxygen molecule, from microwave, submillimetre, and infrared spectroscopy, including some recent measurements. A least-squares analysis was used to fit 25 microwave frequencies and three submillimetre and i.r. frequencies and a new set of parameters for the oxygen molecule has been obtained in this way.

Chlorine and bromine monofluorides have been further examined. Molecular g-values and molecular quadrupole moments have been evaluated from the observed Zeeman effect. The isotopic dependence of the g-values gives the sign of the electric dipole moment for chlorine monofluoride as —ClF+, which is of interest in view of simple arguments based on the idea of electronegativity and also for comparison with conclusions drawn from the chlorine nuclear quadrupole coupling coefficient.

The dipole moment itself has been remeasured

[μ=0.888 12(2) D] and the hyperfine structure examined using a molecular-beam electric resonance spectrometer. Hyperfine structures have been observed for $^{133}Cs^{35}Cl$, ^{133}CS ^{79}Br, and ^{133}Cs ^{127}I. The dependence on vibrational state is summarized in Table 2.CsF has been studied using a molecular-beam electric resonance spectrometer. The analysis of the results includes the following for the nuclear quadrupole coupling for caesium:

$$_{eqv} Q_{cs} = 1245.2—16.2\ (v + ½) + 0.3(v + ½)^2\ \text{kHz}$$

Other alkali-metal halides investigated by molecular-beam spectrometry include LiC, KF, and RbF

Triatomic molecules

A new molecule has been added during the year to the list of linear triatomic molecules investigated by-microwave spectroscopy. Thioborine, HBS, an unstable molecule, which is isoelectronic with methyl-idenephosphine, HCP, shows a rotational spectrum typical of a linear rotor. Rotational and centrifugal distortion constants have been reported for eight isotopic species and *l*-doubling constants for four species. r_B Structures have been calculated taking each isotopic species in turn as the parent molecule and all these calculations give structures failing within a range very similar to the range found for HCN.

The mean r_B values are r(B —H) = 1.1692 and r(S — B) 1.5994Å. A similar study has been made for some of the halogen cyanides. The molecular quadrupole moments (in units of 10^{-26} e.s.u. cm^2) for the various cyanides and for methylidenephosphine are as follows:

^{35}ClN	$^{19}BrCN$	^{127}ICN	HCN	HCP
–3.87 ± 1.0	–6.02 ± 1.1	–7.33 ± 1.1	3.1 ± 0.6	4.4 ± 1.2

The isotopic dependence of the molecular g-values has

also been used to show that for chlorine cyanide the sign of the dipole moment is +ClCN—. For iodine cyanide a detailed re-examination has been made of the microwave spectrum. Rotational constants for $^{127}I\ ^{12}C^{14}\ N$ and $^{127}I^{12}C^{14}N$ have been obtained for nine vibrational states and *l*-doubling constants for three states. This amount of information has made possible the calculation of a number of rotational parameters, and at the same time the change of the iodine nuclear quadrupole coupling coefficient with vibrational state has been examined. Among bent triatomic molecules, H_2O and H_2S have continued to be further studied. Microwave spectra of the radioactive species HTO and T_2O have been observed for the first time. Twenty-six lines have been measured for HTO and five for T_2O, and the rotational constants given in Table 3.

Table 3

Rotational constants/MHz for HTO and T_2O

Species	A	B	C
HTO	677 860.5	198 198.8	150465.3
T_2O	338 808	145 670	100 262

evaluated. Revised rotational and distortion constants have been evaluated for $H_2{}^{16}O$ as a result of a submillimetre microwave study. New transitions have also been reported in the submillimetre region for $H_2{}^{18}O$[27] and the distortion constants obtained for this species have been compared with those calculated on the basis of $H_2{}^{16}O$ data. Excellent agreement is obtained, which is gratifying since the evaluations made for $H_2{}^{16}O$ and $H_2{}^{18}O$ include very different types of i.r. data as well as different higher-order terms in the Hamiltonian.

A very detailed study of centrifugal distortion for $D_2{}^{16}O$ has been made by Steenbeckeliers and Bellet. Twenty-two constants have been determined for the ground state and nine for the v_2 state. The discussion includes an examination of the contribution of the more important distortion terms to the energies of a number of rotational states. Dipole moment measurements have been made for D_2O and HDO.

The dipole moment of D_2O has been determined from the Stark effect on microwave transitions and confirmed by high-resolution Stark spectroscopy using the HCN 337 μm laser. The dipole moment of HDO has also been determined from microwave measurements.

The work indicates that the rotationless dipole of water increases slightly on deuteriation, and this is accounted for in terms of anharmonicity of the bending mode, analogously with the interpretation of a similar effect found for ammonia.

Stark coefficients of millimetre-wave transitions for H_2O, D_2O, and HDO have also been reported. Anharmonic force constants for water have been evaluated using data on H_2O, D_2O, and HDO. Centrifugal distortion has also been investigated for H_2S and D_2S. For H_2S the distortion terms of order P^4 have been obtained and a partial set of order P^6 and P^{10} was found to be necessary in the analysis.

For D_2S a millimetre and submillimetre study has led to the measurement of sixty-six transitions, and these have been analysed with a twenty-two parameter distortion treatment. However, it is found that only a partial set of terms of order P^6 and P^{10} is necessary. Hyperfine structure for deuteriated hydrogen selenide has been investigated by beam maser spectroscopy and quadrupole constants and spin-rotation and spin-spin coupling constants involving deuterium nuclei have been evaluated.

The microwave spectrum has been reported for the first time of two isotopic species of hypofluorous acid, HOF and DOF. The r_B structural parameters are found to be:

r(O—H)	r(O—F)	HOF
0.964±0.01 Å	1.442 ± 0.001 Å	97.2 ±0.6°

The HOF angle is smaller than the angles in either H_2O or F_2O which parallels the finding for HOCl, by comparison with H_2O and Cl_2O. In a further study, more than forty lines each for both HOF and DOF have been measured and a centrifugal distortion treatment has been applied, leading to the quartic distortion constants. The microwave spectrum of the DNO molecule, which has been previously studied by electronic spectroscopy, has been obtained by using a flow technique.

The rotational constants resulting from the analysis are in good agreement with those found for the ground state from the electronic spectrum. The nitrogen nuclear quadrupole coupling coefficients are found to be similar to those for nitrosyl fluoride and nitrous acid, and the dipole moment of deuteriated nitroxyl is found to have a value of 1.70 ± 0.05 D. Following the work on DNO the spectrum of HNO has also been studied. Two independent measurements have been made of the dipole moment of NSCl. A value of 1.83(6) ± 0.036 D has been obtained for $^{15}N^{32}S^{35}Cl$ [38] and 1.87 ± 0.02 D for $^{14}N^{32}S^{35}Cl$.[39] Centrifugal distortion coefficients have been obtained from an analysis or twenty-eight transitions for $^{14}N^{32}S^{35}Cl$ [38].

By combining these with vibrational frequencies and inertial defects force constants have been obtained:

F_{11} — 10.032 mdynÅ^{-1} F_{22} = 1.44 (4) mdynÅ^{-1}

F_{33} — 0.74 mdyn Å and F_{23} =—0.08(6) mdyn

The microwave spectrum of GeF_2 has been further investigated. Rotational constants have been obtained for vibrationally excited states for $^{70}GeF_2$, $^{72}GeF_2$ and $^{74}GeF_2$ and a revised r_e structure has been obtained:

r (Ge—F) = 1.7320(9)Å FGeF = 97.148°

A centrifugal distortion analysis has been made and the question of the best use of centrifugal distortion constants and i.r. data in the calculation of the harmonic force field is discussed. Nuclear quadrupole coupling coefficients have been obtained for $^{73}GeF_2$. A revised calculation has been made of the cubic potential constants for SeO_2 using vibration-rotation interaction constants and new values of vibrational frequencies reported for matrix-isolated SeO_2. The dipole moment has also been measured: μ= 2.62 ± 0.05 D.

The millimetre-wave spectra of KOH and KOD have been examined four ground-state frequencies being measured for the former and three for the latter. These are consistent with a set of rotational constants given in Table 4, but are not consistent with the frequency reported earlier for the J = 1→ 2 transition.

Table 4

Rotational constants/MHz for KOH and KOD

	B_0	D_0
KOH	8208.679 ± 0.010	0.1219 ± 0.00006
KOD	7494.827 ± 0.010	0.009946 ± 0.00006
NaOH	12567.054 ± 0.010	0.02872 ± 0.00005

The pattern of satellites is qualitatively similar to those found previously for CsOH, RbOH and LiOH and is interpreted in the same way. A similar interpretation for NaOH leads to values included in Table 4.

Inorganic molecules

There has been a growth in the number of papers on inorganic compounds, which reflects an increasing interest in applications in this area. A considerable number of phosphorus compounds have been studied, several papers deal with silicon compounds, and a number deal with germanium derivatives.

As well as papers on compounds of the more familiar elements, nitrogen, sulphur, and the halogens, papers have also appeared on compounds of vanadium and tellurium. Some further boron compounds have been studied, including the microwave identification of the molecule BF_2OH. The analysis of the spectrum shows the molecule has a planar structure with the parameters given in Table 5.

Table 5

Structural parameters for BF_2OH

Bond lengths/Å		*Angles/°*	
r(B—F)	1.32 (3)	FBF	118.0
r(B—O)	1.34 (4)	FBO	122.8 and119.2
r(O—H)	0.941	BOH	114.1

The dipole moment $\mu = 1.86 \pm 0.02$ D. As shown in Figure 1, the BF_2 group is tilted away from the OH group in the same way as the NO_2 group is in the nitric acid molecule. For BF_3 itself, *l*-type resonance has been reported and some cubic potential constants have been evaluated. Two further borane adducts have been investigated. Trimethylphosphine-borane, $(CH_3)_3$ P,BH_3, shows a symmetric-rotor spectrum. By using deuterium substitution and ^{10}B and ^{11}B isotopic species, the molecule is found to have the parameters collected in Table 6.

Table 6

Structural parameters for $(CH_3)_3$ P, BH_3

Bond lengths/ Å		*Angles/°*	
r(P—B)	1.901 ± 0.007	CPC	105.0±0.4
r(P—C)	1.819 ± 0.010	HCH	109.3±1.0
r(C—H)	1.08 ± 0.02	HBH	113.5±0.5

The structure of the closely related methylphosphine-borane, CH_3PH_3,BH_3, has also been determined. Substitution co-ordinates were obtained for all the atoms except those of phosphorus which were calculated from first-moment condition.

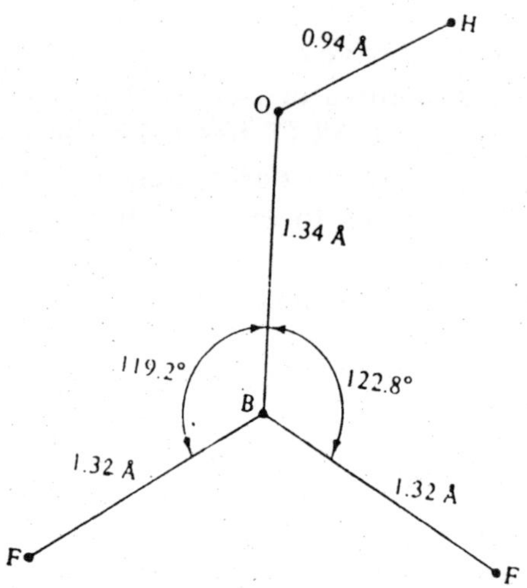

Figure. 1

The resulting structure, which has a plane of symmetry, is shown in Figure 2. The methyl group is tilted towards the borane group and the origin of this tilt is considered in terms of electrostatic interactions. The dipole moments are found to be 4.99 ± 0.2D for $(CH_3)_3P,BH_3$ and 4.66 ± 0.05 D for CH_3PH_2,BH_3.

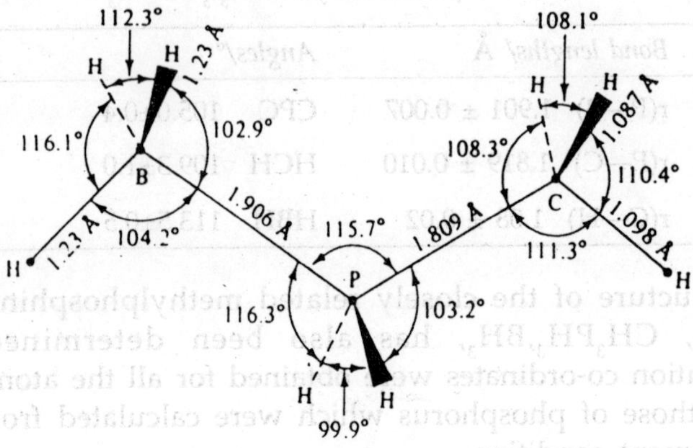

Figure. 2

A number of papers have appeared on isocyanates, and a comparison of structures of isocyanates has been made. Chlorine isocyanate, ClNCO, has been shown to have a planar structure with the parameters listed in Table 7, having Cl and O *trans* to one another. A preliminary report has also appeared on the spectrum of the recently prepared cyanogen isocyanate, NCNCO.

Table 7

Structural parameters for ClCNO

Bond lengths/Å			*Angles*
r(Cl—N)	1.703 ±0.11	NCO	171° 24 ±1°330
r(C—O)	1.165±0.008	ClNC	119° 22 ±1°
r(N—C)	1.218 ±0.012		

Trimethylsily isocyanate, Me_3SiNCO, is found to have a rotational spectrum characteristic of a symmetric totor, indicating that the equilibrium configuration of the Si—N = C = O chain is either linear or very close to linear. There is a very low-frequency bending mode which has been estimated at 64 ± 15 cm^{-1} from the intensities of satellites, and the distinction between linear and non-linear equilibrium configuration is not easily made.

The problem has been discussed in connection with an electron-diffraction study of the large-amplitude vibrations in both H_3SiNCO and H_3SiNCS. for the potential function which is proposed for the thicyanate the energy required to change the Si—N=C angle from 180 to 140° is less than 1 kcal mol^{-1}. The parent molecule of this series of compounds, isocyanic acid, HNCO, has been the subject of a high-resolution molecular-beam maser study. Nitrogen nuclear quadrupole coupling constants were determined and deuteron quadrupole couplings obtained for DNCO. Further lines have been measured in the microwave spectrum of HNCO in connection with radio-astronomical interests. The isomeric linear molecule fulminic acid HCNO, has been the subject of a detailed study of rotational spectra in vibrationally excited states. The analysis has given unperturbed rotational constants B_v, and centrifugal distortion constants D_v for several vibrational states, and vibrational anharmonicity constants have also been obtained.

A potential function containing a hump which disturbs the isotropic two dimensional oscillator potential is proposed for the low-lying degenerate bending mode. Cyanogen azide, NCN_3, has a spectrum consistent with a planar molecule. Independent studies lead to a dipole moment μ = 2.96 ± 0.0 0.03 D. Structural parameters 56 based on certain assumptions are given in Table 8. The

r(C≡N) distance is an r_B value, and the remaining parameters were derived on the assumption that the N_3 chain is linear and that the terminal N—N bond length is 1.133 Å as in hydrazoic acid. Interestingly the N—C≡N chain appears to be bent, which parallels earlier findings for $CH_{2(}CN)_2$ and $S(CN)_2$.

Table 8

Structural parameters for cyanogen azide

Bond lengths/ Å	*Angles*
r_8 (C°N) 1.164 0.005	CNC 120° 13' ± 1°
r_0 (N= N) 1.252 0.01	NCN 176°2' ± 2°

A number of papers have appeared on silicon compounds, leading to further knowledge about silane derivatives in particular. Ground-state rotational constants B_0, D_0^J and D_0^{JK} have been obtained for $^{28}SiH_3D$ from a high-resolution i.r. study. A Zeeman study has been made of methylsilane ($MeSiH_3$ and $MeSiD_3$). It proves not to be possible to decide unambiguously from the Zeeman evidence on the correct quadrupole moment or on the sign of the electric dipole moment.

However, several arguments favour the sign $+CH_3SiH—$, contrary to the relative electronegativities of carbon and silicon, and this conclusion has been supported by non-empirical calculations on the electronic structure. The finding may be understood in terms of the C—H and Si—H bond moments, the octupole moment of methane and silane indicating polarities +H—C— and +Si—H— respectively.

The study of alkylsilanes has been extended from the previously studied methyl-, ethyl-, and dimethyl-silane to include methylethylsilane. This is believed to exist in two rotational isomeric forms, but assignments have so far been made in the microwave spectrum only for the trans-isomer. The rotational constants can be fitted with structural parameters transferred from Me_2SiH_2 and Et_2SiH_2 with small adjustments in the CCSi, CCH, and SiCH angles.

The dipole moment is found to be 0.758 ± 0.005D, which is almost identical with that for dimethylsilane. The spectra of the following halogeno-derivatives of silane have been investigated: CH_3SiF_3 $(CH_3)_3SiCl$, CD_3SiH_2Cl, and $CH_2{=}CHSiF_3$.

A re-investigation of CH_3SiF_3 includes the study of ^{13}C isotopic species and a consequent re-determination of the structural parameters leads to the values listed in Table 9. The dipole moment is found to be 2.33 ± 0.10 D.

Four isotopic species of Me_3SiCl have been examined, viz. the ^{35}Cl and ^{37}Cl species for the normal and the fully deuteriated molecules. The four rotational constants were fitted by a least-squares programme which, with assumed C—H bond distances and HCSi angles as for Me_3SiH, gave the following parameters:

Table 9

Structural parameters for CH_3SiF_3

Bond lngths/Å		*Angles*	
r(C—H)	1.081±0.004	HCSi	110° 1' ± 30'
r(C—Si)	1.812 ± 0.014	FSiC	112° ± 1° 6,
r(Si—F)	1.574 ± 0.007		

r(Si—Cl) = 2.022 ± 0.005 Å ClSiC = 110.5 ± 1°

r(Si—C) = 1.857 ± 0.005 Å

The chlorine nuclear quadrupole coupling coefficient for ^{35}Cl has a value of —46.9 ± 1.5 MHz. The study of the microwave spectra of four isotopic species of CD_3SiHCl ($^{29}Si^{35}Cl$, $^{30}Si^{35}Cl$, $^{28}Si^{35}Cl$, and $^{28}Si^{37}Cl$) has allowed the substitution parameters for Si and Cl to be calculated in two ways, leading to r(Si—Cl) = 2.049 ± 0.013 and 2.052 ± 0.005 Å Centrifugal distortion and chlorine nuclear quadrupole coupling constants have also been reported.

The microwave spectrum of vinyltrifluorosilane, CH_2=$CHSiF_3$, has been analysed to give rotational constants for the ground state and five vibrationally excited states. The dipole moment is found to have a value of 2.33 D. Some further derivatives of germane have also been investigated. For fluorogermane, GeH_3F, the parameters in Table 10 have been reported.

Table 10

Parameters for GeH_3F	
r(Ge—F) = 1.74 ± 0.01 Å	μ= 2.33 ± 0.06 D
r(Ge—H) = 1.47 ± 0.01 Å	*eQq*(^{73} Ge) = -93.0(3) ± 0.10 MHz.

The structure is calculated on the assumption of regular tetrahedral geometry. The microwave spectrum of iodogermane, GeH_3I, has been reported and bromogermane, GeH_3Br, has been re-investigated. Isotopic species for both Ge and Br allow the germanium-bromine bond length to be obtained as *r*(Ge—Br) = 2.2970 ± 0.0002 Å.

Because only a single iodine isotope occurs naturally, the same method cannot be used for GeH_3I. The assumption is made that the Ge—H projection on the symmetry axis is the same as in GeH_3Br and this gives *r*(Ge—I) = 2.5075 ± 0.0005 Å. Nuclear quadrupole coupling constants are also obtained, and the spectrum of GeH_3Br in excited vibrational states has been reported.

The microwave spectrum of trimethylgermane has been analysed and rotational constants have been obtained for Me_3GeH, and with certain assumptions the heavy-atom dispositions have also been determined, giving the parameters in Table 11.

Table 11

Parameters for Me_3GeH and Me_3GeBr

Me_3GeX	r(Ge—C)/Å	r(Ge —X)/Å	CGeX/°
Me_3GeH	1.947 ± 0.006	1.532 ± 0.001	109± 0.1
Me_3 GeBr	1.936 ± 0.006	2.323± 0.001	106.3 ± .01

The structure of trimethylbromogermane has also been obtained 70 from a study of its microwave spectrum and the parameters are included in Table 11.Nitrogen compounds on which papers have appeared include hydroxylamine, methylhydrazine, monochloramine, nitrous acid, and dinitrogen trioxide.

Table 12

Structural parameters for NH2OH

Bond lengths /Å		*Angles*	
r(N—H)	1.016 ± 0.008	HNH	107° 6' ± 30'
r(N—O)	1.453 ± 0.002	HNO	103°15' ± 30'
r(O—H)	0.962 ± 0.005	NOH	101°22 ± 30'

The microwave spectrum of hydroxylamine reveals only the trans-isomer. Only a single rotational spectrum is observed for NHDOH (and for NHDOD) and so it follows that the molecule has a plane of symmetry which bisects the HNH angle and includes the NOH group. The six structural parameters given in Table 12 have been obtained from a least-squares method. Using thirteen observed moments of inertia. The dipole moment is found to be it μ = 0.59 ± 0.05 D and nitrogen nuclear quadrupole coupling coefficients have also been obtained. The observed transitions show no splittings due to inversion, indicating a higher barrier than in ammonia. It appears that electronegative substituents lead to an increased barrier for it has been found previously that no splitting is observed for NHF_2 nor has any been reported for NH_2Cl. A further investigation of NH_2C1 leads to the r_B structure in Table 13. Nitrogen and chlorine nuclear quadrupole coupling constants are also reported.

Table 13

Structural parameteres for NH_2 Cl

Bond lengths/ Å		Angles	
r(N—H)	1.017 ± 0.005	HNCl	103° 41' ± 22'
r(N—Cl)	1.7480 ± 0.0001	HNH	107° ± 2°

A number of theoretical papers on the calculation of the barrier height in ammonia have appeared, including a comparison of NH_3 and CHs–· Further work on the high-resolution spectrum of ammonia obtained by using a beam maser spectrometer shows splittings which are attributed to a difference in molecular *g*-values for the upper and lower inversion states with $J = 3$ and $K = 2$. A reinterpretation of observed hyperfine patterns has also been given.

The potential function hindering the N—N torsional motion in methylhydrazine, $MeNH.NH_2$, has been determined through the use of microwave and far-i.r. spectroscopic data. The microwave work provides the torsion angles of the cis- and trans-rotamers and the energy difference of the two potential minima and the i.r. spectrum provides torsional frequencies. Calculations lead to a trans barrier height of 3.58 ± 0.07 kcal mol^{-1} and a cis barrier of 8.66 ± 0.86 kcal mol^{-1}. Some re-assignment of the far-i.r. spectrum has been made on the basis of the potential function.

A detailed study has been made of centrifugal distortion and its use in the calculation of potential functions for both cis- and trans-forms of nitrous acid, both the HONO and the DONO species being examined in each case. Distortion constants have been obtained for cis- and trans-isomers of each species and have been used together with vibrational frequencies to evaluate the quadratic potential functions. Coriolis coupling constants have been calculated and these, taken with the vibrational frequencies, allow the calculation of average moments of inertia, from which the structures of the average configurations have been determined.

A further examination has also been made of the anhydride of nitrous acid, dinitrogen trioxide, N_2O_3, Nuclear quadrupole coupling coefficients have been evaluated for both nitrogen nuclei and discussed in terms of the bonding in the molecule. Another paper deals with the use of vibration-rotation interaction constants and inertial defects for calculating force constants for nitryl fluoride. An increasing number of papers are appearing on phosphorus compounds. Phosphorous oxytrichloride has been re-investigated, and a number of compounds derived from PF_3 have been studied.

The spectrum of PF_2C1 has been analysed to give rotational constants for both of the chlorine isotopic species and these lead to the structural parameters in Table 14.80 The dipole moment was found to be μ = 0.89 ± 0.01 D and the nuclear quadrupole coupling coefficients have been interpreted to indicate a minimum of 1.5% π-bond character for the P-Cl bond.

Table 14

Structural parameters for PF_2Cl

Bond lengths/Å			Angles/°
r(P—F)	1.571 ± 0.003	FPF	97.3 ± 0.2
r(P—Cl)	2.030 ± 0.006	PFCl	99.2 ± 0.2

The spectrum of the recently prepared aminodifluorophosphine, PF_2NH_2, has also been observed and its analysis Provides strong evidence in favour of a planar PNH_2 configuration. This appears to be the first case of a free molecule in which a planar NH_2 configuration has been found; it is attributed to (*d-p*) π-bonding.

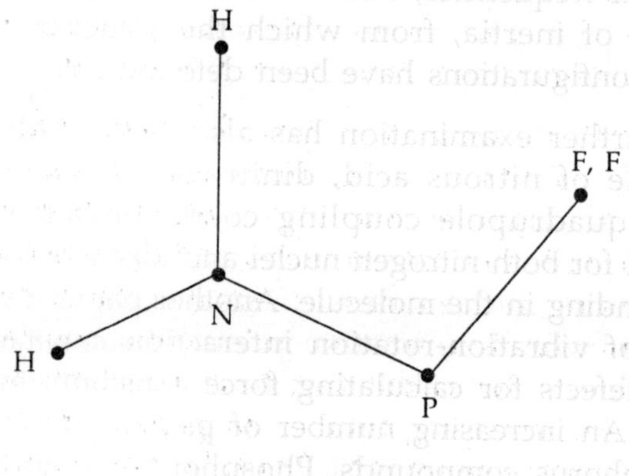

Figure 3

A microwave study has also been made of the dimethyl derivative, dimethylaminodifluorophosphine, PF_2NMe_2, and a Structure similar to that for the parent amino-compound is consistent with the experimental results.

Table 15

Structural parameters for PF_2NH_2

Bond lengths/ Å		*Angles/*	
r(P—F)	1.587± 0.004	FPF	94.6±0.2
r(P—N)	1.650 0.004	PFN	100.6 ± 0.2
r(N—H)(cis)	1.002 ± 0.005	PNH(cis)	123.1± 0.4
r(N—H)(trans)	0.981 ±0.005	PNH(trans)	119.7± 0.4
		HNH	117.2 ± 0.4

Table 16

Structural parameters for PF_2 NMe_2

Bond lengths/Å		*Angles/°*	
r(P—F)	1.57	EPF	95.3
r(P—N)	1.66	NPE	99.8
		PNC (cis)	124.5
		PNC (trans)	121.3

A projection of the molecule in its plane of symmetry is shown in Figure 4 and the structural parameters obtained on the basis of assumed parameters for the methyl group and the N—C bond lengths are given in Table 16.

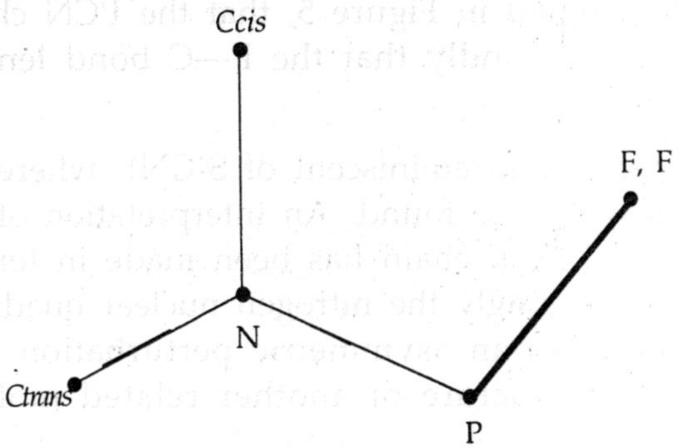

Figure 4

An electron-diffraction study for both of these molecules, PF_2NH_2 and PF_2NMe_2, led to a non-planar gauche structure in eachcase. On the other hand the attempt to get a reasonable fit of the microwave data for F_2PNMe_2 to a gauche conformation did not prove successful.

The microwave spectrum of the cyano-derivative PF_2CN has also been analysed and structural parameters in Table 17 were obtained by making use of ^{13}C and ^{15}N species. This structure has also been investigated by electron-diffraction study.

Table 17

Structural parameters for PF_2 CN

Bond lengths/Å		*Angles/°*	
r(P—F)	1.566 ± 0.007	FPF	99.2 ± 0.2
r(P—C)	1.815 ± 0.005	FPC	96.9 ± 0.2
r(C—N)	1.157 ± 0.003	PCN	171.12 ± 0.8

The parameters obtained by the two methods are in reasonable agreement though not all are within the sum of experimental uncertainties. The assumption of a linear PCN arrangement in the electron-diffraction work probably contributes to this discrepancy. Striking features of the structure as determined spectroscopically are firstly, as illustrated in Figure 5, that the PCN chain is non-linear and secondly that the P—C bond length is unusually short.

The situation is reminiscent of $S(CN)_2$ where quite analogous features are found. An interpretation of these features for the PCN chain has been made in terms of a-bonding; interestingly the nitrogen nuclear quadrupole coupling indicates an asymmetric perturbation to the bonding. The structure of another related molecule, hydrothiophosphonyl difluoride, $SPHF_2$, has been obtained from the microwave spectra of the isotopic species $^{32}SPHF_2$, $^{34}SPHF_2$, and $^{32}SPDF_2$. The S, P, and H atoms define a molecular plane of symmetry as shown in Figure 6, and the parameters listed in Table 18 were obtained.

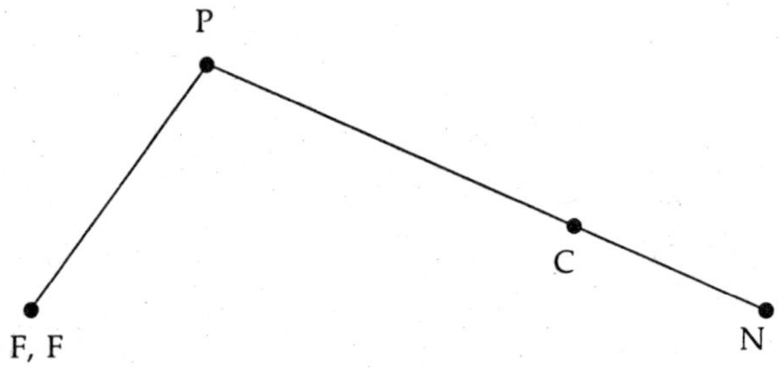

Figure 5

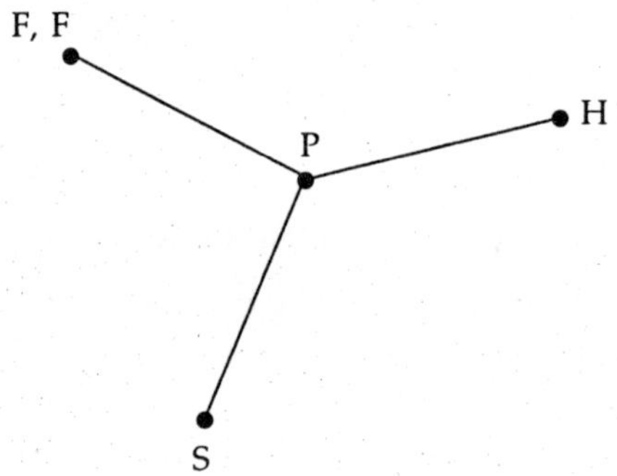

Figure 6

The parameters for the latter molecule were obtained from the spectra of the two symmetric rotor species and the asymmetric rotor $OV^{35}Cl_2\,^{37}Cl$. The vanadium valence angle ClVC1 is about 8° larger than the phosphorus valence angle ClPCl. Among sulphur compounds some detailed studies have been reported on hydrogen persulphide and thionyl halides. An interesting feature to emerge from the analyses of the spectra of HSSH and DSSH is the finding that *K* levels are split by an amount which is several orders of magnitude larger than expected from the asymmetry parameter.

Table 18

Structural for $SPHF_2$

Bond lengths/Å		*Angles/ °Å*	
r(P—H)	1.392 ± 0.005	SPF	117.4 ± 0.2
r(P—F)	1.551 ± 0.005	SPH	119.2 ±0.2
r(S—P)	1.867 ± 0.005	FPF	98.6 ± 0.2

The spectrum of $POCl_3$ has been re-examined, and the structural parameters are listed in Table 19 with those of vanadyl chloride, $VOCl_3$, which has now also been examined by microwave spectroscopy.

Table 19

Structural parameters for $POCl_3$ and $VOCl_3$

Bond lengths/Å		*Angles/°*	
r(P—O)	1.455 ± 0.005	ClPCl	103.7±0.2
r(P—Cl)	1.989 ± 0.002		
r(V—O)	1.595 ± 0.005	ClVCl	118.8 ± 0.2

The origin of the effect is a centrifugal distortion splitting of the *K* levels. Normally asymmetry splitting is much larger than that arising from centrifugal distortion but in these cases not only is splitting of the *K* = 2 levels large but the sequence of levels is reversed as compared with the order expected from asymmetry splitting.

Some 350 lines have been measured and it is found that centrifugal distortion treatment in terms of six quartic constants is sufficient to account for the observations. The spectrum of HSSD has also been observed and analysed in the same way. There is insufficient isotopic information to allow the determination of a complete r_a structure but the parameters in Table 20 have been obtained.

The barrier to internal rotation in hydrogen Peroxide has been discussed from a theoretical point of view.

Table 20

Structural parameters for H_2S_2 and D_2S_2

Bond lengthsÅ		Angles	
r(S—S)	2.055 ± 0.001	SSH	91°20' ±3'
r(S—H)	1.327 ± 0.003	(HSSH)	90°36' ± 3'
r(S—D)	1.324 ± 0.003	(DSSD)	90°14 ± 2'
		(HSSD)	90°25' ± 5'

Thionyl halides have been examined and centrifugal distortion coefficients evaluated. In one study 96 more than 100 transitions observed in the region 40—70 GHz have been used in an attempt to determine quartic and sextic distortion parameters for thionyl fluoride, SOF_2

Another study uses some 250 transitions for thionyl fluoride but advises caution in assessing the significance of the sextic coefficients. It is found that if the sextic coefficients are omitted then the difference between observed and calculated frequencies rises from a few hundredths of a megahertz to several megahertz.

Although inclusion of about four sextics appears to be necessary to fit all the lines measured, various combinations of four sextics are about equally good; measured various combinations of four sextics are about equally good; evidently there is a strong correlation among the individual sextic coefficients.

However, it seems that this does not upset a reliable determination of the quartic coefficients. These quartic coefficients have been used with i.r. data in an attempt to determine the harmonic force fields, and, with some constraints because of lack of data, this has been achieved. The structural parameters (r_0) have also been refined and are given in Table 21. The quoted errors here represent the limits in which the r_0 concept is valid; they are not observational errors but relate to the internal consistency of the I_0 values used in their calculation.

Table 21

Structural parameters for SOF_2

Bond lengths	*Angles/°*
r(S—O) 1.4127± 0.003	FSF 92.83 ± 0.02
r(S—F) 1.5854 ± 0.0002	FSO 106.82 ± 0.03

The microwave spectra of thionyl fluoride in two excited vibrational states has been the subject of another investigation. An observed perturbation is attributed to a Coriolis reasonance between the two levels and an estimate of the coupling parameter has been made.

A centrifugal distortion treatment has also been made for thionyl chloride, $SOCl_2$ some eighty transitions being fitted by a set of quartic and sextic coefficients. The spectrum of a further pentafluoride chloride of a Group VI element has been observed and analysed. Altogether rotational constants have been obtained for twelve isotopic species of TeF_5C. These lead to the first Te—Cl distance for a Te^{VI} molecule.

The bond length is in fact well determined, the mean of thirty r_B values giving r(Te—Cl) 2.250 ± 0.002$Å$. A unique determination of the remaining three parameters is not possible but if the axial and equatorial Te—F bonds are assumed to be of equal length then the structure shown in Figure 7 is obtained, the parameters being given by r(Te—F) = 1,8305 ± 0.0012 $Å$ and $F_{eq}TeF_{ax}$. = 88°15' ± 7'.

There are good reasons for supposing that the angle probably lies between these same limits since implausible differences in the two Te—F bond lengths would be required to take the value outside these limits. Thus the Te—F equatorial bonds are bent away from the chlorine atom, in an analogous way to that proposed in structures for SF_5 Cl and WF_5Cl. A further investigation has been made of BrF_5, which has previously been shown to have C_{4v} symmetry, and a new feature has now been observed. It is Predicted for molecules of C_{4v} symmetry that there should be a splitting of the K = 2 lines, and this effect has now been observed for BrF_5.

The analysis of the spectrum leads to the following values of the centrifugal distortion constants: D_{jk} = 0.57 ± 0.01 kHz; D_{jk} = —0.50 ± 0.02 kHz; and R_6 = 0.07 ± 0.005 kHz. Electron-diffraction studies have been made of BrF_5 and IF_5 and the results combined with microwave data to give the structural parameters in Table 22.

Table 22

Structural parameters for BrF_5 and IF_5

XF_5	r(X—F)$_{eq}$/$Å$	r(X—F)ax/	F_{ax} XFeq/°
BrF_5	1.774 ± 0.003	1.689 ± 0.008	84.8± 0.1
IF_5	1.869 ± 0.005	1.844 ± 0.005	81.9 ± 0.1

The microwave spectrum of chloryl fluoride has been analysed for two isotopic species. The molecule has a pyramidal configuration with chlorine at the apex. The structural parameters which have been obtained are given in Table 23.

Table 23

Structural parameters for $FClO_2$

Bond lengths/Å		*Angles*	
r(Cl—F)	1.664 ± 0.030	OClO	113.5 ± 2.0
r(Cl—O)	1.434 ± 0.005	FClO	103.2 ± 1.5

The hydrogen-bonded dimer formed by hydrogen fluoride has been investigated by the molecular-beam electric resonance method. Parameters obtained for the three isotopic species $(HF)_2$, $(DF)_2$, and HFDF are given in Table 24. The spectrum of DFHF was nor observed. These results are interpreted in terms of a semi-rigid model with large-amplitude motion of the hydrogen and deuterium atoms.

Table 24

Parameters for $FClO_2$

Parameter	*$(HF)_2$*	*$(DF)_2$*	*HFDF*
½(B+C)/ MHz	6504.8 ± 2.0	6252.194±0.002	6500.1 ± 0.1
μ_a/D	2.987 ± 0.003	2.9919 ± 0.0006	3.029 ± 0.003
$[eqQ_D]_a$ kHz		110 ± 8	270 ± 30

Tunnelling motion causes a splitting of the rotational levels for $(HF)_2$ and $(DF)_2$ but not for HFDF. By assuming the H—F bond distance to be the same as in the free monomer it is found that the F—F distance is 2.79 ± 0.05

A and that the end HF unit is bent 60-70° from the F-F axis. The microwave spectrum of hydrogen fluoride has also been examined and lines have been assigned to a hexamer and to a heptamer.

Organic molecules

Acyclic molecules without internal rotation

Matsuura and Overend present an equilibrium structure for methyl iodide. These latter authors have now observed sufficient i.r. bands of methyl iodide under high resolution to ensure that the vibration-rotation constants α^A_i and α^B_i for all of the fundamental modes i are available for sufficient isotopic species from direct spectroscopic observation (microwave and i.r.).

Thus, recourse to assumptions such as the Coriolis sum rule for A_0 values is unnecessary. The results of Matsuura and Overend are r_e(C—H) = 1.084 ± 0.001Å r_e(C—1) = 2.132 ± 0.001Å, and $(HCH)_e$ = 111°12 ± 9, identical within experimental error with those of Duncan. The α_i^B values and the iodine nuclear quadrupole coupling constants for the vibrationally excited states v_2, v_3, v_5, v_6, $2v_3$, and $v_3 + v_6$ of the species CD_3I are reported from a thorough analysis of the $J = 3 \leftarrow 2$ transitions by Kuczkowski.

The degenerate states v_5, v_6, and $v_3 + v_6$ are treated by the method of Grenier-Besson and Amat to give the *l*-doubling constant, among other parameters. The α_i^B values for the fundamentals are in good agreement with those used by Matsuura and Overend in the r_e structure determination. Kukolich and Nelson have carried out high-resolution measurements of the hyperfine structure in the $J = 1 \rightarrow 0$ transitions of $Me^{35}Cl$ and $Me^{37}Cl$, using a molecular-beam maser spectrometer to give very accurate values of the chlorine nuclear quadrupole coupling constants and values for the nuclear spin to molecular rotation magnetic coupling constants.

A comparison of the $eq_{zz}Q(^{35}Cl)$ values along the C—Cl bond direction (z) in the series $CH_3{}^{35}Cl$, $CDH_2{}^{35}Cl$, and $CD_3{}^{35}Cl$ shows a linear decrease; the difference between the first and last (180 kHz) is about fifty times the experimental error. Such a change represents a decrease in electric field gradient along z at the ^{35}Cl nucleus of 0.2%. The authors attribute this reduction to an indirect effect involving changes in the chemical properties of the methyl group on deuterium substitution.

Apparently, the shortening of the C—D distances on deuteriation reduces the electron-withdrawing power of the carbon-hydrogen bonds and thereby decreases the electronegativity of the methyl group, leading to increased ionic character for the C—Cl bond.

Townes-Dailey theory indicates that an increased ionic character of 0.17% for the C—Cl bond in $CD_3{}^{35}Cl$ over that in $CH_3{}^{35}Cl$ is sufficient to account for the decreased nuclear quadrupole coupling in the former. The pure rotational spectra of the [^{79}Br)- and [^{79}Br]-species of methyl bromide have now been resolved in the far-i.r. region between 17 and 43 cm^{-1}. Kukolich and his collaborators have published several other studies involving a molecular beam maser spectrometer.

The inherently high resolution of the technique has been used in methyl isocyanide ($J = 1 \rightarrow 0$ transitions) to obtain the small nitrogen nuclear quadrupole coupling constant ($eq_{zz}Q$), the nitrogen nuclear spin-rotation magnetic coupling constant (C_N), the corresponding quantity (C_H) for the hydrogen nuclei, and the hydrogen spin-spin interaction constant (D_{HH}) with high precision. From a conventional millimetre-wave investigation of transitions of methyl isocyanide up to $J = 7 \leftarrow 6$ in the $v_8 = 1$ and $v_8 = 2$ vibrationally excited states, on the other hand, the quantities $B^* = 10\ 092.3169$, $D_J = 0.00492$, $D_{JK} = 0.2271$, ρ^* 0.05349, and $|q_{8\ \text{eff}^*}| = 6.937$ MHz have been determined by Bauer, Bogey, and Maes using a Grenier-Besson-Amat type of analysis.

The previously reported high-resolution work on the hyperfine structure in fluoroform by Kukolich, Nelson, and Ruben has recently been criticized by Reynders, Ellenbroek, and Dymanus. These latter authors, also using a beam-maser spectrometer, report a sharp difference in the C_F and C_H spin-rotation constants obtained by each group when both use the $J = 1 \rightarrow 0$ transition. Kukolich and Ruben have subsequently re-investigated the hyperfine structure and report results in close agreement with the Netherlands group. In this context, the molecular-beam electric resonance spectrum of methyl fluoride measured in several rotational states is worth reporting.

Spin-rotation constants C_F and C_H for the fluorine and hydrogen nuclei respectively are derived together with an accurate value $\mu = 1.8585(5)$ D for the dipole moment, a result in excellent agreement with the previous value. Another halogenated methane which comes under the scrutiny of Kukolich's molecular-beam maser spectrometer is methylene fluoride. This time the molecular Zeeman effect of the $3_{03} \rightarrow 2_{12}$ rotational transition is observed in emission by placing the spectrometer cavity in a 100 kG magnetic field.

The unusually high resolution possible provides more precise molecular susceptibility anisotropies, $2X_{aa} — X_{bb} — X_{cc} = —4.16 \pm 0.02$ and $2X_{bb} — X_{cc} — X_{aa} = 0.58 \pm 0.01 \times 10^{-7}$ JG $^{-2}$ mol^{-1} than previously available and when these are combined with the previously reported molecular *g*-values, the improved molecular quadrupole tensor components $Q_{aa} = —3.95 \pm 0.14$, $Q_{bb} = 2.05 \pm 0.16$, and $Q_{cc} = 1.90 \pm 0.18$ ($\times 10^{-26}$ e.s.u. cm^2) are obtained. Some further substituted methanes; have also been investigated through more conventional microwave spectroscopic techniques. An essentially complete r_a structure for nitromethane (1) is presented by Cox and Waring from a microwave study of the parent molecule and five isotopically substituted species.

They use the $m = 0$ internal rotation state to obtain accurate rigid-rotor rotational constants by means of a Watson-type centrifugal distortion analysis. This state behaves just like the usual effective rigid rotor except that, because of the almost free internal rotation of the methyl group, I_a derived from the $m = 0$ spectrum corresponds only to the moment of inertia of the NO_2 framework about the molecular symmetry axis.

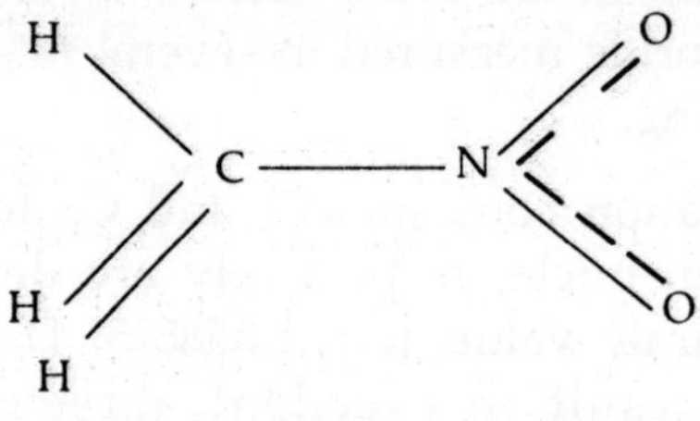

Consequently, the quantity $\Delta = I_e—I_b —I_a(NO_2)$ is analogous to that of a planar asymmetric rotor in that the contribution of the hydrogen atoms to I_e and I_b is the same, and indeed the value 0.2015 a.m.u Å^2 for the parent species and similar values for the heavy-atom isotopically substituted species strongly indicate coplanarity of the heavy atoms. More conclusive evidence of planarity is derived from nuclear-spin statistical-weight effects in transitions of the CH_3NO_2 and CD_3NO_2 species. The quantitative structure which results from isotopic substitution is:

r(N—O) = 1.224 ±0.005 Å	ONO = 125.3 ±0.3°
r(C—H) = 1.088	HCH = 107.2°
r(C—N) = 1.489 ±0.005 Å	

In FNO_2 the fluorine atom is highly electronegative and had previously been assumed to allow important contributions from the ionic valence-bond structure (2) in order to account for the relatively large angle ONO (136°) and the relatively short NO bond (1.180 A).

Table 25

Structural parameters of nitro-groups

Species	*N—O bond length/Å*	*ONO/°*	*O...O distance/Å*	*Electronegativity of attached group*
NO_2	1.240	114.9	2.090	0.8
$C_6H_5NO_2$	1.227	124.4	2.171	2.5
CH_3NO_2	1.224	125.3	2.175	2.5
$ClNO_2$	1.202	130.1	2.181	3.0
NH_2NO_2	(1.206)	1.301	2.181	3.0
N_2O_3	1.210	129.8	2.190	3.0
CH_3ONO_2	1.207	129.5	2.182	3.5
HNO_3	1.205	130.3	2.184	3.5
NO_2	1.193	134.1	2.198	—
FNO_2	1.180	136.0	2.188	4.0
NO_2	1.09	180.0	2.180	>4.0

For nitro-methane the less electronegative CH_3 group is expected to allow important contributions from 'nitrite-ion type' valence-bond structures (3) in addition to the usual structures (4). This is used to rationalize the smaller angle ONO and longer NO bond in nitromethane.

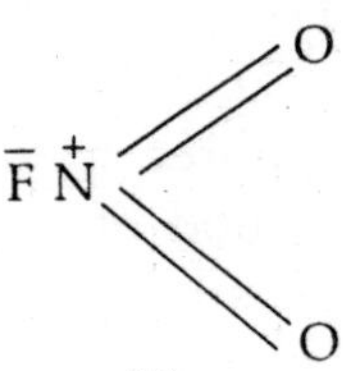

(2)

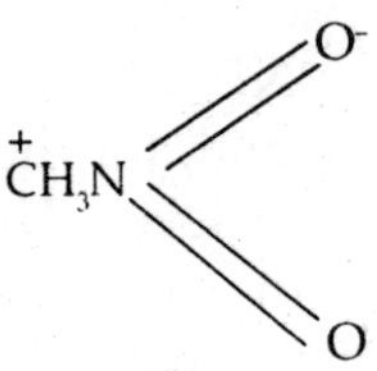

(3)

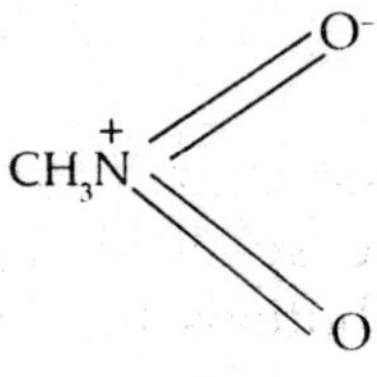

(4)

The intermediate electronegativity of chlorine fits conveniently with the nitro-group structure, which is seen in $ClNO_2$ to be intermediate between those in FNO_2 and CH_3NO_2. McLay and Winnewisser have investigated the millimetre-wave spectrum of deuteriochloroform ($CDCl_3$) in the 100—200 GHz range.

The advantage of the millimetre-wave study is that an accurate rotational constant and centrifugal distortion constants can be obtained. In the conventional microwave region the low-J transitions encountered possess a complicated and only partially resolved nuclear quadrupole hyperfine structure due to the three chlorine nuclei, whereas the K-splitting due to centrifugal distortion is small. Fortunately, for transitions with $J >$ 15 in the millimetre region the hyperfine structure is sufficiently condensed that the individual K components of the transition are well resolved, with no apparent hyperfine broadening.

Then the B_0 value and centrifugal distortion constants can be accurately determined from the K-splitting, which is just like that of a molecule without coupling nuclei. The reported constants are B_0 3250.292 ± 0.0015 MHz, D_J= 1.414 ± 0.005 KHz, and D_{JK} = -2.314 ± 0.006 KHz. The simple but important molecule cyanamide continues to excite considerable interest. A detailed analysis of the conclusions that can be derived from the μ_a spectrum of cyanamide is given by Tyler, Sheridan, and Costain.

Rotational constants B and C have been obtained for the isotopic varieties NH_2CN, NHDCN, ND_2CN, $_{15}NH_2CN$, $NH_2C^{15}N$, $^{15}ND_2CN$, and $ND_2C^{15}N$ for the vibrational ground state and, for the first three species, in the first excited inversion level. The method of analysis of the spectral data in each case is such that the contributions from inversion-rotation interaction to line frequenciesare accounted for in the terms inseparable from one of the centrifugal distortion constants (D_{JK}). No accurate values of the constant A are available since cyanamide approximates closely to a prolate symmetric top. The absence of I_a values from the inertial data presents some difficulties in the structure determination, but relationships are produced which allow essentially r_B co-ordinates for the hydrogen atoms and r_8 a co-ordinates for the nitrogen atoms.

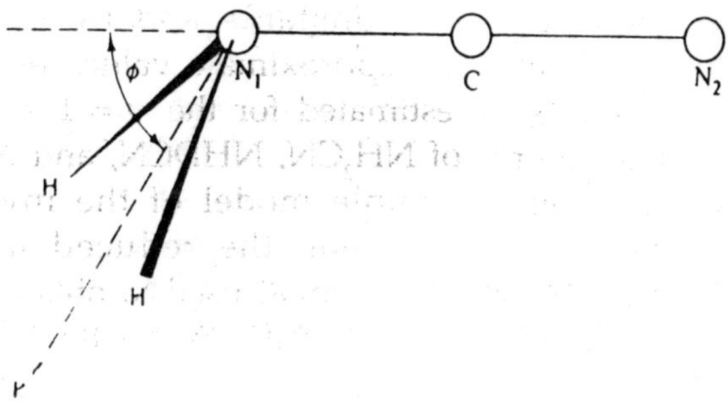

Fig. 7. PN_1—bisector of HN_1H

The first-moment condition then yields a_c. By assumption of collinearity of N(1)—C—N(2) and use of first-moment and product of inertia conditions, the small c co-ordinates of the heavy atoms are obtained. Sufficient isotopic data is also available for the calculation with reference to ND_2CN as the parent species to be carried out. The two structures, the mean of which is shown in Table 26, are in close agreement.

Some discussion of the potential function governing the NH_2 inversion was also possible. Reference to Lide's theory indicates which $v = 0$ state transitions can interact with the $v = 1$ state transitions observed to suffer appreciable perturbations from rigid-rotor behaviour.

Table 26

Structure of cyanamide

r[N(1) —H]	1.001 ± 0.015
r[N(2)—N]	2.506 ± 0.002
r[N(1) —Cl	1.346 ± 0.005
r[C—N (2)	1.160 ± 0.005
HN (1) H	113° 31 ± 2°

Knowing the rotational constants and the pairs of transitions which interact, approximate values of 50, 33, and 15 cm^{-1} have been estimated for the $v = 1 \leftarrow v = 0$ vibrational separations of NH_2CN, NHDCN, and ND_2CN respectively. Given a simple model of the inversion motion at the nitrogen atom, the reduced mass is calculated and a Manning potential used to obtain a best fit to the NH_2CN, NHDCN, and ND_2CN $1 \leftarrow 0$ vibrational separations.

The barrier height to inversion obtained is $V_0 = 710$ cm^{-1}. Although this value is considerable disagreement with $V_0 = 467 \pm 30$ cm^{-1} from the i.r. study, the authors point to the extreme sensitivity of V_0 from the microwave data to the value of the out-of-plane angle corresponding to the minima in the potential function, which is only approximated by ϕ. In consequence of the extra vibrational data used in the derivation of the potential function from the i.r. study, this identification with ϕ is unnecessary and the lower barrier therefrom is to be preferred.

Attanasio, Bauder, and Gunthard have used the exact solution of the rotation-inversion problem by infinite matrix diagonalization as a procedure to attack the cyanamide problem. They employ experimental microwave data consisting of pure rotational transitions in the $v = 0$ and $v = 1$ inversion levels and rotation-inversion transitions between rotational levels in the $v = 0$ and $v = 1$ states of ND_2CN (data collected mainly by Tyler). All of the data could not be fitted by their procedure and the authors conclude that no set of dynamical constants within the semi-rigid model used could reproduce the observed transitions satisfactorily.

Hence, a unique value of V_0 is not possible, but if either $v = 0$ or $v = 1$ rotational transitions only are used with the intersystem transitions the values of V_0 obtained are 735.5 and 700.6 cm^{-1} respectively. The group at the Swiss Federal Institute has also carried out *ab initio* LCAO-MO-SCF calculations on cyanamide in order to determine the molecular electric dipole moment as a function of ϕ and HN(1)H.

The value obtained for HN(1)H = 115° and ϕ = 39° is 4.625 D, in good agreement with μ= 4.32 ± 0.08 . A close relative of cyanamide, difluorocyanamide (NF_2CN), and its phosphorus analogue (PF_2CN) are the subjects of microwave structure determination by Schwendeman and his co-workers. For difluoro-cyanamide the spectra of the isotopic species NF_2CN, $NF_2{}^{13}CN$, $NF_2C^{15}N$, and ${}_{15}NF_2$ CN have been analysed and two types of atomic co-ordinate derived from the observed moments of inertia. First, assuming a plane of symmetry for the molecule, the nine non-zero co-ordinates are fitted to the moments of inertia (excluding the imprecisely determined I_a values for the isotopically substituted species), the two centre of mass relations, and the one product of inertia relation to give an essentially r_0 structure.

Secondly, r_8 co-ordinates (a and c) are derived for the carbon and two nitrogen atoms while the fluorine atom co-ordinates are fixed by auxiliary moment conditions. The dipole moment values measured are μ_a = 1.03 ± 0.02, ϕ_c = 0.39 ± 0. 10, and μ = 1. 10 ± 0.02 D. The similar investigation of PF_2CN $_{84}$ with less isotopic substitution possible, yields the structure shown in Table 27.

There are two noteworthy features of these structures. In both molecules the X—C—N atoms are not collinear but the C ≡ EN group is tilted by about 10° away from the fluorine atoms. This can be explained on the basis of either a bonding interaction between the N or P atom electron]one pair and the CN group π-system or an electrostatic repulsion between the fluorine atoms and the CN group n-system. Similar behaviour has been reported in $S(CN)_2$.

The other significant structural feature is the much more pronounced pyramidal nature of the bonds attached to the nitrogen atom in NF_2CN than in NH_2CN, a change also observed if HNF_2 is compared with ammonia.

The observed rotational microwave spectra of aminoacetonitrile for the isotopic species NH_2CH_2CN, $NHDCH_2CN$, and ND_2CH_2CN, are interpreted in terms of a molecular conformation in which the amino and methylene groups have a trans orientation with respect to each other as in (5). Negative values of X_{aa} observed for both the also has the trans structure, nitrogen nuclei and a quadrupole hyperfine structure for the $1_{01} \leftarrow 0_{00}$ are further evidence.

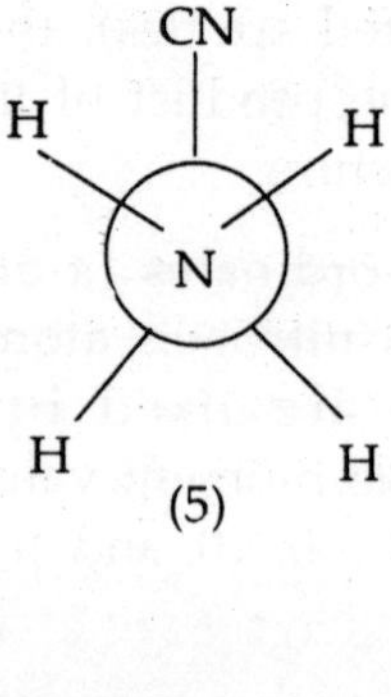

(5)

Table 27

Molecular structures of XF_2CN (X = N or P)

	X =N		X = P
r(C ° N)	1.151 ± 0.004	1.158 ± 0.004	1.157 ± 0.003
r(X —C	1.392 ± 0.009	1.386 ± 0.009 1.815	1.566 ± 0.007
XCN	169.7 ± 2.1	173.9 ± 2.2	171.2 0± 0.8
CXF	104.7 ± 0.6	105.4 ± 0.7	96.9 ± 0.2
FXF	102.9 ± 0.4	102.8± 0.2	99.2 ± 0.2

The measured dipole moment components are transition as in hydroxyacetonitrile, which also has been trans structure, are further evidence. The measured dipole moment components are μ_a =2.55 ± 0.02, μ_b = 0.30 ± 0.02, and μ_{total} = 2.57 ± 0.030 D. Conformations of some ethane derivates existing in a dominant rotameric from have been established recently. The rotational spectrum of but a single isomer of ethyl thiocyanate could be identified by Bjorseth and Marstokk corresponding to the gauche-rotamer(6).

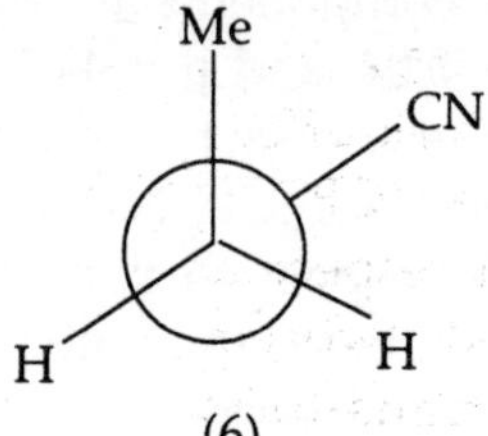

(6)

A rather thorough analysis of the observed μ_a spectrum with a Watson five-constant centrifugal distortion treatment gave rise to rotational constants which could re-produced by assuming structural parameters for the relevant parts of the molecule from *n*-propyl cyanide and methyl thiocyanate if the dihedral angle (measured from the anti-form) for ethyl thiocyanate was 122° (ie. the spectrum corresponds to the gauche-form). The failure to find a spectrum consistent with the anti-form is interpreted to mean that the gauche is the more stable of the two forms by at least 0.8 kcal mol^{-1}.

Vibrational satellites in the spectrum assigned to the methyl-group torsion exhibit no splitting for $v \leq 2$, which places a lower limit of V_3 = 3.8 kcal mol^{-1} on the barrier to internal rotation of the CH_3 group, a value consistent with 4.1 kcal mol^{-1} from the i.r. frequency of the methyl torsion.

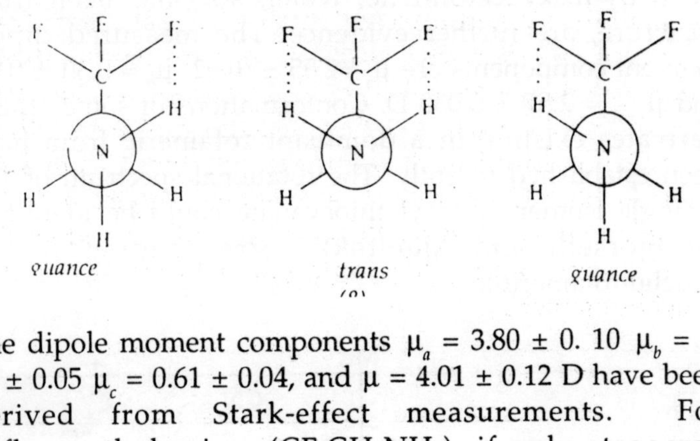

guance *trans* *guance*

The dipole moment components μ_a = 3.80 ± 0. 10 μ_b = 1. 13 ± 0.05 μ_c = 0.61 ± 0.04, and μ = 4.01 ± 0.12 D have been derived from Stark-effect measurements. For trifluoroethylamine, ($CF_3CH_2NH_2$), if only staggered configurations with respect to rotation about the C—N bond are considered, two equivalent gauche-forms, (7) and (9), and one trans-form (8) are possible. In the trans-form stabilisation through two hydrogen bonds is likely whereas only one such interaction need be considered in the gauche-forms.

Warren and Wilson observe and assign near-prolate type spectra belonging to a single rotamer for the $CF_3CH_2NH_2$, CF_2CH_2NHD, and $CF_3CH_2ND_2$ species. No other rotameric form of these molecules could be detected.

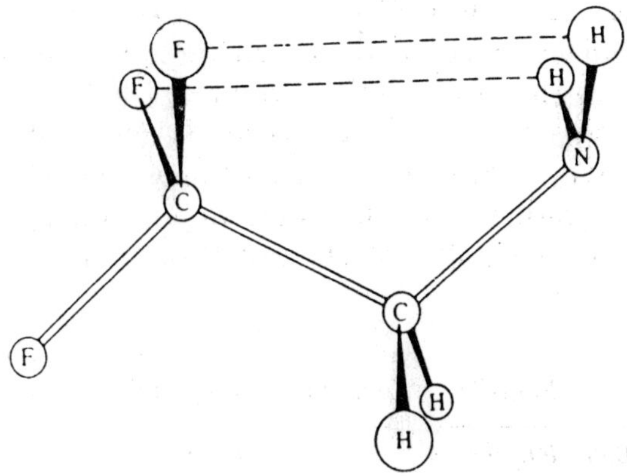

Fig. 8. Trans form of trifluoroethylamine.

Although the isotopic substitution allows the aminoproton co-ordinates to be determined, in order to determine the configuration of the observed rotamer the CF_3 group parameters and the C—C bond distance are assumed from CF_3CH_3 and the CH_2-group, NH_2-group, and C—N-bond parameters are assumed from $CHNH_2$. The angle CCN is varied until the observed rotational constants are re-produced.

Since the amino-proton co-ordinates do not strongly affect the calculated rotational constants, the NH_2-group parameters are subsequently varied to fit the amino-proton co-ordinates so that the plausible structure found for the molecule is the trans-form shown in Table 28 and Figure 9. The measured dipole moment components are $\mu_a = 1.13 \pm \mu_b$, 0.28 ± 0.03 and $\mu_c = 0.0 \pm 0.05$ D . The authors point out that, because of relative dipole moment components, if the *gauche*-form were as populated as in ethylamine the lines of the *gauche*-form of trifluoroethylamine would be stronger than those of the transform.

A stabilisation of the trans-form through interaction of the amino-protons and fluorine atoms is therefore indicated. The contribution of a covalent interaction to this stabilisation is ruled out on the basis of the N—H bond length essentially unchanged from that in methylamine and an F H distance of 2.65 Å which is 0.10 A in excess of the sum of the hydrogen and fluorine van der Waals radii. A dipole-dipole interaction is suggested by the almost parallel N—H and C—F bonds.

Table 28

Plausible structure of trifluroethylamine

Bond lengths/ Å		*Angles*	
r(C—F)	1.335	FCF	108° 30 'a
r(C—C)	1.530	CCF	111° 2'a
r(C—H)	1.093	CCH	109° 28'a
r(C—N)	1.474	HCH	109° 28'a
r(N—H)	1.01 ± 0.02	CCN	113° 50' ± 1°
r(N....F)	2.65 ± 0.02	CNH	110° ± 2°
		HNH	110°30' ± 1°
		NHF	95° ± 5 °
		NH.CF	5° ± 5°

Buckley and Brochu have identified a single dominant conformer of 2-methoxyethanol ($CH_3OCH_2CH_2OH$) from the spectra of the parent and the hydroxy-group-deuteriated species. Six stable conformations of this compound arising from internal rotations about the C—C and C—O(H) bonds are possible, even ignoring those resulting from rotation of the methyl group as a whole about the C—O (ether) bond.

Conformations (10), (11), and (12), referred to rotation about the C—C bond, are described by capital letters whereas (13), (14), and (15), referred to rotation about the C—O(H) bond, are given by lower-case letters. From a consideration of (i) the agreement between the observed rotational constants and those calculated on the assumption of structural parameters for the ether part of the molecule from the dimethyl ether and for the alcohol part from 2-fluoroethanol, (ii) the hydroxyl proton Kraitchman co-ordinates, and (iii) the observed dipole moment components $\mu_a = 2.03 \pm 0.02$, $\mu_b = 1.15 \pm 0.02$, and $\mu_c \approx 0.25$D, Buckley and Brochu assign the observed spectrum to a *GAUCHE*(G)-*gauche*(*g*)-form in which the methyl group has been fixed in its trans position so as to make the COCC chain coplanar.

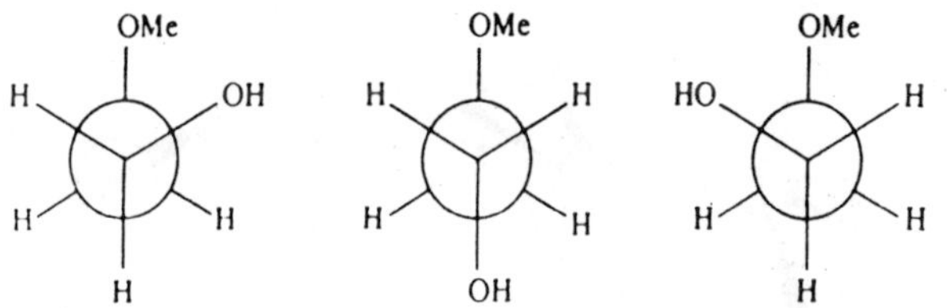

GAUCHE (*G*) *TRANS* (*T*) *GAUCHE* (*G*)

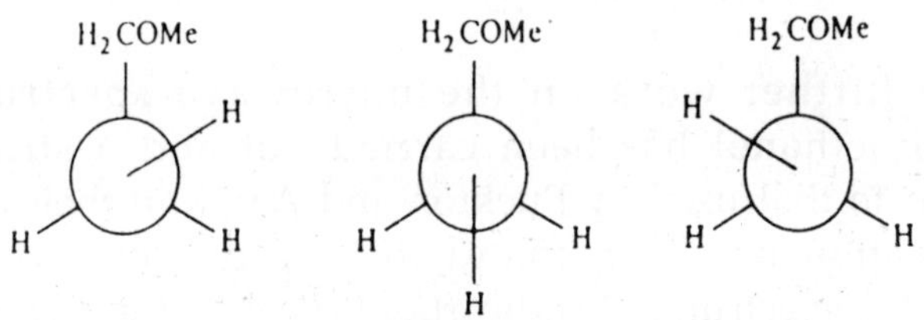

guance (*g*) *trans* (*t*) *guance* (*g*)

(14) (15)

A better fit to the rotational constants, hydroxyl proton co-ordinates, and dipole moment components is obtained if the dihedral angles θ = C (H_3)OC/CCO ϕ = OCC/CCO, and γ = CCO/COH are varied slightly from their standard values $\theta = 0°$, $\phi = 60°$,and $\gamma = 60°$ respectively for the all-gauche-from to give $\theta = 8 \pm 3°$,

$\phi = 57 \pm 3°$, and $\gamma = 45 \pm 5°$. In the assigned conformation, the preferred orientation of the methyl group about its own axis is assumed to be staggered with respect to the nearest methylene group. It should be noted that in the established all-gauche configuration, the hydroxyl hydrogen is approximately aligned with the nearest tetrahedrally disposed sp^3 lone pair of electrons on the ether oxygen atom.

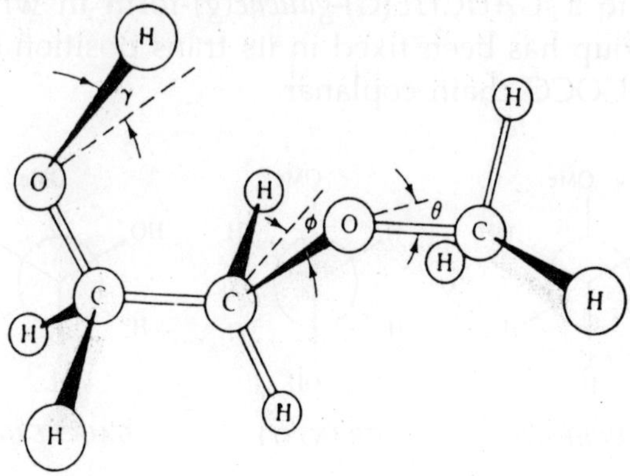

Fig. 9. All gaunce conformation of 2-methoxyethanol

Some further work on the microwave spectrum of 2-fluoroethanol has been carried out and a structure similar to that used by Buckton and Azrak in their earlier publication has been found to be consistent with the observed spectrum. Azodicarbonitrile has the possibility of cis- and trans-isomers, (16) and (17).

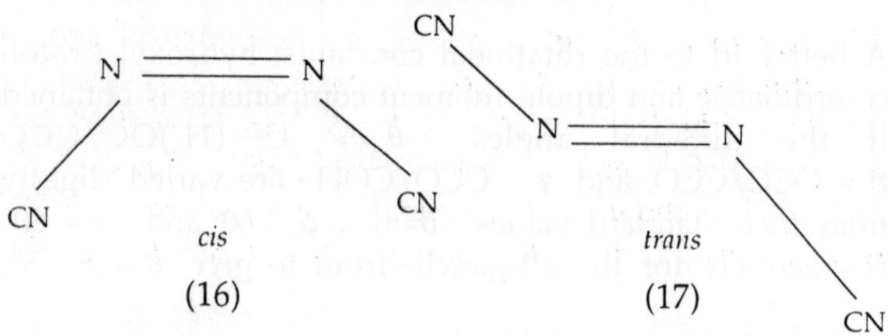

cis (16) *trans* (17)

The i.r. and Raman spectra recorded under a variety of conditions strongly indicate C_{2h} symmetry for the compound. No evidence for the cis-form was found. In the microwave spectrum only seven transitions appeared and these could not be assigned to the cis-isomer, which is thereby restricted to exist in < 1 % abundance.

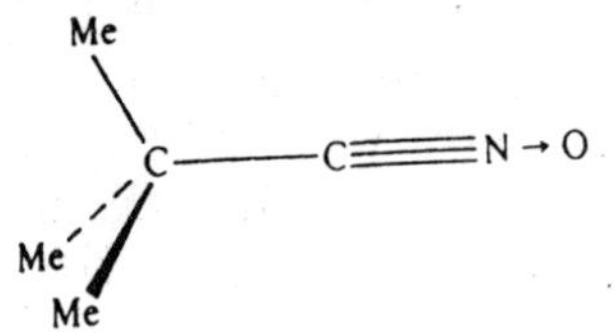

(18)

A preliminary publication concerned with pivalonitrile (18) is adorned with an impressive reproduction of well-resolved *K* structure in the $J = 11 \leftarrow 10$ transition of this symmetric rotor. A strong satellite series of a low-lying bending mode also exhibits such structure in each transition. Of course, the symmetric-top nature of the spectrum establishes collinearity of the C—C≡N→O atoms and by suitable structural assumptions for the —C≡N→O group and the t-butyl group the author derives r(C—C≡) = 1.458 ± 0.01 Å from B_0= 1459.227 MHz. This parameter is longer than in CH_3—CNO (1.442 Å), a change consistent with the family of C—X bond lengthenings, in going from CH_3X to$(CH)_3$ C— X compounds.

Investigations of small molecules containing the C= O group are again in evidence, particularly Zeeman studies. The simplest aldehyde, formadehyde, is the subject of a Zeeman study in which the splittings in the presence of the magnetic field of the radio-frequency K-doublet transitions 2_{20}—2_{21}, 3_{21}—3_{22}, 7_{34}—7_{36} and 8_{35}—8_{36} at 71.143, 355.569, 136.925, and 300.869 MHz respectively are measured and the diagonal elements of the molecular g-tensor obtained.

Of the experimental results, g_{ec} = –2.898 ± 0.005 is in excellent agreement with a previous measurement but g_{bb} = 0.956 and g_{cc} = —0.322 ± 0.003 appear not to be so, presumably because these elements cannot be determined independently from the transitions in the present study. A characteristically thorough study of the molecular rotational Zeeman effect of thioformaldehyde by Rock and Flygare now puts the sulphur analogue of formaldehyde on the same basis.

By observing first-and second-order magnetic field effects for rotational transitions, molecular *g*-values; (g_{aa}= -5.2602 ± 0.0068, g_{bb} = —0. 1337 ± 0.0004, and g_{cc} =—0.0239 ± 0.0004, where a is the symmetry axis and c the out-of-plane axis) and the molecular magnetic susceptibility anisotropies $2X_{aa}$—X_{bb}—X_{cc} = 52.3 ± 1.1 and 2_{Xbb} — X_{aa}— X_{cc} = —5.1 ± 0.7 (10^{-13} J G^{-2} mol^{-1}) are derived. These five magnetic parameters are then combined with the known molecular structure to give the molecular quadrupole moments Q_{aa} = 3.0 ± 0.7, Q_{bb} =—2.4 ± 0.5, and Q_{cc} = —0.6 ± 1.1 (10^{-26} e.s.u cm^2).

The authors are then able to calculate numerous other molecular properties including anisotropies of the second moments of charge distribution, the second moments of the electronic charge distribution themselves (if one of the values, $<C^2>$, is estimated by summing individual free-atom diamagnetic susceptibilities), and the diagonal elements of the diamagnetic and paramagnetic susceptibility tensors. It turns out that g_{aa} =—5.2602 ± 0.0068 is the largest molecular *g*-value yet measured.

Rock and Flygare specifically discussed the reasons for this enhanced value relative to that of formaldehyde smaller separations between the ground-state energy ε_0 and ele ctronically excited-state energies ε_k in thioformaldehyde than in formaldehyde itself since in both molecules g_∞ is given by

$$g_\infty\ 1.00+(2M_p/mI_{aa})\ \Sigma\ [\,|<0|L_a|k>2/\varepsilon_0 - \varepsilon_k]$$

where M_p is the proton mass, m the electron mass, I_{aa} the moment of inertia about the a-axis, and L_a the electronic angular momentum operator projected on the a-axis, and the sum over k includes all electronically excited states. The authors also use this equation to establish rather neatly the absolute signs of the g-values since the second term is always negative and therefore $g_{aa} > 1$. Hence, a value of magnitude 5.2602 can only be negative.

Another interesting point to emerge from the discussion is that the second moments of charge distribution $<a^2>$are 21.1 and 10.4 ($\times 10^{-16}$ cm^2) in thioformaldehyde and formaldehyde respectively, indicating an elongation of the electron cloud in the former, which is a trend also apparent when CO and CS are compared. The recent detection of thioformaldehyde in interstellar space has spurred workers at N.B.S. to attempt a catalogue of all transitions of the molecule within the range of radiotelescopes. As part of this effort, Beers, Klein, Kirchoff, and Johnson have looked at $H_2{}^{12}C^{32}S$ in the millimetre-wave range 100—250 GHz. Twenty-five newly assigned R-branch transitions complement all previously measured transitions in a Watson-type centrifugal distortion treatment.

A high correlation of the τ_{aaaa} value with the rotational constant A dictates that the well-determined value of the former (from a high-resolution i.r. study) should be used as a datum point in the least squares. It is concluded that the rotational and centrifugal distortion constants so obtained should predict all transitions (except for one Q-branch series) with $J \leq 30$ and $v < 300$ GHz with a standard deviation of < 0.5 MHz.

Methyleneimine (CH_2=NH), a molecule isoelectronic with formaldehyde, has been identified as a transient species in the gas phase (half-life ~0.1s at 30 µmHg pressure) through its microwave spectrum. Initially, production of this species was via the mixing of fluorine atoms derived from a microwave discharge of CF_4 or SF_6 with methylamine downstream of the discharge.

A hydrogen atom is abstracted from the methylamine by a fluorine atom. Later, the pyrolysis of methylamine proved to be a useful source of methyleneimine. Twenty-seven transitions, including the $1_{01} \leftarrow 0_{00}$, have been identified and give rotational constants consistent with a reasonable model structure as well as quadrupole coupling constants due to a single nitrogen nucleus.

The quantity $\Delta = I_c^0 - I_b^0 - I_a^0 = 0.05592$ a.m.u Å ^{2} is strong evidence of molecular planarity. Evidence for the existence of the cis-form of glyoxal (19) was recently obtained from an electronic band of glyoxal at 4875 Å by Currie and Ramsay, who also published some rotational constants. With these constants as a starting-point, A small value of the inertia defect $\Delta = -0.193$ a.m.u. Å^2 points to the cis rather than the other dipolar form.

Intensity measurements of satellites associated with the first excited torsional level relative to the ground state give 114 ± 8 cm^{-1} for the $1 \leftarrow 0$ torsion transition, which is to be compared with the value 128 cm^{-1} for the corresponding transition of trans-glyoxal.

The molecular dipole moment is found to be $\mu_b = 4.8 \pm 0.2$ D with the assumption $\mu_a = \mu_c = 0$ on symmetry grounds.

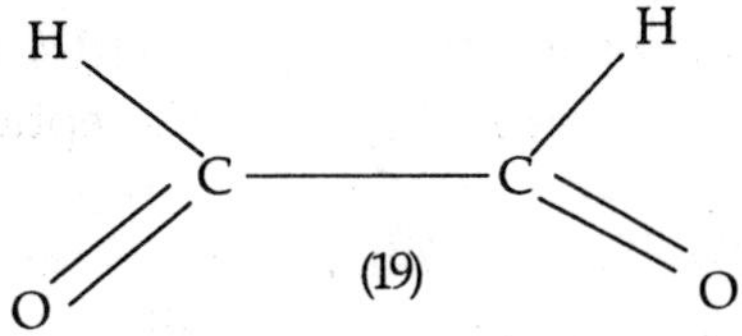

(19)

The very slightly asymmetric rotor keten exhibits an a-type microwave spectrum from which the rotational constant A and the distortion constant D_K are ill determined. Johns, Stone, and Winnewisser remedy this by a high-resolution study of the perpendicular bands v_7 and $(v_2 + v_8)$ in the i.r. spectrum and examination of the millimetre-wave spectrum up to 200 GHz.

Ground-state combination differences from the former and new millimetre transitions from the latter in conjunction with the previously known microwave spectrum lead to a precise set of ground-state molecular constants. As a result the authors confidently predict several microwave and millimetre-wave rotational transitions, as yet unmeasured, which are possibly of use in astrophysical investigations.

An investigation of the rotational Zeeman effect in the microwave spectrum of dimethylketen by the group at Kiel has given the molecular g-values ($g_{aa} = \pm 0.020$, $g_{bb} = \pm 0.0165$, and $g_{cc} = \pm\ 0.0126$) and the molecular magnetic susceptibility anisotropies ($2X_{aa} - X_{bb} - X_{cc} = -1.0 \pm 1.0$ and $2_{xbb} - X_{cc} - X_{aa} = -0.8 \pm 1.2$[$\times\ 10^{-13}$ JG $^{-2}$ mol^{-1}]).

Flygare and Tigelaar have observed the molecular Zeeman effect in transitions of the isotopic species $^{15}NH_2COH$ (the ^{15}N isotope avoids complicating nuclear quadrupole effects) and obtained the molecular g-values ($g_{aa} = -0.2843 \pm 0.0011$, $g_{bb} = -0.0649 \pm 0.0004$, and $g_{cc} = -0.0117 \pm 0.0004$) and the two independent molecular susceptibility anisotropies $2X_{aa} - X_{bb} - X_{cc} = 2.2 \pm 0.7$ and $2X_{bb} - X_{aa} - X_{cc} = 8.0 \pm 0.5$ ($\times\ 10^{-13}$ J G^{-2} mol^{-1}).

They then take formamide as a model for the amide linkage in poly-(L-alanine). This polypeptide (and others) shows two n.m.r. peaks for the α-proton in helix-breaking solvents; the upfield peak, it is agreed, is assigned to α-protons in the helical form whereas controversy surrounds the downfield peak.

Some argue that the downfield peak arises from α-protons in the random coil, the shift being caused by the consequent re-orientation of amide planes adjacent to the proton. Others attribute the shift to solvation of the amide planes. Using the molecular susceptibility anisotropy of formamide as transferable to the amide groups, Flygare and Tigelaar calculate using McConnell's formula that the expected shift caused by the helix to random coil transition in, poly (L-alanine) is slightly upfield rather than the observed downfield shift, thus supporting the solvation theory.

Rotational transitions of formamide have also been observed in emission in space recently. Kirchoff and Johnson have therefore carried out a very accurate centrifugal distortion analysis of transitions in the microwave spectrum of the molecule in order to be able to predict, with low uncertainty, frequencies of transitions of further astrophysical interest. They critically assess the existing microwave data and measure 22 new transitions in the ground state of the $^{14}NH_2{}^{12}CH^{16}O$ species.

The centrifugal distortion constants of the closely related molecule carbarnyl fluoride (NH_2CFO) have also been evaluated recently. The trans-conformer (20) gives rise to a strong microwave spectrum whereas that arising from the cis-conformer (21) is much weaker. Invariance of the quantity $I_a + I_b — I_e$ to isotopic substitution of the hydroxyl hydrogen and the oxygen atoms clearly establishes that both have a plane of symmetry. For both isomers, satellites associated with the torsional vibration and an in-plane skeletal mode where identified.

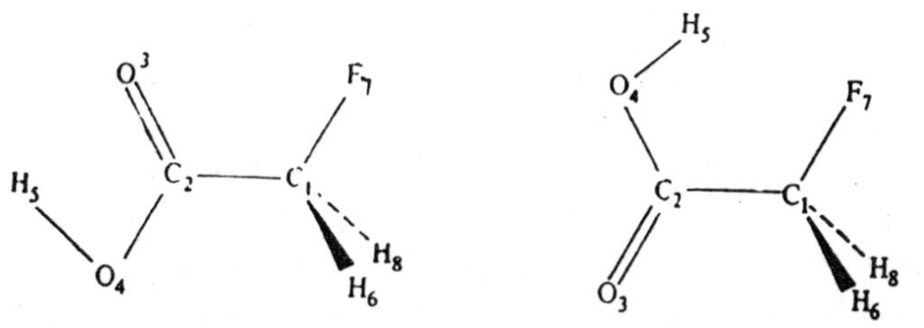

The smooth variation of the rotational constants of the trans-form with the torsional quantum number indicates that the potential function is essentially harmonic in the lower part and relative intensity measurements indicate the equal spacing to be 104 cm^{-1} for the trans-form and 112 cm^{-1} for the cis-form. Stark-effect measurements in the cis- and trans-forms lead to the dipole moments μ_a = 1.582 ± 0.004, μ_b = 2.434 ± 0.007, and μ = 2.903 ± 0.007 D for trans and 2.739 ± 0.007, 0.426 ± 0.010, and 2.772 ± 0.008 D for the corresponding quantities of the cis-isomer.

Table 29

Molecular parameters for fluoroacetic acid [H' is projection of H (6) and H (8) on the molecular plane

Band lengths / Å	trans	cis-trans
C(2) = C (3)	1.202 ± 0.004	0 (ass)
C(2) —C(4)	1.344 ± 0.010	0 (ass)
C(1) —C(2)	1.534 ± 0.008	0 (ass)
C(1)—F(7)	1.387 ± 0.010	0 (ass)
O(4)—H(5)	0.971 ± 0.004	—0.043 ± 0.008
C(1)—H(6, 8)	1.073	0 (ass)

Angles/ °		
C(1)—C(2) = O (3)	126.1± 0.7	-6.3 ± 0.7
C(1)—C(2) —O(4)	108.8 ± 0.4	+ 6.3 ± 0.7
C(2)—C(1)—C(7)	109.2 ± 1.0	+2.5 ± 0.4
C(2) —O(4)—H(5)	105.9 ± 0.5	+ 3.0 ± 0.8
C(2)—C(1) —H'	125° (ass)	0° (ass)

Four conformers of fluoroacetic acid with a plane of symmetry are possible but calculated dipole moments using the addition of bond moments and also the CNDO/2 method show quite clearly that the indicated trans-and cis-forms should be chosen by virtue of their observed dipole components. Agreement between calculated and observed principle axis co-ordinates of the hydroxyl hydrogen also confirms this choice.

The molecular structures of both isomers are determined by a combination of microwave spectral data with electron-diffraction data. Each bond length, except *r*(O—H), is taken to be the same in both conformations and some assumptions about the CH_2-group parameters are made. The resulting structures are recorded in Table 29. The energy difference between the cis- and trans-forms from relative intensities in the microwave spectra is estimated as 604 ± 28 cal mol^{-1}, corresponding to 70 ± 2% of the trans-form at 385 K. A potential energy function based on a simple model for cis-trans conversion and fitted to the estimated torsional frequencies of each form and to the cis-trans energy difference gives

$$V_1 = 1155 \pm 180 \text{ cal mol}^{-1},\ V_2 = 5300 \pm 350 \text{ call mol}^{-1}, \text{ and}$$

$$V_3 = —580 \pm 180 \text{ cal. mol}^{-1}$$

for the first three terms in the Fourier expansion. The energy barrier separating the two forms based on the three-term function is 5.7 kcal mol^{-1}. Glyoxylic acid has three likely conformations in which the heavy atoms are coplanar, viz. trans-1 (22), trans-2 (23), and cis (24). The microwave spectrum of one conformer has been detected by Marstokk and Mollendal.

The observed rotational constants agree closely with those of the trans-forms calculated from structural parameters transferred from oxalic acid and glyoxal. The observed inertia defect $\Delta = 0.075\ 78$ a.m.u. Å is suggestive of a planar arrangement of the atoms, and the smooth variation of rotational constants derived from satellites assigned to successive states of the C—C torsional mode confirms a planar equilibrium configuration.

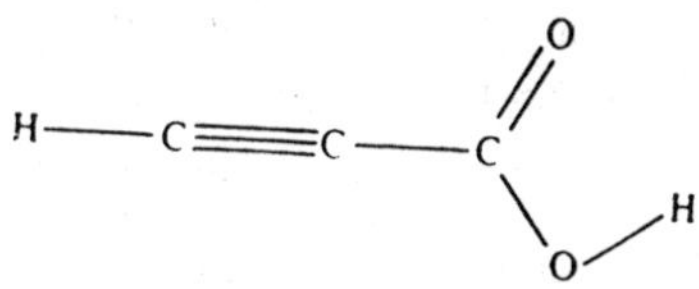

Relative intensity measurements give the 1← 0 separation in the torsional mode as 167 ± 12 cm^{-1}, a value to be compared with 122 cm^{-1} from an i.r. combination band. The dipole moment components of the observed conformer are $\mu_a = 1.85 \pm 0.03$, $\mu_b = 0.20 \pm 0.10$, and $\mu = 1.86 \pm 0.04$ D. The isotopic species OHC—CO_2D was studied in order to differentiate between the two trans-forms. The principal axis co-ordinates of the carboxyl hydrogen atom point unequivocally to the trans-1 form, presumably stabilized by an intramolecular hydrogen bond as well as conjugation.

Propiolic acid (25) is a planar molecule as indicated

by the inertia defects Δ = 0.2430,0.2369, and 0.2496 a.m.u. Å of the isotopic species $HC{\equiv}CCO_2H$, $HC{\equiv}CCO_2D$, $DC{\equiv}COO_2H$, and derived from a study of their microwave spectra by Lister and Tyler.

The principal axis co-ordinates of the hydrogen atoms derived from the isotopic moments of inertia are in excellent agreement with those calculated from an assumed structure based on the accurately determined microwave structures of propynal and formic acid and show without doubt that the hydroxyl proton adopts the cis configuration with respect to the carbonyl group as in formic acid. The dipole moment components are measured from the $1_{11} \leftarrow 0_{00}$ and $3_{21} \leftarrow 3_{12}$ transitions of $HC{\equiv}CCO_2H$ and the $2_{12} \leftarrow 1_{01}$ and $3_{21} \equiv 3_{12}$ transitions of $HC{\equiv}CCO_2D$.

The values are $\mu_a = 0.80 \pm 0.02$ and $\mu_b = 1.38 \pm 0.02$D for the former species and $\mu_a = 0.76 \pm 0.02$ and $\mu_a = 1.40 \pm 0.02$ D for the latter; is 1.59 ± 0.03 D.

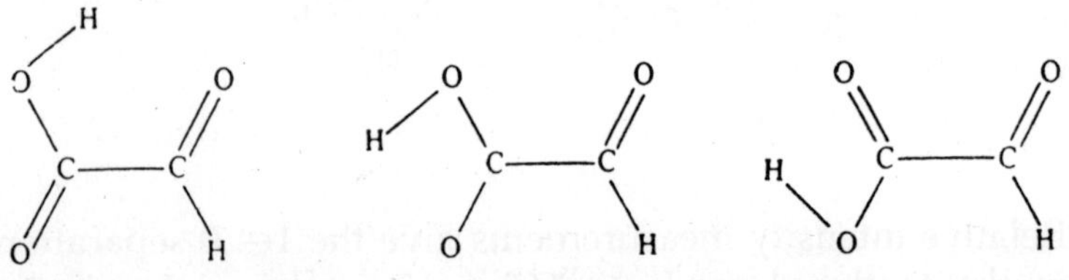

A planar s-trans-form has been established for the one geometrical isomer of acryloyl chloride (26) detected by its microwave spectrum by Kewley, Hemphill, and Curl. A small positive inertia defect (e.g. Δ= 0.0333 a.m.u. Å^2 for Cl) derived for both ^{35}Cl and ^{37}Cl isotopic species is consistent with planar geometry. Using the structure of the vinyl group as in acrolein and assuming the remaining parameters from acetyl fluoride, the observed rotational constants demonstrably correspond with those calculated for the s-trans-form, Unlike acryloyl fluoride the s-cis-form is as yet unidentified. A partial structure is determined by allowing four of the assumed parameters to vary until a best fit to the rotational constants of the ^{35}Cl and ^{37}Cl species is achieved.

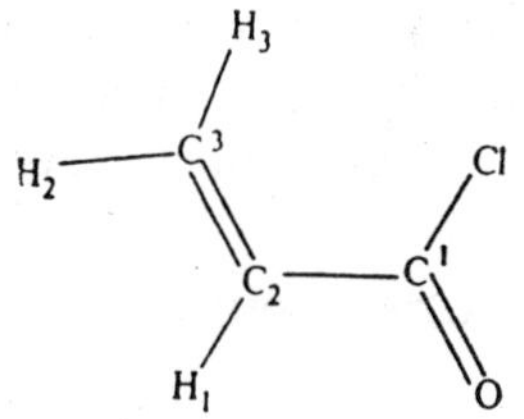

The final parameters, *r*[C(2)– C(1) = 1.476Å, *r*[C(1)–Cl] = 1.816 A, C(3) = C(2)– C(1) = 122.6°, and C(2)–C(1)–Cl = 116.3°, do not differ greatly from those assumed initially. Relative intensity measurements lead to 95 cm^{-1}for the 1 ← 0 separation associated with the C—C torsion, a value in excellent agreement with that estimated from Δ(94 cm^{-1}) but, as expected, lower than that of acryloyl fluoride (115 cm^{-1}). Dipole moment components are $\mu_a = 2.76 \pm 0.02$, $\mu_b = 1.45 \pm 0.03$, and $\mu_{total} = 3.12 \pm 0.04$ D. A large number of *a*- and *b*-type transitions with $J \leq 40$ in vinyl fluoride have been analysed using a Watson-type centrifugal distortion treatment including quartic and sextic distortion constants.

The observed quartic coefficients agree quite well with those calculated from a valence force field of vinyl fluoride published previously while the observed inertia defect (Δ = 0.0894 a.m.u. Å^2) is in moderate agreement with the value Δ = 0.0592 a.m.u. Å^2 calculated on the basis of a Urey-Bradley force field. A preliminary report of the microwave spectrum of the four-atom cumulene chlorobutatriene shows the rotational constants to be entirely consistent with a planar model in which the bond lengths are transferred from an electron-diffraction study of butatriene and a microwave study of vinyl chloride. Three halogenated acetylenes have come under investigation. Allen and Flygare examined the high-field molecular Zeeman effect of the $J \leftarrow 0$ transitions of the ^{35}Cl and ^{37}Cl species of chloroacetylene to give the molecular *g*-values, $^{35}g_{\perp}$ = —0.00630 ± 0.00014 and $^{37}g_{\perp}$ = —0.00601 ± 0.00008, the magnetic susceptibility anisotropy $(X_{\|}-X_{\perp}) = (9.3 \pm 0.5)\times10^{-13}$ JG^{-2} mol^{-1}, and the molecular quadrupole moment $Q_{\|}$ = (8.8 ± 0.4) × 10^{-2} e.s.u. cm^2.

The *g*-values of the ^{35}Cl and ^{37}Cl isotopes and the shift of centre of mass between these two isotopic species are combined to give a magnitude 0.3 ± 0.2 D for the electric dipole moment (cf. 0.44 D from the Stark effect) and an unambiguous direction ClC_2H +. A similar study of bromoacetylene has been made. As a result of their work on 1-chloro-3,3,3-trifluoropropyne (27), Bjorseth and Marstokk present a profusion of parameters for this molecule. For the most abundant species, ClC≡ C—CF_3, the chlorine nuclear quadrupole coupling constant is *eqQ* = —79.4 ± 3 MHz and the α-values for three vibrational satellite series are α_1= –1.740 ± 0.007, α_2 = -1 -05 ± 0.02, and α_3 = —0.71 ± 0.02 MHz.

For the mode v_1 five quanta are observed and from the *l*-doubling in the v_1= 1 state, the *l*-type doubling constant is q_1= 0.586 ± 0.004 MHz, which leads to v_1= 97 ± 6 cm^{-1} from the familiar expression $q = B_e^2 a'/\omega$. On the other hand, v_2 = 300 ± 50 cm^{-1} and v_3 = 380 ± 60 cm^{-1}, according to relative intensity measurements.

Rotational constants for the isotopic species allow the r_e parameters r_e [C(1) —Cl] = 1.629 ± 0.006Å and derived.

CF_3—C≡C—^{37}Cl, $^{13}CF_3$—C≡C—^{37}Cl, and CF_3—C≡^{13}C—^{37}Cl

The latter value is short compared with those in Me_3C—C≡C —Cl and Me—C≡Cl and indicates that either C(3) —C(2) or C(2)—(1) (or both) is short. Alternatively, given the assumption of FCF = 107.0 ± 1.0°, the following r_0 structure can be determined by fitting all the rotational constants:

r_0 [C(1) —Cl] = 1.627 ± 0.009, r_0[C(1)C(2) = 1.199 ± 0.005,

r_0[C(2) —C(3)] = 1.453 ± 0.002, and r_0[C(3) —F] = 1.336 ± 0.006Å

Stark-effect measurements lead to μ = 1.73 0.20 D, which is reproduced within experimental error by taking the difference of the moments of CF_3—C≡C—H (2.36) and H—C≡C—H—C≡C—Cl (0.44 D).

Acyclic molecules with internal rotation

Hydrocarbons and Halogenoderivatives—A zero-point average structure for isobutane, $(CH_3)_3CH$, has been obtained by combining new electron-diffraction data with microwave spectroscopic rotational constants obtained previously. The results show that the tertiary C—H distance (r_g = 1.122 ± 0.006 Å) is substantially longer than the average methyl C—H distance (r_g = 1.113 ± 0.002 Å). Other structural parameters are:

r_g (C—C) = 1.535 ± 0.001Å and CCC = 110.8 ± 0.2°

and for the methyl groups the average CCH = 111.4 ± 0.2° A similar investigation has also been made for t-butyl chloride, $(CH_3)_3CCl$. In this case an r_z structure has resulted from the previously obtained microwave constants using a calculation based on a harmonic force field. The parameters calculated in this way are in excellent agreement with those obtained directly from electron-diffraction work. A detailed study has been made of rotational isomerism in pent-1-yne,

$CH_3CH_2CH_2C{\equiv}CH$. The spectrum can be attributed to two rotational isomers, one having the methyl group trans with respect to the acetylene group, as shown in Figure 11, and the other the gauche conformation.

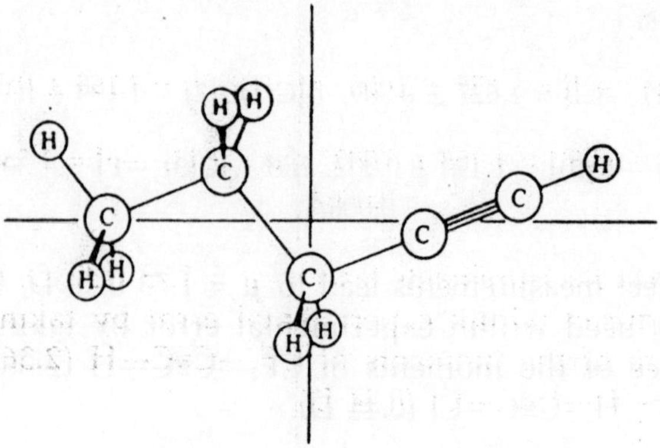

Fig. 10. Trans-pent -1 -yne

The latter, which has a dihedral a ngle of 115° ± 3° from the trans position, is slightly more stable than the trans-form, its ground state falling 27 ± 36 cm^{-1} lower. The potential barrier between the two wells is estimated to be 3.0 ± 1.3 kcal mol^{-1} from a potential function derived from the torsional frequencies found for both trans- and gauche-forms.

Some plausible structural parameters are put forward and the dipole moments μ_{trans} = 0.842 ± 0.010 and μ_{gauche} = 0.769 ± 0.028 D. The microwave spectrum of the related molecule *trans*-pent-3-en-1-yne shown in Figure 12 has been analysed. The dipole moment is found to be 1.06 ± 0.05 D and the barrier to internal rotation of the methyl group is 1.903 ± 0.050 kcal mol^{-1}.

New information has been obtained about both 1, 1, 1-trichloroethane, CH_3CCl_3, and 1,1,1-tribromoethane, CH_3CBr_3. From the relative intensities of satellite lines, torsional-mode frequencies of 276 and 199 cm^{-1} were found for the CH_3CCl_3 and CD_3CCl_3 Molecules respectively.

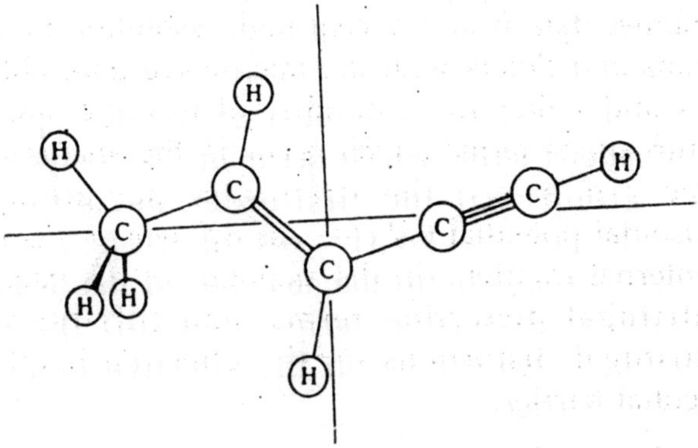

Fig. 11. Trans-pent-3-en-1-yne

From these frequencies the barrier to internal rotation for the chloride was calculated to be 5.1 kcal mol^{-1}. For CH_3CBr_3 a torsional frequency of 304 cm^{-1} has been obtained from an i.r. and Raman study of the solid, leading to a barrier of 6.0 kcal mol^{-1} in this case. From a microwave study it was found that *r*(C—Br) = 1.927 Å and CCBr = 107.7° with an assumed methyl group structure and *r*(C—C) distance.

The microwave spectra of all the deuteriummono substituted species of 2-chloropropene have been analysed to give rotational constants and nuclear quadrupole coupling constants. Substitution co-ordinates were determined for the chlorine and hydrogen atoms and the structure of the molecule, shown in Figure 13, was obtained on the assumptions *r*(C=C) = 1.338, r(C—C) = 1.512, and *r*(C—Cl) = 1.735 Å. The equilibrium conformation of the methyl group was established unambiguously from measurements on the two rotational isomers of the species with a singly deuteriated methyl group.

Alcohols

A detailed analysis has appeared of the torsion-rotation spectra of isotopic methanol molecules. This analysis combines data from a recent high-resolution i.r. study by Woods and Peters with the microwave data obtained by Lees and Baker for a number of isotopic species. The perturbations terms which occur in the analysis fall into three groups: (i) the first-order deviation from a sinusoidal potential $\frac{1}{2}V_6(1 - \cos 6\gamma)$, where γ is the angle of internal rotation, (ii) the analogue of the usual quartic centrifugal distortion terms, and (iii) the effect of centrifugal distortions on the effective height of the potential barrier.

The evaluation of the perturbation constants is dependent on information relating to excited states of the torsional oscillation, and for the species CD_3OD Lees has recently reported frequencies for the $J = 0 \leftarrow 1$ transition up to the fourth excited torsional state. The result of the analysis by Kwan and Dennison is a set of ten constants for each of four isotopic species. The interrelation of these constants has been examined and a set of twenty-one constants has been derived which provide a good fit for the data on the four isotopic species.

An interesting feature to emerge from the analysis is that the torsional barrier is highly sinusoidal in form, with $V_6/V_3 = -0.0002 \pm 0.0006$. Lees has also recently determined the barrier height for two excited vibrational states of methanol. For the first excited state of the C—O stretching mode the barrier height is found to be 397.9 ± 3 cm^{-1}. For an excited state at 933 ± 150cm^{-1}, which is most probably the CH_3 in-plane rocking mode, $V_3 = 557 \pm 35 cm^{-1}$, an increase of 50% above the ground-state value of 376 cm^{-1}. Centrifugal distortion constants have also been reported for four isotopic species of methanol, and spin-rotation and spin-spin coupling constants have been obtained by beam maser spectroscopy of three transitions for CH_3OH. A further investigation has been made of the spectrum of the gauche-rotamer of ethanol.

In addition to a-type lines, some c-type lines have also been observed. The latter lead to a direct determination of the tunnelling frequency between the equivalent gauche configurations, and the barrier hindering internal rotation has been calculated on the assumption that the threefold term is dominant, giving $V_3 = 420.8\ cm^{-1}$. Rotational isomerism in propanol has been further discussed and frequencies and relative intensities of lines have been reported for t-butyl alcohol.

The determination of zero-point average structures of molecules which contain a symmetric internal rotor has been examined, and it is shown how microwave and electron-diffraction data may be combined for this purpose. Application of the method has been made to acetaldehyde and the zero-point average structure has been determined. Similar treatments have been applied to acetone, acetyl chloride, and acetyl bromide. The methyl group is tilted towards the oxygen atom by 1.3 ± 1.0° for the chloride, by 1.9 ± 1.0° for the bromide, and by 2.0 ± 0.5° in acetone.

The barriers V_3 to internal rotation have been revised to 1.260 and 1.256 kcal mol^{-1} for the chloride and bromide respectively. The structure and dipole moment of dimethyl sulphone, $(CH_3)2SO_2$, have been determined. With the assumption that the methyl groups have the same structure as in dimethyl sulphide the parameters given in Table 30 have been obtained. The value of the dipole moment is found to be 4.432 ± 0.041 D.

The microwave spectrum of a molecule having two non-equivalent methyl groups, namely trans-N-methykthylidencimine, $CH_3CH{=}NCH_3$, has been analysed in detail. The theory for overall and internal rotation has been extended to cover molecules with two non-equivalent symmetric internal rotors and internal rotation splittings have been calculated using the internal axis method (IAM).

Table 30

Strucural parameters for $(CH_3)_2SO_2$

Bond length/Å	*Angles*
r(C—S 1.77 ± 0.006	CSCX 103° 17' ±10'
r(S—O) 1.431 ± 0.004	OSO 121° 1' ± 15'

The following values are reported for the methyl-group barriers: C—CH_3, 1.642 ± 0.019, and N—CH_3 2.109 ± 0.084 kcal mol^{-1}. The molecular dipole moment is found to be 1.499 ± 0.007 D and nitrogen nuclear quadrupole coupling coefficients are also reported. The barrier to internal rotation in dimethyl ether has been obtained as 2.50 kcal mol^{-1} by treating CH_3OCD_3 as single-top problem. The inertial defect of dimethylnitrosamine shows the nuclear framework to be planar, in agreement with earlier electron-diffraction results, and the dipole moment is found to be 4.22 ± 0.02 D.

The microwave spectrum of trifluoro (trifluoromethyl) silane, CF_3SiF_3, has been analysed and the barrier to internal rotation found to be 489 ± 50 cm^{-1}, corresponding to a torsional frequency of 37.0 ± 2.0 cm^{-1}. The theory of coupling between internal rotation and a degenerate vibration in a symmetric rotor has been re-examined and revised expressions have been obtained for *l*-type doubling. The treatment has been used to refine the analysis of the spectrum of methylsilane, CH_3SiH_3.

PART 2
Analytical Spectroscopy

Chapter 5

Introduction to Spectrochemical Analysis

The important parameter to be selected is how fast, or at what rate, the input signal should be digitized. One answer to the problem of selecting an appropriate sampling rate would be to digitize the signal at as high a rate as possible. With modern high-speed, analogue-to-digital converters, however, this would produce so much data that the storage capacity of the computer would soon be exceeded. Instead, it is preferred that the number of values recorded is limited.

The analogue signal is digitally and discretely sampled, and the rate of sampling determines the accuracy of the digital representation as a time discrete function. Figure 1 illustrates a data path in a typical ratio-recording, dispersive infrared spectrometer. The digitization of the analogue signal produced by the detector is a critical step in the generation of the analytical spectrum.

Sampling theory dictates that a continuous time signal can be completely recovered from its digital representation if the original analogue signal is band-limited, and if the sampling frequency employed for digitization is at least twice the highest frequency present in the analogue signal. This often quoted statement is

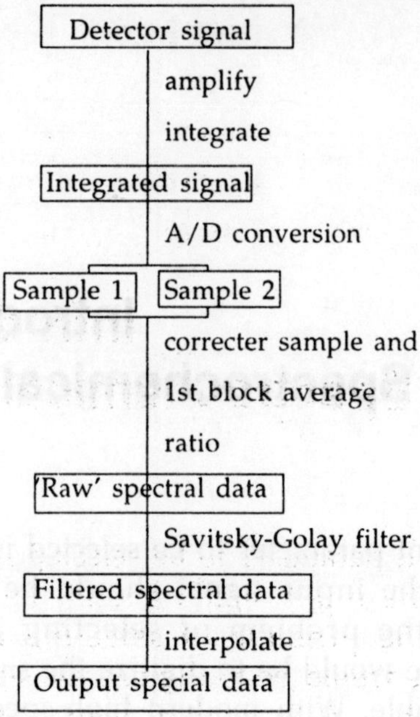

Fig. 1 Data path of a ratio-recording, dispersive IR spectrometer

fundamental to digitization and is worth examining in more detail.

The process of digital sampling can be represented by the scheme shown in Figure 2. The continuous analytical signal as a function of time, x_t, is multiplied by a modulating signal comprising a train of pulses of equal magnitude and constant period, p_t. The resultant signal is a train of similar impulses but now with amplitudes limited by the spectral envelope x_t. We wish the digital representation accurately to reflect the original analogue signal in terms of all the frequencies present in the original data.

Not only that, it is necessary that the difference, $(f_s - f_m)$, must be greater than f_m, i.e.

$$(f_s - f_m) > f_m \text{ or } f_s > 2f_m \tag{1}$$

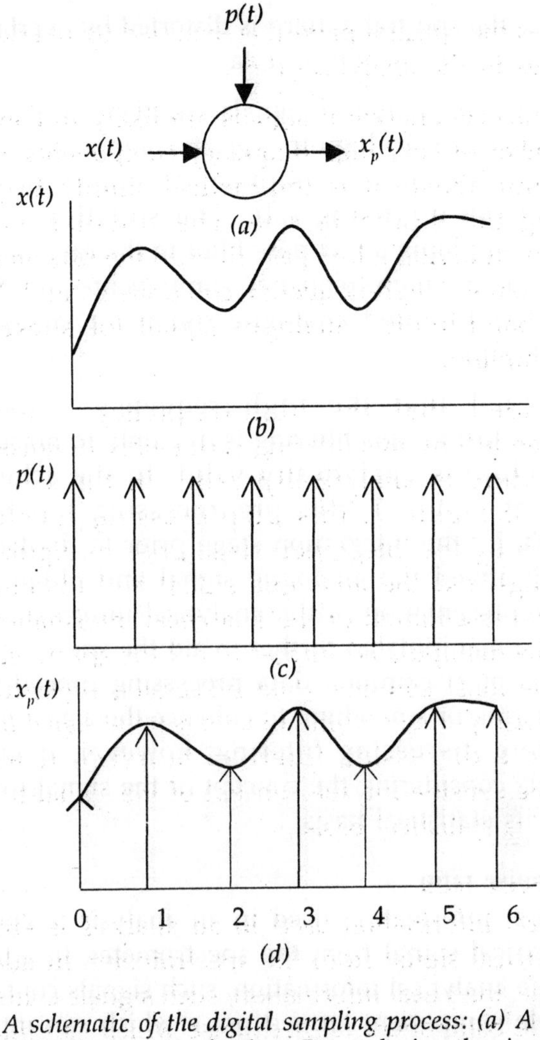

Fig. 2 A schematic of the digital sampling process: (a) A signal, x_t, is multiplied by a train of pulses, Pt, producing the signal $x_{p,t}$; (b) The analetical signal, x_t; (c) The carrier signal, p_t; (d) the resultant sampled signal is a train pulses with amplitudes limited by x_t

$f_s = 2f_m$ is referred to as the minimum or *Nyquist sampling frequency*. If the sampling frequency, f_s, is less than the Nyquist value then aliasing arises. At low sampling frequencies the spectral pattern is distorted by overlapping frequencies in the analytical data.

In practice, analytical signals are likely to contain a large number of very high-frequency components and, as pointed out above, it is impractical simply to go on increasing the digitizing rate. The situation may be relieved by applying a low pass filter to the raw analogue signal to remove high-frequency components and, hence, derive a band-limited analogue signal for subsequent digital sampling.

Provided that the high-frequency analogue information lost by this filtering is due only to noise, then the procedure is analytically valid. In the schematic diagram of Figure 1, this preprocessing function is undertaken by the integration stage prior to digitization. Having digitized the analogue signal and obtained an accurate representation of the analytical information, the data can be manipulated further to aid the spectroscopist. One of the most common data processing procedures is digital filtering or smoothing to enhance the *signal-to-noise ratio*. Before discussing filtering, however, it will be worthwhile considering the concept of the signal-to-noise ratio and its statistical basis.

Signal-to-noise ratio

The spectral information used in an analysis is encoded as an electrical signal from the spectrometer. In addition to desirable analytical information, such signals contain an undesirable component termed noise which can interfere with the accurate extraction and interpretation of the required analytical data. There are numerous sources of noise that arise from instrumentation, but briefly the noise will comprise flicker noise, interference noise, and white noise. These classes of noise signals are characterized by their frequency distribution.

Flicker noise is characterized by a frequency power spectrum that is more pronounced at low frequencies than at high frequencies. This is minimized in instrumentation by modulating the carrier signal and using a.c. detection and a.c. signal processing, *e.g.* lock-in amplifiers. Interference from power supplies may also add noise to the signal. Such noise is usually confined to specific frequencies about 50 Hz, or 60 Hz, and their harmonics. By employing modulation frequencies well away from the power line frequency, interference noise can be reduced, and minimized further by using highly selective, narrow-bandpass electronic filters. White noise is more difficult to eliminate since it is random in nature, occurring at all frequencies in the spectrum.

It is a fundamental characteristic of all electronic instruments. In recording a spectrum, complete freedom from noise is an ideal that can never be realized in practice. The noise associated with a recorded signal has a profound effect in an analysis and one figure of merit used to describe the quality of a measurement is the signal-to-noise ratio, S/N, which is defined as,

$$S/N = \frac{\text{average signal magnitude}}{\text{rms noise}} \quad (2)$$

The rms (room mean square) noise is the square root of the average deviation of the signal, x_i, from the mean noise value, i.e.

$$\text{rms noise} = \sqrt{\frac{\Sigma(\tilde{x} - x_i)^2}{n-1}} \quad (3)$$

This equation should be recognized as equating rms noise with the standard deviation of the noise signal, σ. S/N can, therefore, be defined as $\tilde{x}/\sigma$.

In spectrometric analysis S/N is usually measured in one of two ways. The first technique is repeatedly to sample and measure the analytical signal and determine the mean and standard deviation using Equation (3). Where a chart recorder output is available, then a second method may be used.

Assuming the noise is random and normally distributed about the mean, it is likely that 99% of the random deviations in the recorded signal will lie within T 2.5σ of the mean value. By measuring the peak- to-peak deviation of the signal and dividing by 5, an estimate of the rms, noise is obtained. Whichever method is used, the signal should be sampled for sufficient time to allow a reliable estimate of the standard deviation to be made. When measuring S/N it is usually assumed that the noise is independent of signal magnitude for small signals close to the baseline or background signal. Noise, as well as affecting the appearance of a spectrum, influences the sensitivity of an analytical technique and for quantitative analysis the S/N ratio is of fundamental importance.

Analytical terms dependent on the noise contained in the signal are the decision limit, the detection limit, and the determination limit. These analytical figures of merit are often quoted by instrument manufacturers and a knowledge of their calculation is important in evaluating and comparing instrument performance in terms of analytical sensitivity.

Detection limits

The concept of an analytical detection limit implies that we can make a qualitative decision regarding the presence or absence of analyte in a sample. In arriving at such a decision there are two basic types of error that can arise (Table 1). The Type I error leads to the conclusion that the analyte is present in a sample when it is known not to be, and the Type II error is made if we conclude that the analyte is absent, when in fact it is present. The definition of a detection limit should address both types of error.

Table 1

The Type I and Type II errors that can be made in accepting or rejecting a statistical hypothesis

	Hypothesis is correct	Hypothesis is incorrect
Hypothesis is accepted	Correct decision	Type II Error
Hypothesis is rejected	Type 1 Error	Correct decision

Consider an analytical signal produced by a suitable blank sample, with a mean value of μ_b. If we assume that noise in this background measurement is random and normally distributed about μ_b, then 95% of this noise will lie within $\mu_b + 1.65\sigma$. With a 5% chance of committing a Type I error, then any analysis giving a response value greater than $\mu_b + 1.645\sigma$ can be assumed to indicate the Presence of the analyte. This measure is referred to as the decision limit,

$$\text{Decision Limit} = Z_{0.95} \cdot \sigma_b = 1.65\sigma_b \tag{4}$$

If the number of measurements made to calculate s_b is small, then the appropriate value from the *t*-distribution should be used in place of the z-value as obtained from the normal distribution curve. We may ask, what if a sample containing analyte at a concentration equivalent to the decision limit is repeatedly analysed? In such a case, we can expect that in 50% of the measurements the analyte will be reported present, but in the other half of the measurements the analyte will be reported as not present.

This attempt at defining a detection limit using the decision limit defined by Equation (4) does not address the occurrence of the Type II error. If, as with the Type I error, we are willing to accept a 5% chance of committing a Type II error, then the relationship between the blank signal and sample measurement is as indicated in Figure 3(b). This defines the detection limit,

$$\text{Detection Limit} = 2z_{0.95}\sigma_b = 3.3\sigma_b \quad (5)$$

Under these conditions, we have a 5% chance of reporting the analyte present in a blank solution, and a 5% chance of reporting the analyte absent in a sample actually containing analyte at the concentration defined by the detection limit.

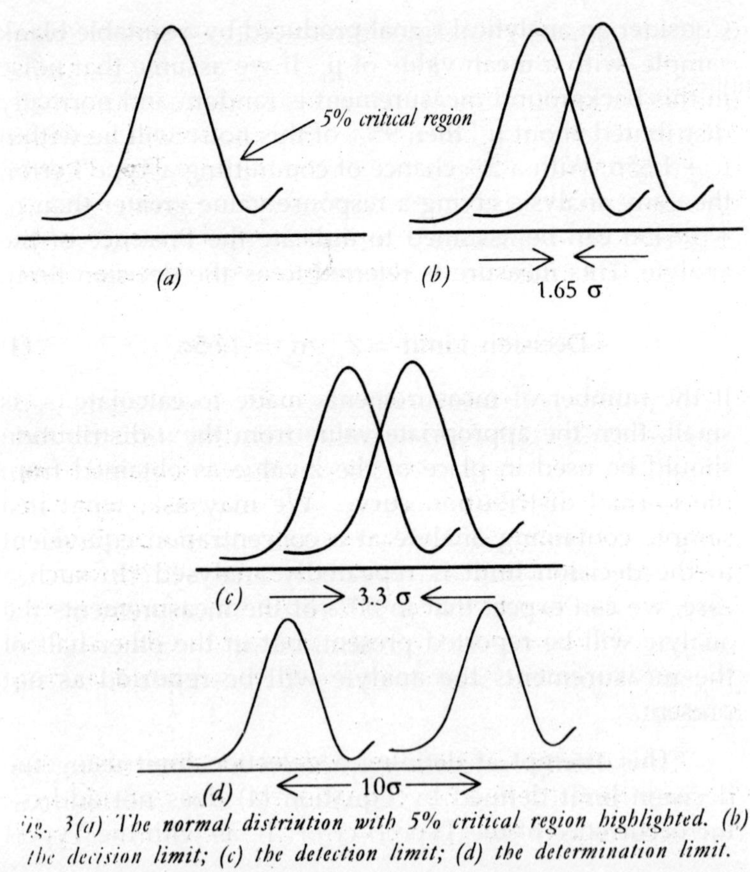

Fig. 3(a) The normal distriution with 5% critical region highlighted. (b) the decision limit; (c) the detection limit; (d) the determination limit.

We should examine the precision of measurements made at this limit before accepting this definition of detection limit. The relative standard deviation, RSD, of such measurements is given by

$$\mathrm{RSD} = 100\sigma/\mu = 100/(2z_{0.95}) = 30.3\% \qquad (6)$$

For a RSD of 10%, a further term can be defined called the determination limit, Figure 5(d),

$$\text{Determination Limit} = 10\sigma_b \qquad (7)$$

Signal averaging

The process of *signal averaging* is conducted by repetitively scanning and co-adding individual spectra. Assuming the noise is randomly distributed, then the analytical signals which are coherent in time are enhanced, since the signal grows linearly with the number of scans, N,

$$\text{signal magnitude} \propto N$$

$$\text{signal magnitude} = k_1 N \qquad (8)$$

To consider the effect of signal averaging on the noise level we must refer to the *propagation of errors*. The variance associated with the sum of independent errors is equal to the sum of their variances, *i.e.*

$$\sigma_N^2 = \sum_{i=1}^{N} \sigma_i^2 = N\sigma_i^2 \qquad (9)$$

Since we can equate rms noise with standard deviation then,

$$\sigma_N = \sqrt{(N\sigma_i^2)} \qquad (10)$$

Thus the average magnitude of random noise increases at a rate proportional to the square root of the number of scans,

$$\text{noise magnitude} \propto N^{1/2}$$

$$\text{noise magnitude} = k_2N^{1/2} \quad (11)$$

Therefore,

$$\frac{\text{signal}}{\text{noise}} = \frac{k_1N}{k_2N^{1/2}} = kN^{1/2} \quad (12)$$

and the signal-to-noise ratio is improved at a rate proportional to the square root of the number of scans. Infrared spectrum and the effect of signal averaging 4, 9, and 16 spectra. The increase in signal-to-noise ratio associated with increasing the number of co-added repetitive scans is evident. For signal averaging to be effective, each scan must start at the same place in the spectrum otherwise analytical signals and useful information will also cancel and be removed.

The technique is widely used but is most common in fast scanning spectrometers, particularly Fourier transform instruments such as NMR and IR. Even with a fast scan, say 1 s, the time required to perform 10000 scans and aim to achieve a 100-fold improvement in signal-to-noise ratio may be unacceptable.

Signal smoothing

A wide variety of mathematical manipulation schemes are available to smooth spectral data, and in this section we shall concentrate on smoothing techniques that serve to average a section of the data. They are all simple to implement on personal computers. This ease of use has led to their widespread application, but their selection and tuning is somewhat empirical and depends on the application in-hand. One simple smoothing procedure is *boxcar averaging*. Boxcar averaging proceeds by dividing the spectral data into a series of discrete, equally spaced, bands and replacing each band by a centroid average value. The greater the number of points averaged, the greater the degree of smoothing, but there is also a corresponding increase in distortion of the signal and subsequent loss of spectral resolution. The technique is derived from the use of electronic boxcar integrator units. It is less widely used in modern spectrometry than the methods of moving average and *polynomial smoothing*.

As with boxcar averaging, the moving average method replaces a group of values by their mean value. The difference in the techniques is that with the moving average successive bands overlap. Which is comprised of transmission values, denoted x_i. By averaging the first five values, $i = 1 \ldots 5$, a mean transmission value is produced which provides the value for the third data point, x'_3, in the smoothed spectrum. The procedure continues by incrementing i and averaging the next five values to find X'_4 from original data X_2, X_3, X_4, X_5, and X_6. The degree of smoothing achieved is controlled by the number of points averaged, *i.e.* the width of the smoothing window. Distortion of the data is usually less apparent with the moving average method than with boxcar averaging.

The mathematical process of implementing the moving average technique is termed convolution. The resultant spectrum, x' (as a vector), is said to be the result of convolution of the original spectrum vector, x, with a filter function, w, i.e.

$$x' = w \otimes x \tag{13}$$

For the simple five-point moving average, $w = [1,1,1,1,1]$. The mechanism and application of the convolution process can be visualized graphically. In 1964 Savitzky and Golay described a technique for smoothing spectral data using convolution filter vectors derived from the coefficients of least-squares-fit polynomial functions. This chapter, with subsequent

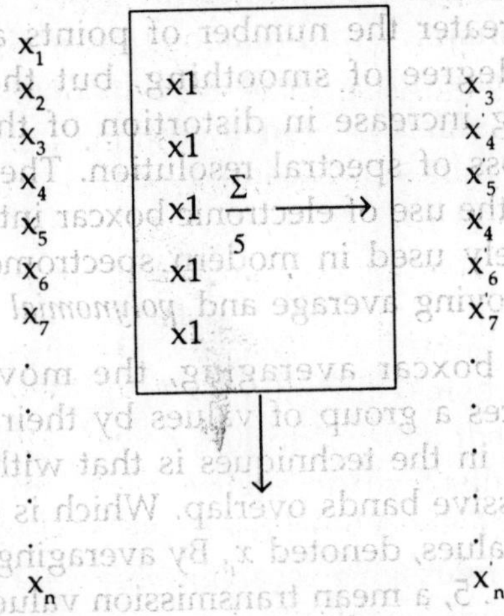

Fig. 4: Convolution of a spectrum with a filter is achieved by pulling the filter function across the spectrum

arithmetic corrections, has become a classic in analytical signal processing and least-squares polynomial smoothing is probably the technique in widest use in spectral data processing and manipulation. To appreciate its derivation and application we should extend our discussion of the moving average filter. The simple moving average technique can be represented mathematically by

$$x_i = \sum_{j=-n}^{n} x_{i+j}\omega_j \Big/ \sum_{j=-n}^{n} \omega_j \qquad (14)$$

where x_i and x'_i are elements of the original and smoothed data vectors respectively, and the values ω_j are the weighting factors in the smoothing window. For a simple moving average function, $\omega_j = 1$ for all j and the width of the smoothing function is defined by (2n + 1) points. The process of polynomial smoothing extends the principle of the moving average by modifying the weight vector, ω, such that the elements of ω describe a convex polynomial.

The central value in each window, therefore, adds more to the averaging process than values at the extremes of the window. Consider five data points forming a part of a spectrum described by the data set x recorded at equal wavelength intervals. Polynomial smoothing seeks to replace the value of the point xj by a value calculated from the least-squares polynomial fitted to x_{j-2}, x_{j-1}, x_j, x_{j+1}, and x_{j+2} recorded at wavelengths denoted by λ_{j-2}, λ_{j-1}, λ_j, λ_{j+1}, and λ_{j+2}. For a quadratic curve fitted to the data, the model can be expressed as

$$x' = a_0 + a_1\lambda + a_2\lambda_2 \tag{15}$$

where x' is the fitted model data and a_0, a_1 and a_2 are the coefficients or weights to be determined. Using the method of least squares, the aim is to minimize the error, ε, given by the square of the difference between the model function, Equation (13) and the observed data, for all data values fitted, *i.e.*

$$\varepsilon = \Sigma(x_j' - x_j)^2 \left[a_0 + a_1 \sum_{j=-n}^{n} \lambda_j + a_2 \sum \lambda_j^2 - \sum x_j \right] \tag{16}$$

and, by simple differential calculus, this error function is a minimum when its first derivative is zero.

Differentiating Equation (16) with respect to a_0, a_1, and a_2 respectively, provides a set of so-called *normal equations*,

$$a_0 \sum_{j=-n}^{n} (1) + a_1 \sum \lambda_j + a_2 \sum \lambda_j^2 = \sum x_j$$

$$a_0 \sum \lambda_j + a_1 \sum \lambda_j^2 + a_2 \sum \lambda_j^3 = \sum x_j \lambda_j \tag{17}$$

$$a_0 \sum \lambda_j^2 + a_1 \sum \lambda_j^3 + a_2 \sum \lambda_j^4 = \sum x_j \lambda_j^2$$

Because the λ_j values are equally spaced, $\Delta\lambda = \lambda_j - \lambda_{j-1}$ is constant and only relative λ values are required for the model,

$$\lambda_j = j.\Delta\lambda \tag{18}$$

Hence, for $j = -2 \ldots +2$ (a five-point fit),

$$\Sigma\lambda j^1 = \Delta\lambda.\Sigma j^1 = 0$$

$$\Sigma\lambda j^2 = \Delta\lambda.\Sigma j^2 = 10\mathrm{Dl}$$

$$\Sigma\lambda j^3 = \Delta\lambda.\Sigma j^3 = 0 \tag{19}$$

$$\Sigma\lambda j^4 = \Delta\lambda.\Sigma j^4 = 34\Delta\lambda$$

which can be substituted into the normal equations, Equations (17), giving

$$5a_0 + 10\Delta\lambda^2.a_2 = \Sigma x_j = x_{j-2} + x_{j-1} + x_j + x_{j+1} + x_{j+2}$$

$$10\Delta\lambda.a_1 = \Sigma x_j.\lambda_j = -2x_{j-2} - x_{j-1} + x_{j+1} - 2x_{j+2}$$

$$10a_0 + 34\Delta\lambda^2.a_2 = \mathrm{S}x_j.\lambda_j^2 = 4x_{j-2} + x_{j-1} + x_{j+1} + 4x_{j+2} \tag{20}$$

which can be rearranged,

$$a_0 = (-3x_{j-2} + 12x_{j-1} + 17x_j + 12x_{j+1} - 3x_{j+2}).1/35$$
$$a_1 = (-2x_{j-2} - x_{j-1} + x_{j+1} - 2x_{j+2}).1/10\Delta\lambda$$
$$a_2 = (2x_{j-2} - x_{j-1} - 2_{xj} - x_{j+1} + 2x_{j+2}).1/14\Delta\lambda^2 \tag{21}$$

At the central point in the smoothing window, $\lambda_j = 0$ and $x'_j = a_0$ from Equation (15). The five weighting coefficients, ω_i, are given by the first equation in Equation (21),

$$\omega = [-3, 12, 17, 12, -3] \tag{22}$$

Savitzky and Golay published the coefficients for a range

of least-squares fit curves with up to 25-point wide smoothing windows for each.

Table 2 presents the weighting coefficients for performing 5, 9, 13, and 17-point quadratic smoothing and the results of applying these functions to the infrared spectral data. When choosing to perform a Savitzky-Golay smoothing operation on spectral data. The final choice is largely empirical, the quadratic function is the most commonly used, with the window width selected according to the scanning conditions.

Table 2

Savitzky-Golay coefficients, or weightings, for 5-, 9-, 13-, and 17-point quadratic smoothing of continuous spectral data

Points	17	13	9	5
– 8	– 21			
– 7	– 6			
– 6	7	– 11		
– 5	18	0		
– 4	27	9	– 21	
– 3	34	16	14	
– 2	39	21	39	– 3
– 1	42	24	54	12
0	43	25	59	17
1	42	24	54	12
2	39	21	39	– 3
3	34	16	14	
4	27		9	– 21
5	18	0		
6	7	– 11		
7	– 6			
8	– 21			
Norm	323	143	231	35

Filtering in the frequency domain

The smoothing operations discussed above have been presented in terms of the action of filters directly on the spectral data as recorded in the time domain. By converting the analytical spectrum to the frequency domain, the performance of these functions can be compared and a wide variety of other filters designed.

Time-to-frequency conversion is accomplished using the Fourier transform. Its use was introduced earlier in this chapter in relation to sampling theory, and its application will be extended here. The electrical output signal from a conventional scanning spectrometer usually takes the form of an amplitude-time response, *e.g*, absorbance *vs.* wavelength. All such signals, no matter how complex, may be represented as a sum of sine and cosine waves. The continuous function of composite frequencies is called a Fourier integral. The conversion of amplitude-time, t, information into amplitude-frequency, w, information is known as a Fourier transformation. The relation between the two forms is given by

$$F(w) = \int_{-\infty}^{\infty} f(t)[\cos(wt) + \mathrm{i}.\sin(wt)]dt \qquad (23)$$

or, in complex exponential form,

$$F(w) = \int_{-\infty}^{\infty} f(t)\mathrm{e}^{-2\pi iwt} dt \qquad (24)$$

The corresponding reverse, or inverse, transform, converting the complex frequency domain information back to the time domain is

$$f(t) = \int_{-\infty}^{\infty} F(w)\mathrm{e}^{-2\pi iwt} dw \qquad (25)$$

The two functions $f(t)$ and $F(w)$ are said to comprise *Fourier transform pairs*. With regard to sampling theory, real analytical signals are band-limited. The Fourier equations therefore should be modified for practical use as we cannot sample an infinite number of data points. With this practical constraint, the discrete forward complex transform is given by

$$F(n) = \sum_{k=0}^{N-1} f(k)e^{-2\pi ikn/N} \tag{26}$$

and the inverse is

$$f(k) = \frac{1}{N} \sum_{n=0}^{N-1} F(n)e^{-2\pi ikn/N} \tag{27}$$

A time domain spectrum consists of N points acquired at regular intervals and it is transformed to a frequency domain spectrum. This consists of $N/2$ real and $N/2$ imaginary data points, with $n = -N/2 \ldots 0 \ldots N/2$, and k takes integer values from 0 to $N - 1$. Once a frequency spectrum of a signal is computed then it can be modified mathematically to enhance the data in some well defined manner.

The suitably processed spectrum can then be obtained by the inverse transform. Several Fourier transform pairs are shown pictorially in Figure 5. An infinitely sharp amplitude-time signal, Figure 5(a), has a frequency response spectrum containing equal amplitudes at all frequencies. This is the white spectrum characteristic of a random noise amplitude-time signal. As the signal becomes broader, the frequency spectrum gets narrower. The higher frequencies are reduced dramatically and the frequency spectrum has the form $(\sin x)/x$, called the sinc function, Figure 5 (b). For a triangular signal, Figure 5 (c), the functional form of the frequency spectrum is $(\sin^2 x)/x^2$, the sinc^2 function.

The sinc and sinc' forms are common filtering functions in interferometry, where their application is termed *apodisation*. The frequency response spectra of

Lorentzian and Gaussian shaped signals are of particular interest since these shapes describe typical spectral profiles. The Fourier transform of a Gaussian signal is another Gaussian form, and for a Lorentzian signal he transform takes the shape of an exponentially decaying oscillator.

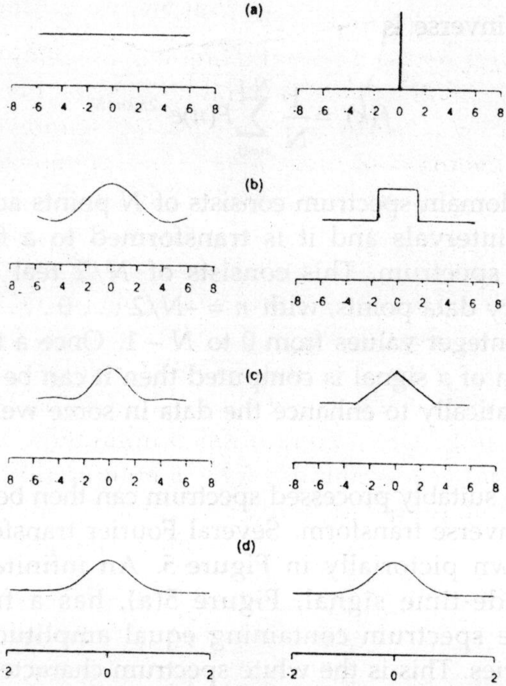

Fig. 5. Some well characterised fourier pairs. The white spectrum and the impulse function (a), the boxcar and sinc functions (b), the triangular and sinc 2 functions (c), and the Gaussian pair (d).

One of the earliest applications of the Fourier transform in spectroscopy was in filtering and noise reduction. This technique is still extensively employed. The Fourier transform of arl infrared spectrum, before and after applying the 13-point quadratic Savitzky-Golay function. The effect of smoothing can clearly be seen as reducing the high-frequency fluctuations, hopefully due to noise, by the polynomial function serving as a low-pass filter. Convolution provides an important technique for smoothing and processing spectral data, and can be undertaken in the frequency domain by simple multiplication. Thus smoothing can be accorbplished in the frequency domain, following Fourier transformation of the data, by multiplying the Fourier transform by a rectangular or other truncating function.

The low-frequency Fourier coefficients should be relatively unaffected, whereas the high-frequency components characterizing random noise are reduced or zeroed. The subsequent inverse transform then yields the smoothed waveform. The rectangular window function is a simple truncating function which can be applied to transformed data. This function has zero values above some pre-selected cut-off frequency, f_c, and unit values at lower frequencies. Although the selection of an appropriate cut-off frequency value is somewhat arbitrary, various methods of calculating a suitable value have been proposed in the literature.

The method of Lam and Isenhour is worth mentioning, not least because of the relative simplicity in calculating f_c. The process relies on determining what is termed the equivalent width, EW, of the narrowest peak in the spectrum. For a Lorentzian band the equivalent width in the time domain is given by

$$EW_t = \omega_{1/2}.\pi/2 \tag{28}$$

where $\omega_{½}$ is the full-width at half-maximum, the half-width, of the narrowest peak in the spectrum. The equivalent width in the frequency domain, EW*f*, is simply the reciprocal of EW_t. Assuming the spectrum was acquired in a single scan taking 10 s and it comprises 256 discrete points, then the sampling interval, At, is given by

$$\Delta t = 10/256 = 0.039 \text{ s} \tag{29}$$

and the maximum frequency, f_{max}, by

$$f_{max} = 1/(2\Delta t) = 12.75 \text{ Hz} \tag{30}$$

The IR spectrum was synthesized from two Lorentzian bands, the sharpest having $\omega_{½} = 1.17$ s. Therefore EW^t = 1.838 s and EW_f = 0.554 Hz.

The complex interferogram of 256 points is composed of 128 real values and 128 imaginary values spanning the range 0-12.75 Hz. According to the EW criterion, a suitable cut-off frequency is 0.554 Hz and the number of significant points, N, to be retained may be calculated from

$$N = (128)(0.554)/12.75 \cong 6 \tag{31}$$

Obviously, to use the technique, it is necessary to estimate the half-width of the narrowest band present. Where possible this is usually done using some sharp isolated band in the spectrum. All the smoothing functions discussed in previous sections can be displayed and compared in the frequency domain, and in addition new filters can be designed. Bromba and Ziegler have made an extensive study of such 'designer' filters.

The Savitzky-Golay filter acts as a low-pass filter that is optimal for polynomial shaped signals. Of course, in spectrometry Gaussian or Lorentzian band shapes are the usual form and the polynomial is only an approximation to a section of the spectrum defined by the width of the filter window. There is no reason why filters other than the polynomial should not be employed for smoothing spectral data. Use of the Savitzky-Golay procedure is as much traditional as representing any theoretical optimum. Bromba and Ziegler have defined a general filter with weighting elements defined by the form

$$\omega_j = \frac{2\alpha+1}{2n+1} - \frac{\alpha|j|}{n(n+1)} \tag{32}$$

where ω is the vector of coefficients, $j = -n \ldots n$, and a is a shape parameter. The frequency-response curves of three 15-point filters with α = 0.5, 1, and 2. The case of the filter constructed with α = 2 is of particular interest as its frequency response increases beyond zero frequency and then falls off rapidly.

The effect of convoluting a spectrum with this function is apparently to enhance resolution. The practical use of such filters should be undertaken with care, however, and they are best used in an interactive mode when the user can visibly assess the effects before proceeding to further data manipulation. Whatever smoothing technique is employed, the aim is to reduce the effects of random variations superimposed on the analytically useful signal. This transform can be simply expressed as

$$\text{Spectrum (smoothed)} = \text{Spectrum (raw)} - \text{noise} \tag{33}$$

Assuming all noise is removed then the result is the true spectrum. Conversely, from Equation (33), if the smoothed spectrum is subtracted from the original, raw data, then a noise spectrum is obtained. The distribution of this noise as a function of wavelength may provide information regarding the source of the noise in spectrometers. The procedure is analogous to the analysis of residuals in regression analysis and modelling.

Interpolation

Not all analytical data can be recorded on a continuous basis; discrete measurements often have to be made and they may not be at regular time or space intervals. To predict intermediate values for a smooth graphic display, or to perform many mathematical manipulations, e.g. Savitzky-Golay smoothing, it is necessary to evaluate regularly spaced intermediate values. Such values are obtained by *interpolation*. If the true underlying mathematical relationship between the independent and dependent variables is known then any value can be computed exactly. Unfortunately, this information is rarely available and any required interpolated data must be estimated. The data in Table 3, shown consist of magnesium concentrations as determined from river water samples collected at various distances from the stream mouth. Because of the problems of accessibility to sampling sites, the samples were collected at irregular intervals along the stream channel and the distances between samples were calculated from aerial photographs.

Table 3

Concentration of maganesium (mg kg-) from a stream sampled at different locations along its course. Distances are from stream mouth to sample locations

Distance (m)	Mg (mg kg^{-1})
1800	4.0
2700	10.1
4500	11.5
5200	10.2
7100	8.4
8500	8.6

To produce regularly spaced data, all methods for interpolation assume that no discontinuity exists in the recorded data. It is also assumed that any intermediate, estimated value is dependent on neighbouring recorded values. The simplest interpolation technique is *linear interpolation*. If y_1 and y_2 are observed values at points x_1 and x_2, then the value of y' situated at x' between x_1 and

x_2 can be calculated from

$$y' = y_1 + \frac{(y_2 - y_1)(x' - x_1)}{(x_2 - x_1)} \tag{34}$$

For a value of x' of 2500 m the estimated magnesium concentration, y', is 8.74 mg kg^{-1}. The difference between values of adjacent points is assumed to be linear function of the distance separating them. The closer a point is to an observation, the closer its value is to that of the observation.

Despite the simplicity of the calculation, linear interpolation should be used with care as the abrupt changes in slope that may occur at recorded values are unlikely to reflect accurately the more smooth transitions likely to be observed in practice. A better, and graphically more acceptable, result is achieved by fitting a smooth curve to the data. Suitable polynomials offer an excellent choice. Polynomial interpolation is simply an extension of the linear method.

The polynomial is formed by adding extra terms to the model to represent curved regions of the spectrum and using extra data values in the model. If only one pair of measurements had been made, say (y_1, x_1), then a zeroth order equation of the type $y' = y_1$, for all y' would be the only possible solution. With two pairs of measurements, (y_1, x_1) and (y_2, x_2), then a first-order linear model can be proposed,

where

$$a_0 = (y_2 - y_1)/(x_1 - x_1) \tag{36}$$

$$= 6.77 \times 10^{-3} \text{ for the magnesium data.}$$

This, of course, is the model of linear interpolation and for $x' = 2500$ m, $y' = 8.74$ mg kg^{-1}. To take account of more measured data, higher order polynomials can be employed. A quadratic model will fit three pairs of points,

$$y' = y_1 + a_0(x' - x_1) + a_1(x' - x_1)(x' - x_2) \qquad (37)$$

with the quadratic term being zero when $x' = x_1$ or $x' = x_2$ = When $x' = x_3$ then substitution and rearrangement of Equation (37) allows the coefficient a_1 to be calculated,

$$y_3 = y_1 + \frac{(y_2 - y_1)(x_3 - x_1)}{(x_2 - x_1)} + a_z(x_3 - x_1)(x_3 - x_2) \qquad (38)$$

and

$$a_1 = \frac{\frac{(y_3 - y_1)}{(x_3 - x_1)} - \frac{(y_2 - y_1)}{(x_2 - x_1)}}{(x_3 - x_2)} \qquad (39)$$

$= -2.2 \times 10^{-6}$, for the magnesium data.

Substituting for a_1 and $x' = 2500$ m into Equation (37), the estimated value of y' is 9.05 mg kg^{-1} Mg.

The technique can be extended further. With four pairs of observations, a cubic equation can be generated to pass through each point,

$$y' = Y_1 + a_0(x' - x_1) + a_1(x' - x_1)(x' - x_2) + a_2(x' - x_1)(x' - x_2)(x' - x_3) \qquad (40)$$

and by a similar process, at x_4 the coefficient a_2 is given by

$$a_2 = \frac{\frac{\frac{(y_4 - y_1)}{(x_4 - x_1)} - \frac{(y_2 - y_1)}{(x_2 - x_1)}}{(x_4 - x_2)} - \frac{\frac{(y_3 - y_1)}{(x_3 - x_1)} - \frac{(y_2 - y_1)}{(x_2 - x_1)}}{(x_3 - x_2)}}{(x_4 - x_3)} \qquad (41)$$

$= -4.28 \times 10^{-10}$, for the magnesium data.

and substituting into Equation (40), for $x' = 2500$ m, then $y' = 8.93$ mg $kg^{-1}Mg$. As the number of observed points to be connected increases, then so too does the degree of the polynomial required if we are to guarantee passing through each point.

The general technique is referred to as providing *divided difference* polynomials. The coefficients a_2, a_3, a_4, etc. may be generated algorithmically by the *'Newton forward formula'*, and many examples of the algorithms are available. To fit a curve to n data points a polynomial of degree (n – 1) is required, and with a large data set the number of coefficients to be calculated is correspondingly large. Thus 100 data points could be interpolated using a 99-degree polynomial.

Polynomials of such a high degree, however, are unstable. They can fluctuate wildly with the high-degree terms forcing an exact fit to the data. Low-degree polynomials are much easier to work with analytically and they are widely used for curve fitting, modelling, and producing graphic output. To fit small polynomials to an extensive set of data it is necessary to abandon the idea of trying to force a single polynomial through all the points. Instead different polynomials are used to connect different segments of points, piecing each section smoothly together.

One technique exploiting this principle is *spline interpolation*, and its use is analogous to using a mechanical flexicurve to draw manually a smooth curve through fixed points. The shape described by a spline between two adjacent points, or knots, is a cubic, third-degree polynomial. For the six pairs of data points representing our magnesium study, we would consider the curve connecting the data to comprise five cubic polynomials. Each of these take the form

$$s_i(x) = a_i x^3 + b_i x^2 + C_i x + a_i, \qquad i = 1 \ldots 5 \qquad (42)$$

To compute the spline, we must calculate values for the 20 coefficients, four for each polynomial segment. Therefore we require 20 simultaneous equations, dictated by the following physical constraints imposed on the curve.

Since the curve must touch each point then

$$s_i(x_i) = y_i, \qquad i = 1 \ldots 5$$
$$s_i(x_{i+1}) = y_{i+1}, \qquad i = 1 \ldots 5 \qquad (43)$$

The spline must curve smoothly about each point with no sharp bends or kinks, so the slope of each segment where they connect must be similar. To achieve this the first derivatives of the spline polynomials must be equal at the measured points.

$$\frac{ds_{i-1}(x_i)}{dx} = \frac{ds_i(x_i)}{dx} \qquad (44)$$

We can also demand that the second derivatives of each segment will be similar at the knots.

$$\frac{d^2 s_{i-1}(x_i)}{dx^2} = \frac{d^2 s_i(x_i)}{dx^2} \qquad (45)$$

Finally, we can specify that at the extreme ends of the curve the second derivatives are zero:

$$\frac{d^2 s_1(x_1)}{dx^2} = 0$$
$$\frac{d^2 s_5(x_6)}{dx^2} = 0 \qquad (46)$$

From Equations (43) to (46) we can derive our 20

simultaneous equations and, by suitable rearrangement and substitution of values for x and y, determine the values of the 20 coefficients a_i, b_i, c_i, and d_i, $i = 1 \ldots 5$. This calculation is obviously laborious and the same spline can be computed more efficiently by suitable scaling and substitution in the equations." If the value of the second derivative of the spline at x_i is represented by p_i,

$$p_i = \frac{d^2 s_{i-1}(x_i)}{dx^2} = \frac{d^2 s_i(x_i)}{dx^2}, \; i = 2 \ldots 5 \tag{47}$$

then if the values of $p_1 \ldots p_5$ were known, all the coefficients, a, b, c, d, could be computed from the following four equations,

$$S_i(x_i) = y_i$$

$$s_i(x_{i+1}) = y_{i+1}$$

$$\frac{d^2 s_i(x_i)}{dx^2} = p_i$$

$$\frac{d^2 s_i(x_{i+1})}{dx^2} \tag{48}$$

If each spline segment is scaled on the x-axis between the limits [0, 1], using the term $t = (x - x_i)/(x_{i+1} - x_i)$, then the curve can be expressed as

$$s_i(t) = \frac{ty_{i+1} + (1-t)y_i + (x_{i+1} - x_i)^2\{(t^3 - t)p_{i+1} - [(1-t)^3 - (1-t)]p_i\}}{6} \tag{49}$$

To calculate the values of p_i, we impose the constraint that the first derivatives of the spline segments are equal at their endpoints. The resulting equations are

$$v_2 p_2 + u_2 p_3 = w_2$$

$$u_2p_2 + v_3p_3 + u_3p_4 = w_3$$
$$u_3P_3 + v_4P_4 + u_4p_5 = w_4$$
$$u_4p_5 + v_5P_5 = w_s \tag{50}$$

or in matrix form,

$$\begin{bmatrix} v_2 & u_2 & 0 & 0 \\ u_2 & v_3 & u_3 & 0 \\ 0 & u_3 & v_4 & u_4 \\ 0 & 0 & u_4 & v_5 \end{bmatrix} \cdot \begin{bmatrix} p_2 \\ p_3 \\ p_4 \\ p_5 \end{bmatrix} = \begin{bmatrix} w_2 \\ w_3 \\ w_4 \\ w_5 \end{bmatrix} \tag{51}$$

Equation (51) can be solved for pi by conventional elimination methods. Once the p_i values have been computed, the value of t for any segment can be calculated. From this the spline, $s_i(x)$, can be determined using Equation (49) and the appropriate values for p_i and p_{i+1},

For the magnesium in river water data, after scaling the distance data to km, we have,

$$\begin{bmatrix} 5.4 & 1.8 & 0.0 & 0.0 \\ 1.8 & 5.0 & 0.7 & 0.0 \\ 0.0 & 0.7 & 5.2 & 1.9 \\ 0.0 & 0.0 & 1.9 & 6.6 \end{bmatrix} \cdot \begin{bmatrix} p_2 \\ p_3 \\ p_4 \\ p_5 \end{bmatrix} = \begin{bmatrix} -36 \\ -16 \\ 5.5 \\ 6.5 \end{bmatrix} \tag{53}$$

with the result $p_2 = -6.314$, $p_3 = -1.058$, $p_4 = 0.939$, and $p_5 = 0.714$.

To estimate the magnesium concentration at a distance x = 2.5 km, a value of t is calculated,

$$t = (x' - x_1)/(x_2 - x_1) = 0.778 \tag{54}$$

and this, with values for $p_1 = 0$ and $p_2 = -6.314$, is substituted into Equation (49),

$$s_1(t) = ty_2 + (1 - t)y_1 + (x_2 - x_1)^2(t^3 - t)\ p_2/6 \qquad (55)$$

$$s_1(t) = 9.008 \text{ mg kg}^{-1} \text{ Mg}$$

The resultant cubic spline curve for the complete range of the magnesium data. Spline curve fitting has many important applications in analytical science, not only in interpolation but also in differentiation and calibration.

The technique is particularly useful when no analytical model of the data is available. Having acquired our chemical data, it is now necessary to analyse the results and extract the required relevant information.

Electromagnetic radiation

Radiant energy is transferred in waves which consist of electric and magnetic components. These components are at right angles to each other as well as at right angles to the direction of propagation of the wave. Because of the existence of the two components radiant energy is frequently termed as *electromagnetic radiation.*

Electromagnetic radiation does not need any supporting media; in fact, it more readily passes in vacuum than in a supporting medium such as air. In contrast to this, other waves, such as sound do require a supporting medium. The *frequency* of radiation of any wave may be defined as the number of oscillations which occur within a given period of time. It is designated by the Greek letter v and is dependent solely upon the source. It is variant with regard to the media through which the radiation travels.

The most common unit is the hertz, Hz, and has the unit of cycles/second. The crest to crest distance of a wave is called the wavelength, λ. It possesses lines units, usually centimeters. The wave number, v refers to the reciprocal of the wavelength, i.e., it is the number of wavelengths which occur in a given unit of distance and has the units of cm^{-1}. The amplitude, *a*, refers to the height of the wave are functions of the square of the amplitude. The *velocity*, *v*, in constant to frequency, is dependent upon the medium through which radiation is passing. It possesses the units of cm/sec. The product of the wavelength and frequency is equal to the velocity of the wave in that medium, i.e.,

$$\text{wavelength} \times \text{frequency} = \text{velocity}$$

$$\lambda\left(\frac{cm}{cycle}\right) \times v\left(\frac{cycles}{\text{sec}}\right) = v\left(\frac{cm}{\text{sec}}\right)$$

As the density of the medium through which electromagnetic radiation is passing decreases the wavelength and velocity of the radiation increase, reaching constant maximum vales in a vacuum. At this point the velocity is 3×10^{10} cm/sec and is designated, *c*. As the frequency must remain constant, the relationship between the wavelength, frequency, and velocity of light in a vacuum is given as follows:

$$\lambda v = c$$

With dimensions and substitution of the value of the speed of light a vacuum this becomes as follows:

$$\lambda\left(\frac{cm}{cycle}\right) \times v\left(\frac{cycles}{\text{sec}}\right) = 3.00 \times 10^{10}\ cm/\text{sec}$$

More correctly, the units are centimeters per cycle for wavelength and cycles per second for frequency, but the cycles unit is often assumed. In place of cycles/sec., the unit *hertz* (Hz) is now commonly used.

Example 1

What is the velocity, in meters/minute, of a wave which

has a length of 7.5 m and a frequency of 0.45 cycles/sec?

Solution: $\lambda v = \text{v}$

$$7.5\ \frac{\text{m}}{cycle} \times 0.45 \frac{cycles}{\text{sec}} \times 60 \frac{\text{sec}}{\text{min}} = 203\ m\,/\,\text{min}$$

Example 2

What is the wave number of electromagnetic radiation which has a wavelength of 620 nm in vacuum?

Solution: $v = \frac{1}{\lambda}$

$$v- = \frac{1}{620\ \text{nm}} \times \frac{10^9\ \text{nm}}{\text{m}} \times \frac{\text{m}}{10^2\ \text{cm}} = 1.61 \times 10^4\ \text{cm}^{-1}$$

Example 3

What is the frequency and wave number of electromagnetic radiation which has a wavelength of 1.58×10^{-6} cm in vacuum?

Solution: $v = \frac{c}{\lambda}$

$$v = \frac{3.00 \times 10^{10}\ \text{cm / sce}}{1.58 \times 10^{-6}\ \text{cm / cycle}} = 1.90 \times 10^{16}\ cycles\,/\,\text{sec}$$

Whereas wave parameters are primarily discussed so as to establish nomenclature, the energy properties must be considered in order to understand the nature of the radiant processes which are measured by the instruments. The energy consists of small bundles called photons or quanta which are minute, discrete quantities like matter itself. Every photon of a specific wavelength possesses exactly the same energy as every other photon of that wavelength and is different for different wavelengths. The relationship between the energy of particles and their wave nature is given as follows:

$$E = hv$$

Where *E* denotes the energy of a photon in ergs, *v* frequency in cycles per second and *h* a universal constant known as Plank's constant (6.62 x erg sec or 6.62 x 10-34 Js.) When this equation is combined with the previous one which related the frequency, velocity, and wavelength ($v = c/\lambda$) of light in a vacuum, a third equation which shows the interdependence of wavelength and energy properties more clearly is obtained.

$$E = h \times \frac{c}{\lambda}$$

Hence the energy of photon increases linearly with its frequency and is inverse to its wavelength.

Table 4: Radiation parameters and equations

Parameter	*Symbol*	*Units*	*Value*
Wavelength	λ	*cm*	
Amplitude	a	*cm*	
Wave number	v	*cm*$^{-1}$	
Frequency	v	*cycles sec-1* *Hz*	
Velocity	v	*cm sec-1*	
Velocity of light	c	cm sec-1	3.00 x 10^{10}
		m sec-1	3.00 x 10^{8}
Energy	E	ergs	
Plack's constant	h	ergs sec	6.62 x 10^{-27}
		Js	6.62 x 10^{-34}

Electromagnetic radiation consists of small bundles of energy, called *photons*. These particles travel with wave-like motions and each wave consists of electric and magnetic displacements. Electromagnetic radiation may be characterized by wavelength, wave number, frequency, or energy parameters. A list of the nomenclature, units, and interrelationships of the wave parameters is given in Table 4. Many of these functions may be expressed in other units. However, the tabulated set is consistent within itself.

Example 4

Calculate the wave number in cm^{-1}, the frequency in sec^{-1}, and the energy of a photon in ergs of electromagnetic radiation which has a wavelength of 1.24×10^{-6} cm in a vacuum.

Solution:

$$\text{wave number} = \bar{v} = \frac{1}{\lambda} = \frac{1}{1.24 \times 10^{-6}\ \text{cm}} = 8.1 \times 10^{5}\ \text{cm}^{-1}$$

$$\text{frequency} = v = \frac{c}{\lambda} = 3.00 \times 10^{10}\ \frac{\text{cm}}{\text{sec}} \times \frac{1}{1.24 \times 10^{-6}}$$

$$v = 2.42 \times 10^{16}\ \text{sec}^{-1}$$

$$\text{energy} = E = hv$$

$$= 6.62 \times 10^{-27}\ \text{erg sec} \times 2.42 \times 10^{16}\ \text{sec}^{-1}$$

$$= 1.60 \times 10^{-10}\ \text{erg.}$$

Electromagnetic spectrum

Electromagnetic radiation, for purposes can be considered a from of radiant energy that is propagated as a transverse wave. It vibrates perpendicular to the direction to propagation and this imparts a wave motion to the radiation.

The wavelength of electromagnetic radiation varies

from a few angstroms to several meters. The units used to describe the wavelength are as follows:

Å = angstrom = 10^{-10} meter = 10^{-8} centimeter = 10^{-4} micrometer

nm = nanometer = 10^{-9} meter = 10 angstroms = 10^{-3} micrometer

mm = micrometer = 10^{-6} meter = 10^{4} angstroms

The wavelength unit preferred for the *ultraviolet* and *visible* regions of the spectrum is nanometer, while the micrometer is preferred for the *infrared* region. Nanometer (nm) is the preferred term over millimicron (mμ) the unit used extensively prior to this.

In the infrared region, micrometer (μm) is the preferred term in place of the previously used term micron (μ). In infrared region wave numbers are often used in place of wavelength and the unit is cm^{-1}. The electromagnetic spectrum is arbitrarily broken down into different regions according to wavelength. We will not be concerned with the gamma-ray and X-ray regions in this chapter, although these high-energy radiations can be used in principle in the same manner as lower-energy radiations.

The ultraviolet region extends from about 10 to 380 nm, but the most analytically useful region is from 200 to 380nm, called the *near-ultraviolet region*. Below 200 nm, the air absorbs appreciably and so the instruments are operated under a vacuum; hence, this wavelength region is called the *vacuum-ultraviolet region*. The *visible region* is actually a very small part of the electromagnetic spectrum, and it is the region of wavelength that can be seen by the human eye, that is the where the light appears as colour.

The visible region extends from the near-ultraviolet region (380nm) to about 780nm. The *infrared region* extends from about 0.78 um (780nm) to 300 um, but the range from 2.5 to 15 um is the most frequently used for analysis. The 0.8 to 2.5 um range is known as the *near-infrared region,* the 2.5 to 15um region as the *mid-or NaCI-infrared region,* and longer wavelengths as the *far-infrared region.*

Nuclear magnetic resonance spectroscopy involves the interaction of low-energy microwave radiation with the nuclei of atoms. Table 5 summarizes the approximate colours associated with different wavelengths in the visible spectrum. As an example, a solution of potassium permanganate absorbs light in the green region of the spectrum with an absorption maximum of 525 nm, and the solution is purple.

Table 5 Colours of different wavelength regions

Wavelength Absorbed, nm	*Absorbed colour*	*Transmitted colour (Complement)*
380-450	Violet	Yellow-green
450-495	Blue	Yellow
495-570	Green	Violet
570-590	Yellow	Blue
590-620	Orange	Green-blue
620-750	Red	Blue-green

The visible region is a very small of the total. In fact, if a linear scale is used and the visible region allocated 1 inch, a sheet of paper approximately 10^{18} miles long would be needed to waves. It must be emphasized that the electromagnetic radiation itself is fundamentally the same over the entire electromagnetic spectrum and that even the boundaries between the instrumentally based divisions are diffuse.

Absorption of radiation

There are three basic processes by which a molecule can absorb radiation; all involve raising the molecule to a higher internal energy level, the increase in energy being equal to the energy of the absorbed radiation (*hv*). The three types of internal energy are *quantized;* that is; they exist at discrete levels.

First, the molecule rotates about various axes, the energy of rotation being at definite energy levels, so the molecule may absorb radiation and be raised to a higher rotational energy level, in a *rotational transition.*

Second, the atoms or groups of atoms within a molecule vibrate relative to each other and the energy of this vibration occurs at definite quantized levels. The molecule may then absorb a discrete amount of energy and be raised at a higher vibrational energy level, in a *vibrational transition.*

Third the electrons of a molecule may be raised to a higher electron energy, corresponding to an *electronic transition.*

Since each of these internal energy transitions is quantized, they will occur only at *definite wavelengths* corresponding to an energy *hv* equal to the quantized jump in the internal energy. The relative energy levels of the three transition processes are in the order: electronic > vibrational > rotational, each being about an order of magnitude different in its energy level. Rotational transitions thus can take place at very low energies (long wavelengths, that is the microwave or far-infrared region), but vibrational transitions require higher energies in the near-infrared region, while electronic transitions require still higher energies (in the visible and ultraviolet regions). Purely rotational transitions can occur in the *far-infrared* and *microwave* regions (ca, 100 μm to 10 cm), where the energy is insufficient to cause vibrator electronic transitions. The molecule at room temperature, is usually in its lowest electronic energy state, called the *ground state* (E).

Thus, the pure rotational transition will occur at the ground-state electronic level although it is also possible to have an appreciable population of *excited states* of the molecule. When only rotational transitions occur, discrete absorption *lines* will occur in the spectrum the wave length of each corresponding to a particular transition. Hence, funda-mental information can be obtained about rotational energy levels of molecules. This region has been of little use analytically, however. As the energy is increased (the wavelength decreased), vibrational transitions occur *in addition* to the rotational transitions, with different combinations of vibrational-rotational transitions.

Each rotational level of the lowest vibrational level can be excited to different rotational levels of the excited vibrational level. In addition, there may be several different excited vibrational levels, each with a number of rotational levels. This leads to numerous discrete transitions.

The result is a spectrum of peaks or "envelops" of unresolved fine structure. The wavelengths at which these peaks occur can be related to vibrational modes within the molecules. These occur in the mid-and far-infrared regions. At still higher energies (visible and ultraviolet wavelengths), different levels of electronic transition take place, and rotational and vibrational transitions are superimposed on these. This results in an even larger number of possible transitions.

Although all the transitions occur in quantized steps corresponding to discrete wavelengths, these individual wavelengths are too numerous and too close to resolve into the individual lines or vibrational peaks, and the net result is a spectrum of broad bands of absorbed wavelengths. Not all molecule can absorb in the infrared region. For absorption to occur there must be a change *in the dipole moment* (polarity) *of the molecule.* A diatonic molecule must have a permanent dipole (polar covalent bond in which a pair of electrons is shared unequally) in order to absorb, but larger molecules do not. For example, nitrogen, N $\equiv$ N, cannot exhibit a dipole and will not absorb in the infrared region.

An unsymmetrical diatomic molecule such as carbon monoxide does have a permanent dipole and hence will absorb. Carbon monoxide, O $\Rightarrow$ C $\Rightarrow$ O, does not have a permanent dipole, but by vibration it may exhibit a dipole moment. Thus, in the vibration mode O $\Leftarrow$ C $\Leftarrow$ O there is a dipole moment. But in the mode O $\Rightarrow$ C $\Rightarrow$ O, there is a dipole moment and the molecule can absorb infrared radiation, that is,via an induced dipole.

The types of absorbing groups and molecules for the infrared and other wavelength regions will be discussed below. Our discussions are being confined to molecules, since neatly all absorbing species in solution are molecular in nature. In the case of single atoms (which occur in a flame or an electric arc) that do not vibrate or rotate, only electronic transitions occur.

These occur as sharp lines corresponding to definite transitions. The lifetimes of excited states of molecules are rather short, and the molecules will lose their energy emitting this energy as a photon of the same wavelength as absorbed, most of them will be deactivated by collisions processes in which the energy is lost as heat; the heat will be too small to be detected in most cases. This is the reason for a solution or a substance being coloured. If the light were remitted, then it would appear colourless. In some cases, light will be emitted, usually at longer wavelength. For this, see fluorescence.

Interaction of radiation energy with matter

Prior to any discussion regarding specific radiant energy instruments, it becomes necessary to get a broad overview of a number of processes by which radiation may react with matter. Some of these are later used to explain the chemical and physical reactions within the system being measured, and some are needed to explain the components of the instruments. Specific instruments have been developed to measure each interactive property. A requisite process in one instrument might contribute to an error in another. For ease of explanation the properties have been paired:

1. Absorption and transmission
2. Emission and fluorescence
3. Refraction and dispersion
4. Scattering and reflection.

It is not to be inferred that these are the only reactions of energy with matter. The listing includes only those which are most prominent in instrumental analysis.

Absorption and transmission: The electrons in chemical particles such as atoms, or molecules have a limited number of discrete energy levels which they may occupy in the particle. When electromagnetic energy such as light gets impinged upon these particles, the electrons may be promoted from the lower energy (*ground*) state to one of a higher energy (*excited*) state provided the energy of the impinging radiation corresponds to one of the energy differences between the ground and excited states.

During the process the energy of the incoming radiation gets transferred to the particles at wavelengths corresponding to these discrete energy differences and the electromagnetic radiation at these wavelengths is decreased or *absorbed*. If the intensity of the incoming radiation is in excess of that required at any particular wavelength ($E = hc/\lambda$) the reminded is *transmitted*.

Due to the limited number of permissible atomic energy levels atoms can absorb at only a few selected frequencies. The plot of absorbance vs. Wavelength exhibits a *line absorption spectrum* where each line corresponds to a permitted transition.

This type of spectrum is utilized for atomic analysis in atomic absorption and X-ray absorption instruments. On the other hand, the number of possible energy transitions in molecule is much greater than in atoms. More electrons are present in molecules and the number of possible electronic transitions is vastly increased. In addition, energy is also needed for *vibration* of the atoms within the molecule and *rotation* of the molecule around its gravitational center, the total energy of the molecule being.

$$E_{\text{total}} = E_{\text{electronic}} + E_{\text{rotational}} + E_{\text{vibrational}}$$

Because of the number of permissible combinations of three components and because the energies of these various combination are frequently close to each other, they cannot be resolved by the instrument and the plot of absorbance vs. Wavelength appears as a *band absorption spectrum*.

Emission and fluorescence: After electrons in the chemical entities are excited the energy of excitation will subsequently be released and the electrons will be returned to their respective ground or stable states. This excess energy release is generally dissipated as heat when the particles collide, but it might also be released in photonchemical reactions or as radiantly energy. It is not uncommon for several of these processes to take place simultaneously.

If the excited particles are gaseous atom a limited number of discrete energy transitions which correspond to specific wavelengths may take place and a discontinuous emission line spectrum is obtained. *Emission line spectra* are used as qualitative and quantitative tools in flame photometry, emission spectroscopy, and x-ray spectroscopy. An *emission band spectrum* is obtained if the energy states of the sample are so close to each other and so numerous, as in an excited molecule, that the energies of the various transitions to the ground state cannot be separated.

This principle is used in molecular fluorescence and phosphorescence instruments. Molecular fluorescence may be roughly considered the reverse process of molecular absorption. If the emitting energy is quantitatively equal to the excitation energy, the emission process is designated as *resonance fluorescence.* However, in most fluorescence processes some of the energy is lost as heat, and the resulting *emission spectrum* will be at longer wavelengths (lower energies) than will be corresponding *excitation spectrum.*

Refraction and Dispersion: Even if no absorption occurs, an interaction of electromagnetic radiation with the matter through which it get transmitted will occur. It has previously been stated that the velocity of electromagnetic radiation is less matter than in a vacuum. The exact relationship is

$$n = \frac{c}{v}$$

where n refers to the *refractive index*, c the velocity in vacuum, and v the velocity in the medium. The refractive index of a medium may be defined as the ratio of the velocity of light in a vacuum to its velocity in the medium. As the velocity is dependent on the wavelength (energy) of radiation, the refractive index will also be dependent upon the wavelength as well as upon the composition of the matter through which it is passing.

The direction of a light path changes as the composition of the matter through which the light is passing changes. This change in direction is designated *refraction*. It is a function of the velocities in the media and of the angle of incidence. It will not occur if the angle of incidence is at right angles to the media. The relationships between the velocities, incident and refractive angles, and refractive indices of electromagnetic radiation are stated as follows:

$$\frac{n_1}{n_1} = \frac{v_1}{v_2} = \frac{\sin \theta_1}{\sin \theta_2}$$

where n_1 and n_2 refer to the respective refractive in the first and second media v_1 and v_2 the respective velocities, and θ_1 the angle of incidence at the medium boundaries while θ_2 the angle (perpendicular to the normal) at which the wave travels in the second medium. The change in refractive index which occurs with a change in the wavelength (frequency) of the transmitted light is *dispersion*.

In normal dispersion a gradual increase in refractive index with decreasing wavelength will be exhibited. If the radiation frequency corresponds to a natural vibrational frequency of a portion of the molecule atom, or ion, the energy of the radiant beam will be transferred to the molecule, atom, or ion, and a sharp discontinuity in a plot of the refractive index against wavelength will result. This phenomenon is known as *anomalous dispersion*. Refractive indices and dispersion values are obtained with a *refractometer*. These quantities are fundamental physical constants and may be used for qualitative and quantitative identification purposes. In addition a knowledge of these properties is necessary in order to design or evaluate other radiant energy instruments.

Scattering and reflection: If incoming radiant energy is impinged upon particles which are suspended in a medium which has a refractive index different from that of the suspended particles, the light which is transmitted at angles other than 180° from the incident light is said to be *scattered* as the radiation passes through the sample. If as is usually the case, the wavelength of the impinging radiation is larger than the particle size, the emitted radiation is removed by destructive interference and the path of the light beam appears to be unchanged. If the wavelength is decreased the particle size increased or both the fraction of light which is scattered may become significant.

Nephelometry and turbidimetry are based upon this ability of particles of scatter light. The size, shape, and concentration of colloidal particles and suspensions may be determined from this property.

Reflection takes place as a ray of light strikes a boundary between two different media. It is dependent upon the refractive indices of the two media and increases as these differences in the refractive indices increases. Specular reflectance occurs as in a mirror and is a true and equal reflectance of all the wavelengths of the impinging light. In diffuse reflectance some of the of the incoming light may be absorbed or scattered practices appear coloured.

Reflectance measurements are characterization of suspensions as well as in the quality of fabrics and paints. Both scattering and reflectance must be regarded as possible interferences in absorption and fluorescence measurements. The number of intensities of lines which may appear in a spectrum can be determined by three factors,

1. the populations of the energy levels from which the transitions originate
2. the values of individual transition moments or transition probabilities
3. quantum mechanical selection rules.

In brief, the statistical probability for the occurrence of a transition can be calculated and lies between zero and one. It can be shown that weak spectral lines have small transition moments while strong lines have values approaching one.

One factor which determines the value of a transition moment is the magnitude of the change in dipole moment associated with the transition. In addition, the selection rules may show that a particular transition is *forbidden*. As a consequence of these conditions spectra often have fewer lines or bands than might be expected, a fact which facilitates interpretation. A detailed discussion of transition moments and selection rules, which are mathematical concepts, is beyond the scope of this book and the known selection rules will therefore be assumed.

Spectral line widths also affect the appearance of the spectrum. Lines arising from transitions in atoms and gaseous molecules are characteristically narrow as are those due to electron and nuclear spin transitions which involve only small energy changes. Molecule absorption spectra in the infrared visible and ultraviolet regions consist of sets of very closely spaced lines which are not normally resolved by the instrumentation used.

They are not broadened by collisions between solute and solvent molecules so that the overall appearance is of a number of broad overlapping band envelopes. The relative populations of energy levels, that is the proportion of the analyze species occupying them, have a direct bearing on line intensities and are determined by the spacing of the levels and the thermodynamic temperature. The relation is expressed in the *Maxwell-Boltzmann* equation,

$$\frac{n_2}{n_1} = \frac{g_2}{g_1}\left(-\frac{\Delta E}{kT}\right) \tag{56}$$

Table 6: Analytical spectroscopic techniques

Name of Technique	*Principle*	*Major Application*
arc/spark spectroscopy		qualitative and quantitative
or spectrography		determination of metails,
plasma emission	atomic	largely as minor or trace
spectrometry	emission	constituents
flame photometry		quantitative determination of
		metals as minor or trace
		constituents.
X-ray fluorescence		qualitative and quantitative
spectroscopy	atomic	determination of elements
	flourescence	heavier than nitrogen as trace
atomic fluorescence	emission	to major constituents
spectroscopy		
atomic absorption	atomic	quantitative determination of
	absorption	metals at minor or trace
		constituents
y-spectroscopy	nuclear	qualitative and quantitative
	emission	determination of elements at
		trace levels.
ultraviolet spectroscopy		quantitative determination of
		elements and compounds
		mainly at trace levels.
visible spectroscopy	molecular	quantitative determination of
	absorption	elements and compounds
		mainly as trace and minor
infrared spectroscopy		constituents.
		Identification and structural
		analysis of organic compounds
nuclear magnetic	nuclear	identification and structural
resonance spectroscopy	absorption	analysis of organic compounds
mass spectroscopy	structural	identification and structural
	fragmentation	analysis of organic compunds

where n_1 and n_2 are the numbers of species in energy states E_1 and E_2 separated by ΔE, g_1 and g_2 are statistical weighting factors, k is the Boltzmann constant (1.38×10^{-23} J K^{-1}) and T is the thermodynamic temperature. Calculations show that at room temperature and when ΔE exceeds 10^3 J mol^{-1} only the lowest level of a set will be populated to a significant extent.

Thus, absorption spectra recorded in the infrared, visible, ultraviolet regions and beyond arise from transitions from the ground state only. For atomic emission spectra to be observed, a considerable increase in temperature (to more than 1500 K) is required to give appreciable population of the higher energy levels. Indeed the practical importance of the Maxwell Boltzmann excitation conditions on the intensity of atomic emission spectra. It is possible to have some measure of control over the sensitivity of atomic emission techniques but little or no such control over molecular absorption.

Chapter 5

Techniques of Chemometrics

Many of these procedures are based on multivariate numerical data processing and before the methods can be successfully applied it is usual to perform some pre-processing on the data. There are three main aims of this pre-processing stage in data analysis.

— to reduce the amount of data and eliminate data that are irrelevant to the study being undertaken,

— to preserve or enhance sufficient information within the data in order to achieve the desired goal,

— to extract the information in, or transform the data to, a form suitable for further analysis.

One of the most common forms of pre-processing spectral data is *normalization*. At its simplest this may involve no more than scaling each spectrum in a collection so that the most intense band in each spectrum is some constant value. Spectra could be normalized to constant area under the curve of the absorption or emission profile.

A more sophisticated procedure involves constructing a covariance matrix between variates and extracting the *eigenvectors* and *eigenvalues*. Eigen analysis yields a set of new variables which are linear combinations of the original variables. This can often lead to representing the original information in fewer new variables, thus reducing the dimensionality of the data and aiding subsequent analysis. The success of pattern recognition techniques can frequently be enhanced or simplified by suitable prior treatment of the analytical data, and *feature selection* and *feature extraction* are important stages in chemometrics.

Feature selection refers to identifying and selecting those features present in the analytical data which are believed to be important to the success of calibration or pattern recognition. Techniques commonly used include *differentiation*, *integration*, and *peak identification*. Feature extraction, on the other hand, changes the dimensionality of the data and generally refers to processes combining or transforming original variables to provide new and better variables.

Methods widely used include Fourier transformation and *principal components analysis*. In this chapter the popular techniques pertinent to feature selection and extraction are introduced and developed. Their application is illustrated with reference to spectrochemical analysis.

Differentiation

The technique has been used for many years in many branches of analytical spectroscopy. Derivative spectra are usually obtained by differentiating the recorded signal with respect to wavelength as the spectrum is scanned. Whereas early applications mainly relied on hard-wired units for electronic differentiation, modern derivative spectroscopy is normally accomplished computationally using mathematical functions. First-, second-, and higher-order derivatives can easily be generated. Analytical applications of derivative spectroscopy are numerous and generally owe their popularity to the apparent higher resolution of the differential data compared with the original spectrum.

The effect can be illustrated with reference to the example shown in Figure 1. The zero' the, first-, and second-order derivatives of a spectrum, comprised of the sum of two overlapping Gaussian peaks, are presented. The presence of a smaller analyte peak can be much more evident in the derivative spectra. In addition, for determining the intensity of the smaller peak in the presence of the large neighbouring peak, derivative spectra can be more useful and may be subject to less error.

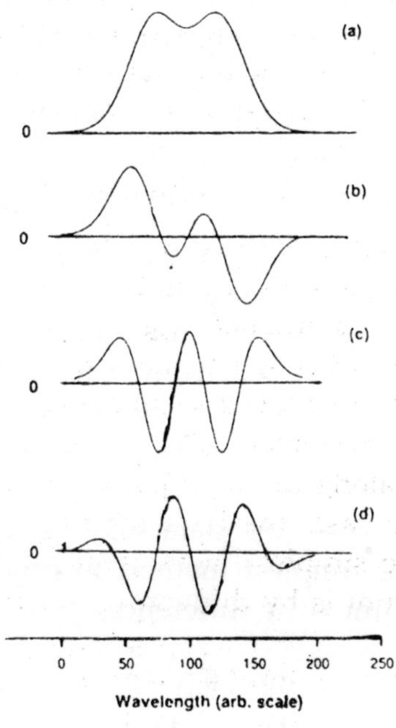

Fig. 1. A pair of overlapping Gaussian peaks (a), and the first (b), second (c), and third-order (d) derivative spectra.

If we assign unit peak height to the analyte in the normal, zero'th-order, spectrum, then for the same band with the interfering band present, a peak height of 55 units is recorded. Using a tangent baseline in order to attempt to correct for the overlap fails as there is no unique or easily identified tangent, and a not unreasonable value of 12 units for the peak height could be recorded, a 20% error.

The situation is improved considerably if the first derivative spectrum is analysed.

A value of one is assigned to the peak-to-peak distance of the lone analyte spectrum. In the presence of the overlapping band a similar measure for the analyte is now 1.04, a 4% error. This example, however, oversimplifies the case of using derivative spectroscopy as it gives no indication of the effects of noise on the results. Derivative spectra tend to emphasize changes in slope that are difficult to detect in the zero'th-order spectrum. Unfortunately, as we have seen in previous chapters, noise is often comprised of high-frequency components and thus may be greatly amplified by differentiation.

It is the Presence of noise which generally limits the use of derivative spectroscopy to UV-visible spectrometry and other techniques in which a high signal-to-noise ratio may be obtained for a spectrum. Various mathematical procedures may be employed to differentiate spectral data. We will assume that such data are recorded at evenly spaced intervals along the wavelength, λ, or other x-axis. If this is not the case, the data may be interpolated to provide this. The simplest method to produce the first-derivative spectrum is by difference,

$$\frac{dy}{d\lambda} = \frac{y_{i+1} - y_i}{\Delta\lambda} \tag{1}$$

or,

$$\frac{dy}{d\lambda} = \frac{y_{i+1} - y_{i-1}}{2\Delta\lambda} \tag{2}$$

and for the second derivative,

$$\frac{d^2y}{d\lambda^2} = \frac{y_{i+1} - 2y_0 - y_{i-1}}{\Delta\lambda^2} \tag{3}$$

where y represents the spectral intensity, the absorbance, or other metric.

Various other methods have been proposed to compute derivatives, including the use of suitable polynomial derivatives as suggested by Savitzky and Golay. An array can be specified which on convolution produces the first, or higher degree differential spectrum. Using a quadratic polynomial and a five-point moving window, the first derivative is given by

$$\frac{dy}{d\lambda} = \frac{1}{10\Delta\lambda}\,(-2y_{i-2} - y_{i-1} + y_{i+1} + 2y_{i+2}) \tag{4}$$

and for the second derivative,

$$\frac{d^2y}{d\lambda^2} = \frac{1}{7\Delta\lambda^2}\,(2y_{i-2} - Y_{i-1} - 2y_i - y_{i+1} + 2Y_{i+2}) \tag{5}$$

Equations (4) and (5) are similar to Equations (2) and (3). The difference is in the use of additional terms using extra points from the data in order to provide a better approximation. The relative merits of these different methods can be compared by differentiating a known mathematical function.

Table 1
Derivative model data, $y = x+x^2/2$ + noise

x	0	1	2	3	4	
Noise	0.200	0.000	0.200	−0.200	0.200	
y	0.000	1.500	4.000	7.500	12.000	
y + Noise	0.200	1.500	4.200	7.300	12.200	Data 1
y + (Noise/2)	0.100	1.500	4.100	7.400	12.100	Data 2
y + (Noise/4)	0.050	1.500	4.050	7.450	12.050	Data 3
y + (Noise/8)	0.025	1.500	4.025	7.475	12.025	Data 4

The model we will use is $y = (x + x^2/2)$ at the point $x = 2$. Various levels of noise are imposed on the signal y, as shown in Table 1. The resulting derivatives are shown in Table 2. As the noise level reduces and tends to zero, the derivative results from applying the five-point polynomial converge more quickly towards the correct

Table 2

Derivatives of $y = x + x^2/2$ + noise (from Table 1) determined by difference formulae

		Data			
		1	2	3	4
$dy/d\lambda$	by Equation (1)	3.1 or 2.7	3.3 or 2.6	3.4 or 2.55	3.45 or 2.525
$dy/d\lambda$	by Equation (2)	2.9	2.95	2.98	2.9875
$dy/d\lambda$	by Equation (4)	2.980	2.990	2.995	2.9975
$d^2y/d\lambda^2$	by Equation (3)	0.4	0.7	0.85	0.925
$d^2y/d\lambda^2$	by Equation (5)	**1.0857**	**1.0429**	**1.0214**	**1.0107**

noise-free value of 3 for the first derivative, and 1 for the second derivative. As with polynomial smoothing, the Savitzky-Golay differentiation technique is available with many commercial spectrometers. Just as smoothing can be undertaken in the frequency domain, so too can differentiation following Fourier transformation of the amplitude-time spectrum. Obtaining a derivative in the Fourier domain is quite simple and is achieved by multiplying the transform by a linear function.

The original spectrum, comprising two overlapping bands and random noise, is first converted by Fourier transformation to the frequency domain. The susceptibility of differentiation to high-frequency noise is clearly demonstrated in this example. The high-frequency components present in the Fourier domain data are heavily weighted by the filter function compared with low-frequency data, and the signal-to-noise ratio of the differential spectrum is severely degraded. This problem can be partly alleviated by combining a smoothing function along with the differential filter.

High frequencies are eliminated by the zero weighting of the function. The result of multiplying our transformed data by this new filter function. For many applications the digitization of a full spectrum provides far more data than is warranted by the spectrum's information content. This represents such a dramatic decrease in dimensionality of the spectral data that it is not surprising that peak tables are commonly employed to describe spectra.

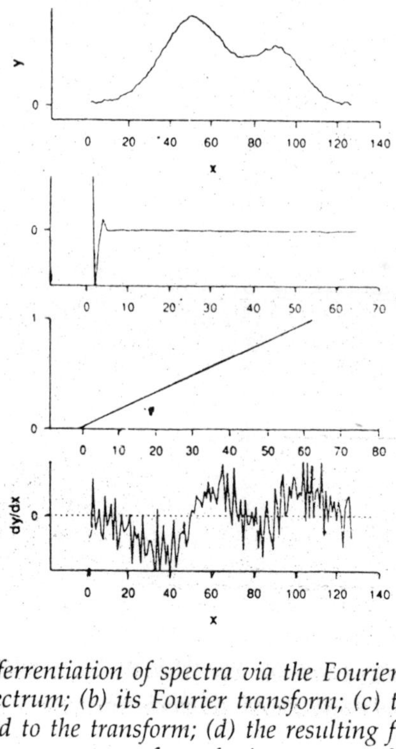

Fig. 2: Differrentiation of spectra via the Fourier transform: (a) the original spectrum; (b) its Fourier transform; (c) the differential filter applied to the transform; (d) the resulting first derivative spectrum from the inverse transform

The determination of spectral peak positions from digital data is relatively straightforward and the facility is offered on many commercial spectrometers. Probably the most common techniques for finding peak positions involve analysis of derivative data. In Figure 2 a single Lorentzian function is illustrated along with its first, second, third, and fourth derivatives with respect to energy. At peak positions the following conditions exist,

$$Y' = 0 \qquad y'' < 0$$

$$Y''' = 0 \qquad y'''' > 0 \tag{6}$$

where y' is the first derivative, y'' the second, and so on.

Thus, the presence and location of a peak in a spectrum can be ascertained from a suitable subset of the rules expressed mathematically in Equation (6):

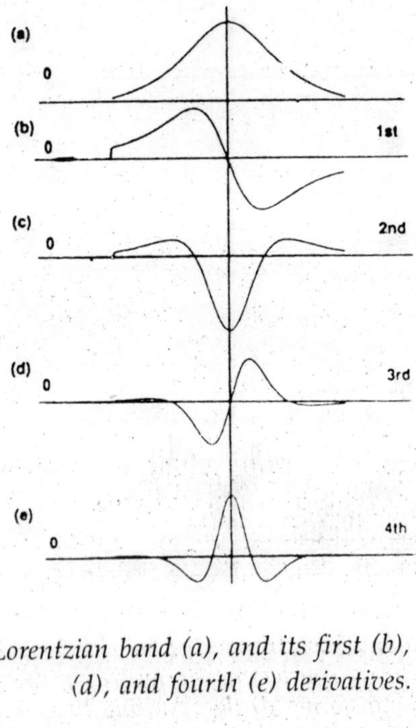

Fig. 3. A Lorentzian band (a), and its first (b), second (c), third (d), and fourth (e) derivatives.

Rule 1, a peak centre has been located if the first derivative value is zero and the second derivative value is negative, *i.e.*

$$(y' = 0) \text{ AND } (y'' < 0), \text{ or}$$

Rule 2, a peak centre has been located if the third derivative is zero and the fourth derivative is positive, *i.e.*

$$(y''' = 0) \text{ AND } (y'''' > 0)$$

Whereas Rule 2 is influenced less by adjacent, overlapping bands than Rule 1, it is affected more by noise in the data. In practice some form of Rule 1 is generally used. A peak-finding algorithm may take the following form:

Step 1: Convolute the spectrum with a suitable quadratic differentiating function until the computed central value changes sign.

Step 2: At this point of inflection compute a cubic, least-squares function. By numerical differentiation of the resultant equation determine the true position of zero slope (the peak position).

With any such algorithm it is necessary to specify some tolerance value below which any peaks are assumed to arise from noise in the data. The choice of window width for the quadratic differentiating function and the number of points about the observed inflection to fit the cubic model are selected by the user. These factors depend on the resolution of the recorded spectrum and the shape of the bands present. Results using a 15-point quadratic differentiating convolution function and a nine-point cubic fitting equation.

Integration

Integration is complementary to differentiation and computing the integral of a function is a fundamental operation in data processing it occurs frequently in analytical science in terms of determining the area under a curve, e.g. the integrated absorbance of a transient signal from a graphite furnace atomic absorption spectrometer.

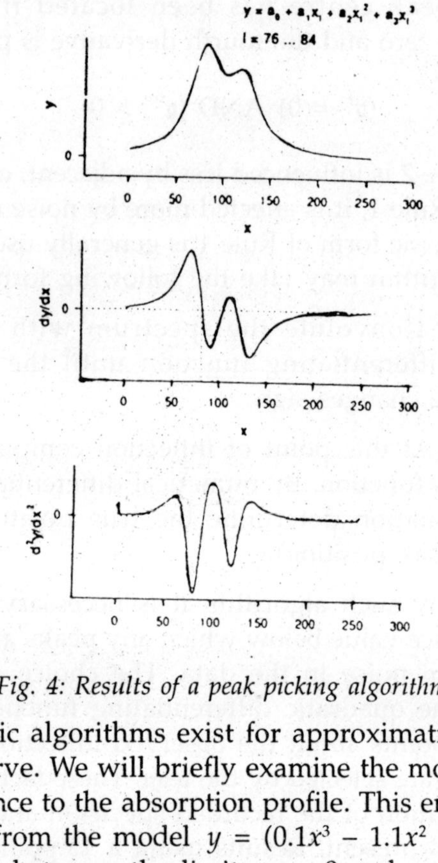

Fig. 4: Results of a peak picking algorithm

Many classic algorithms exist for approximating the area under a curve. We will briefly examine the more common with reference to the absorption profile. This envelope was generated from the model $y = (0.1x^3 - 1.1x^2 + 3x + 0.2)$. Its integral, between the limits $x = 0$ and $x = 6$, can be computed directly.

The area under the curve is 8.400. One of the simplest integration techniques to implement on a computer is the method of summing rectangles that each fit a portion of the curve. For $N + 1$ points in the interval $x_1, x_1 \ldots x_{N+1}$, we have N rectangles of width $(x_{i+1} - x_i)$ and height, h_{mi}, given by the value of the curve at the mid-point between xi and x_{i+1}. The approximate area under the curve, A, between x_1 and x_{N+1} is therefore given by

$$A = \sum_{i=1}^{N} (x_{i+1} - x_i) h_{mi} \tag{7}$$

As N gets larger, the width of each rectangle becomes is more accurate:

for $N = 5$, $A = 8.544$

$N = 10$, $A = 8.436$

$N = 15$, $A = 8.388$

A second method of approximating the integral is to divide the area under the curve into trapezoids. The area of each trapezoid is given by one-half the product of the width $(x_{i+1} - x_i)$ and the sum of the two sides, h_i and h_{i+1}. The area under the curve can be calculated from

$$A = \sum_{i=1}^{N} (x_{i+1} - x_i)(h_i + h_{i+1}) / 2 \tag{8}$$

For our absorption peak, the trapezoid method using different widths produces the following estimates for the integral:

for $N = 5$, $A = 8.112$

$N = 10$, $A = 8.328$

$N = 15$, $A = 8.368$

In general the trapezoid method is inferior to the rectangular method.

A more accurate method can be achieved by combining the rectangular and trapezoid methods into the technique referred to as *Simpson's method*,[5]

$$A = \sum_{i=1}^{N} (x_{i+1} - x_i)(4h_{mi} + h_{i+1})/6 \quad (9)$$

For our absorption profile this gives

for $N = 5, \quad A = 8.400$

$N = 10, \quad A = 8.400$

$N = 15, \quad A = 8.400$

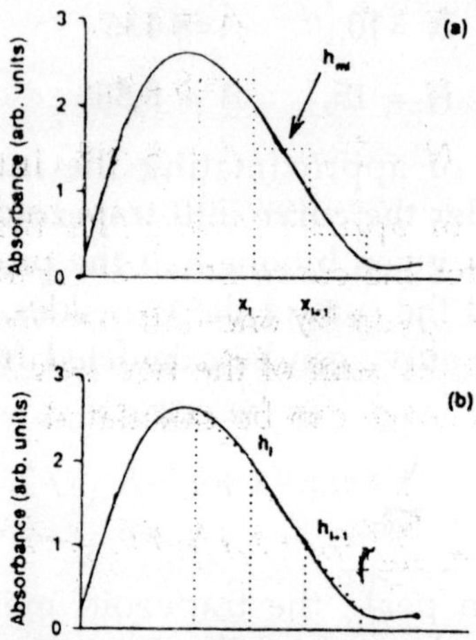

Fig. 5: The area under the AAS profile using (a) rectangular and (b) trapezoidal integration

Combining variables

Many analytical measures cannot be represented as a time-series in the form of a spectrum, but are comprised of discrete measurements, e.g. compositional or trace analysis. Data reduction can still play an important role in such cases.

The interpretation of many multivariate problems can be simplified by considering not only the original variables but also *linear combinations* of them. That is, a new set of variables can be constructed each of which contains a sum of the original variables each suitably weighted. These linear combinations can be derived on an *ad hoc* basis or more formally using established mathematical techniques.

Whatever the method used, however, the aim is to reduce the number of variables considered in subsequent analysis and obtain an improved representation of the original data. The number of variables measured is not reduced. An important and commonly used procedure which generally satisfies these criteria is Principal components analysis. Before this specific topic is examined it is worthwhile discussing some of with linear combinations of variables.

Linear combinations of variables

In order to consider the effects and results of combining different measured variables the data set shown in Table 3 will be analysed. Table 3 lists the mean values, from 11 determinations, of the concentration of each of 13 trace metals from 17 different samples of heart tissue. The data in Table 3 indicate that the trace metal composition of cardiac tissue derived from different anatomical sites varies widely.

However, it is not immediately apparent by visual examination of these raw data alone, what order, groups, or underlying patterns exist within the data. The correlation matrix for the 13 variables is shown in Table 4 and, as is usual in multivariate data, some pairs of variables are highly correlated. Consider, in the first instance, the concentrations of chromium and nickel. We shall label these variables $X1$ and $X2$. Also shown are projections of the points on to the $X1$ and $X2$ concentration axes, providing one-dimensional frequency distributions (as bar graphs) of the variables X1 and X2. This single new variable or axis would contain more variance or potential information than either of the two original variables on their own. For example, a new variable, X3 could be identified which can be defined as the sum of the original variables, *i.e.*

$$X3 = a.X1 + b.X2 \tag{10}$$

and its value for the 17 samples calculated. The values of a and b could be chosen arbitrarily such that, for example, $a = b$. As for the actual values of the coefficients a and b, the simplest case is described by $a = b = 1$, but any value will provide the same angle of projection and the same form of the distribution of data on this new line. In practice, it is usual to specify a particular linear combination referred as the *normalized linear combination* and defined by

$$a^2 + b^2 = 1 \tag{11}$$

Normalization of the coefficients defining our new variable scales it to the range of values used to define the X1 and X2 axes of the original graph. In our example, this implies $a = b = 1/\sqrt{2}$. The variance of X3 derived from substituting a and b into Equation 10 for the concentration of chromium and nickel for each of the 17 samples is 5.22 compared with $\sigma^2 = 3.07$ and $\sigma^2 = 2.43$ for X1 and X2 respectively. Thus X3 does indeed contain more potential information than either X1 or X2.

This reorganization or partitioning of variance associated with individual variates can be formally addressed as follows.

For any linear combination of variables defining a new variable X given by

$$X = a_1\ x_2 + a_2x_2 + \ldots + a_nx_n \qquad (12)$$

The variance, s_x^2, of the new variable can be calculated from

$$s_x^2 = \sum_{j=1}^{n}\sum_{k=1}^{n} a_j.a_kCov_{jk} \qquad (13)$$

which, from the definition of covariance, can be rewritten as

$$s_x^2 \sum_{j=1}^{n} a_j^2.s_j^2 + \sum_{j=1}^{n}\sum_{k=j+1}^{n} a_j.s_j.a_k.s_k.r_{jk} \qquad (14)$$

where R_{JK} is the correlation coefficient between variables x_j and X_k.

It should be noted that for statistically independent variables, $r_{jk} = 0$ and Equation (14) reduces to the more common equation stating that the variance of a sum of variables is equal to the sum of the variances for each variable. The calculated value for the variance of our new variable $X3$ confirms that there is an increased spread of the data on the new axis. As well as this algegbraic notation, it is worth pointing out that the coefficients of the normalized linear combination may be represented by the trigonometric identities

$$a = \cos\ \alpha$$

$$b = \sin\ \alpha \qquad (15)$$

where α is the angle between the projection of the new axis and the original ordinate axis. If $\alpha = 45^0$, then $a = b = 1/\sqrt{2}$, the normalized coefficients as derived from Equation (11). This trigonometric relationship is often

Table 3

Heart-tissue trace metal data

	Cu	*Mn*	*Mo*	*Zn*	*Cr*	*Ni*	*Cs*	*Ba*	*Sr*	*Cd*	*Al*	*Sn*	*Pb*
1. AO	38.4	5.1	1.9	300	2.3	1.8	3.9	9.9	5.4	7.1	31.0	15.2	8.8
2. MPA	47.6	3.8	2.1	774	1.2	1.7	2.3	4.0	3.7	9.7	13.7	15.9	8.8
3. RSCV	112.0	9.8	4.6	521	3.0	.9	4.9	7.3	4.4	11.8	35.9	32.8	20.1
4. TV	52.7	3.7	3.2	358	3.0	2.7	3.7	6.6	3.6	17.6	28.6	18.5	25.2
5. MV	42.0	3.6	3.2	327	2.1	3.5	3.1	5.1	3.7	9.7	22.0	15.4	15.1
6. PV	102.0	21.9	5.9	744	7.6	8.4	47.3	54.4	16.4	33.9	280.0	36.9	55.0
7. AV	61.2	12.8	4.2	224	5.7	5.2	21.9	31.7	7.8	13.8	126.0	25.2	32.5
8. RA	140.0	6.4	3.3	429	2.2	2.8	2.0	2.3	2.3	7.5	5.0	33.9	12.2
9. LAA	137.0	7.9	3.2	353	0.7	2.8	1.1	0.7	1.2	7.9	6.5	33.5	9.5
10. RV	163.0	6.7	3.8	433	2.0	2.2	0.8	0.7	1.6	7.5	6.3	38.9	6.7
11. LV	171.0	7.2	4.6	396	1.7	2.8	0.7	0.8	1.5	7.3	6.4	44.2	7.6
12. LV-PM	170.0	7.8	5.3	330	1.8	2.6	0.9	0.8	2.1	6.8	7.6	41.6	9.3
13. IVS	171.0	6.8	4.6	248	1.1	2.8	1.4	0.9	1.5	7.0	9.5	39.6	10.3
14. CR	161.0	6.9	4.1	493	1.5	2.9	1.3	1.6	1.9	7.7	17.8	35.6	12.5

15.	SN	145.0	6.6	4.2	548	1.7	2.9	1.1	1.5	2.2	7.7	8.6	31.5	12.4
16.	AVN + B	144.0	6.5	4.2	284	1.3	2.5	1.3	1.3	3.3	6.5	5.4	32.8	7.5
17.	LBB	164.0	7.7	5.4	449	1.5	2.8	1.5	1.2	2.1	7.6	12.8	39.7	12.6

AO Aorta; MPA Main pulmonary artery; RSCV : Right superior vena cava; TV Tricuspid valve; MV Mitral valve; PV Pulmonary valve; AV Aortic valve; RA Right atrium; LAA atrial appendage; RV Right ventricle; LV Left ventricle; LV-PM Left ventricle, muscle; IVS Interventricular septum; CR Crista supraventricularis; SN sinus node; AVN + B Atrioventicular node; LBB Left bundle branch.

Table 4

The matrix ofcorrelations between the analytes determined from heart-tissue data

	Cu	*Mn*	*Mo*	*Zn*	*Cr*	*Ni*	*Cs*	*Ba*	*Sr*	*Cd*	*Al*	*Sn*	*Pb*
Cu	1												
Mn	0.08	1											
Mo	0.61	0.65	1										
Zn	–0.14	0.33	0.08	1									
Cr	–0.36	0.83	0.36	0.25	1								
Ni	–0.13	0.93	0.57	0.34	0.90	1							
Cs	–0.27	0.91	0.40	0.38	0.94	0.95	1						
Ba	–0.38	0.87	0.32	0.34	0.96	0.92	0.99	1					
Sr	–0.42	0.83	0.28	0.42	0.93	0.88	0.97	0.98	1				
Cd	–0.34	0.78	0.34	0.48	0.88	0.88	0.92	0.89	0.91	1			
Al	–0.28	0.91	0.40	0.39	0.94	0.94	0.99	0.99	0.97	0.93	1		
Sn	0.94	0.36	0.77	–0.07	–0.07	0.14	0.01	–0.10	–0.16	–0.08	–0.01	1	
Pb	0.34	0.83	0.41	0.37	0.95	0.94	0.95	0.94	0.92	0.96	0.95	–0.07	1

employed in determining different linear combinations of variables and is used in many principal component algorithms.

Values of α, or a and b, employed in practice depend on the aims of the data analysis. Different linear combinations of the same variables will produce new variables with different attributes which may be of interest in studying different problems. The linear combination which produces the greatest separation between two groups of data samples is appropriate in supervised pattern recognition. Considering our samples or objects as a single group or cluster, we may wish to determine the minimum number of normalized linear combinations having the greatest proportion of the total variance, in order to reduce the dimensionality of the problem.

Principal components analysis

The aims of performing a principal components analysis (PCA) on multivariate data are basically two-fold. Firstly, PCA involves rotating and transforming the original, n, axes each representing an original variable into new axes. This transformation is performed in a way so that the new axes lie along the directions of maximum variance of the data with the constraint that the axes are *orthogonal, i.e.* the new variables are uncorrelated. It is usually the case that the number of new variables, p, needed to describe most of the sample data variance is less than n. Thus PCA affords a method and a technique to reduce the dimensionality of the parameter space.

Secondly, PCA can reveal those variables, or combinations of variables, that determine some inherent structure in the data and these may be interpreted in chemical or physico-chemical terms.

As in the previous section, we are interested in linear combinations of variables, with the goal of determining that combination which best summarizes the n-dimensional distribution of data. We are seeking the linear combination with the largest variance, with normalized coefficients applied to the variables used in the linear combinations. This axis is the so-called first principal axis or *first principal component*.

Once this is determined, then the search proceeds to find a second normalized linear combination that has most of the remaining variance and is uncorrelated with the first principal component. The procedure is continued, usually until all the principal components have been calculated. In this case, $p = n$ and a selected subset of the principal components is then used for further analysis and for interpretation. Before proceeding to examine how principal components are calculated, it is worthwhile considering further a graphical interpretation of their structure and characteristics. From our heart tissue, trace metal data, the variance of chromium concentration is 3.07, the variance of nickel concentration is 2.43, and their covariance is 2.47. This variance-covariance structure is represented by the variance-covariance matrix,

$$Cov_{X1.X2} = \begin{array}{c|cc} & X1 & X2 \\ X1 & 3.07 & 2.47 \\ X2 & 2.47 & 2.43 \end{array} \qquad (16)$$

As well as this matrix form, this structure can also be represented diagrammatically. The variance of the chromium data is represented by a line along the $X1$ axis with a length equal to the variance of $X1$. Since the concentration of chromium is correlated with the concentration of nickel, $X1$ values vary with variable $X2$ axis. The length of this line is equal to the covariance of $X1$ with $X2$ and represents the degree of interaction or *colinearity* between the variables. In a similar manner, the variance and covariance of $X2$ are drawn along and from the second axis. For a square (2×2) matrix, these elements of the variance-covariance matrix lie on the system. The slope of the major axis is the *eigenvector* associated with the first principal component, and its corresponding *eigenvalue* is the length of this major axis.

The second principal component is defined by the second eigenvector and eigenvalue. It is represented by the minor axis of the ellipse and is orthogonal, 90^0, to the first principal component. For a 3 × 3 variance-covariance matrix the elements lie on the surface of a three-dimensional ellipsoid. For larger matrices still, higher-dimensional elliptical shapes apply and can only be imagined. Fortunately the mathematical operations deriving and defining these components remain the same whatever the dimen-sionality.

Thus, principal components can be defined as the eigenvectors of a variance-covariance matrix. They provide the direction of new axes (new variables) on to which data can be projected. The size, or length, of these new axes containing our projected data is proportional to the variance of the new variable. How do we calculate these eigenvectors and eigenvalues? In practice the calculations are always performed on a computer and there are many algorithms published in mathematical and chemometric texts.

For our purposes, in order to illustrate their derivation, we will limit ourselves to bivariate data and calculate the eigenvectors, manually. The procedure adopted largely follows that of Davis and Healy.

Consider a set of simultaneous equations, expressed in matrix notation,

$$A.x = .x \tag{17}$$

which simply states that matrix **A**, multiplied by vector

x, is equal to some constant, the eigenvalue 1, multiplied by x. To determine these eigenvalues, Equation (17) can be rewritten as

$$A.x - 1.x = 0 \qquad (18)$$

or

$$(A - 1.I).x = 0 \qquad (19)$$

where I is the identity matrix, which for a 2 × 2 matrix is

$$I = \begin{bmatrix} 1 & 0 \\ 0 & 1 \end{bmatrix} \qquad (20)$$

If x is not 0 then the determinant of the coefficient matrix must be zero, *i.e.*

$$|A \ / \ 1.I| = 0 \qquad (21)$$

For our experimental data with $X1$ and $X2$ representing chromium and nickel concentrations, and $A = Cov$, then

$$|Cov - 1.I| = \begin{vmatrix} s_{x1}^2 - 1 & Cov \\ Cov & s_{x2}^2 - 1 \end{vmatrix} \qquad (22)$$

where Cov is the covariance between $X1$ and $X2$. Expanding Equation (22) gives the quadratic equation,

$$(s_{x1}^2 - l)(s_{x2}^2 - l) - Cov^2 = 0 \qquad (23)$$

and substituting the values for our Cr and Ni data,

$$(3.07 - 1)(2.43 - 1) \ / \ 2.47^2 = 0 \qquad (24)$$

which simplifies to

$$1^2 - 5.51 + 1.36 = 0 \qquad (25)$$

This is a simple quadratic equation providing two characteristic roots or eigenvalues, *viz.* $l_1 = 5.24$ and $l_2 = 0.26$.

As a check in our calculations, the sum of the eigenvalues should be equal to the sum of diagonal elements, the *trace*, of the original matrix (*i.e.* 3.07 + 2.43 = 5.24 + 0.26).

Associated with each eigenvalue (the length of the new axis in our geometric model) is a characteristic vector, the eigenvector, $v = [v_1, v_2]$ defining the slope of the axis. Our eigenvalues, l, were defined as arising from a set of simultaneous equations, Equation (19), which can now be expressed, for a 2 × 2 matrix, as,

$$\begin{bmatrix} A_{11} - l_1 & A_{12} \\ A_{21} & A_{22} - l_2 \end{bmatrix} \cdot \begin{bmatrix} X_1 \\ X_2 \end{bmatrix} = \begin{bmatrix} 0 \\ 0 \end{bmatrix} \tag{26}$$

and the elements of x are the eigenvectors associated with the first eigenvalue, l_1. For our 2 × 2, Ni-Cr variance-covariance data, substitution into (26) leads to

$$\begin{vmatrix} s_{x1}^2 - l_1 & Cov \\ Cov & s_{x2}^2 - l_1 \end{vmatrix} \cdot \begin{bmatrix} v1_1 \\ v1_2 \end{bmatrix} = 0 \tag{27}$$

$$\begin{vmatrix} s_{x1}^2 - l_2 & Cov \\ Cov & s_{x2}^2 - l_2 \end{vmatrix} \cdot \begin{bmatrix} v2_1 \\ v2_2 \end{bmatrix} = 0 \tag{28}$$

with $v1_1$ and $v1_2$ as the eigenvectors associated with the first eigenvalue, and $v2_1$ and $v2_2$ defining the slope of the second eigenvalue.

Solving these equations gives

$$v1 = [0.751, 0.660] \tag{29}$$

which defines the slope of the major axis of the ellipse, and

$$v2 = [-0.660, 0.751] \tag{30}$$

which is perpendicular to v1 and is the slope of the ellipse's minor axis.

Having determined the orthogonal axes or principal components of our bivariate data, it remains to undertake the projections of the data points on to the new axes. For the first principal components *PC*1,

$$PC1_i = 0.751\ X1_i + 0.660 X2_i \tag{31}$$

and for the second principal component *PC*2,

$$PC2_i = -0.660 X1_i + 0.751 X2_i \tag{32}$$

Thus, the elements of the eigenvectors become the required coefficients for the original variables, and are referred to as *loadings*. The individual elements of the new variables (*PC*1 and *PC*2) are derived from *X*1 and *X*2 and are termed the *scores*. The principal components scores for the chromium and nickel data are given in Table 5.

The total variance of the original nickel and chromium data is 3.07 + 2.43 = 5.5 with *X*1 contributing 56% of the variance and *X*2 contributing the remaining 44%. The calculated eigenvalues are the lengths of the two principal axes and represent the variance associated with each new variable, *PC*1 and *PC*2. The first principal component, therefore, contains 5.24/5.50 or more than 95% of the total variance, and the second principal component less than 5%, 0.26/5.50.

If it were necessary to reduce the display of our original bivariate data to a single dimension using only one variable, say chromium concentration, then a loss of

44% of the total variance would ensue. Using the first principal component, however, and optimally combining the two variables, only 5% of the total variance would be missing.

Table 5

The PC scores for chromium and nickel concentrations

Sample	*PC1*	*PC2*
AO	2.91	–0.17
MPA	2.02	0.48
RSCV	4.82	0.94
TV	4.03	0.04
MV	3.89	1.24
PV	11.25	1.28
AV	7.71	0.14
RA	3.50	0.65
LAA	2.37	1.64
RV	2.95	0.33
LV	3.12	0.98
LV-PM	3.06	0.76
IVS	2.67	1.37
CR	3.04	1.18
SN	3.19	1.05
AVN+B	2.62	1.02
LBB	2.97	1.11

We are now in a position to return to the complete set of trace element data in Table 3 and apply principal components analysis to the full data matrix. The techniques described and used in the above example to extract and determine the eigenvalues and eigenvectors for two variables can be extended to the more general, multivariate case but the procedure becomes increasingly difficult and arithmetically tedious with large matrices.

The eigenvalues are usually found by matrix manipulation and iterative approximation methods using appropriate computer software. Before such an analysis is undertaken, the question of whether to transform the original data should be considered. Examination of Table 3 indicates that the variates considered have widely differing means and standard deviations. Rather than standardizing the data, since they are all recorded in the same units, one other useful transformation is to take logarithms of the values.

The result of this transformation is to scale all the data to a more similar range and reduce the relative effects of the more concentrated metals. Having performed the log-transformation on our data, the results of performing PCA on all 13 for the 17 samples are as given in Table 6. According to the eigenvalue results present in Table 6(b), and displayed in the *scree plot.* Over 84% of the total variance in the original data can be accounted for by the first two principal components.

The transformation of the 13 original variables to two new linear combinations represents considerable reduction of the data presented whilst retaining much of the original information. A scatter plot of the first two principal components scores. Patterns to the samples according to the distribution of the trace metals in the data are evident. Three tissues, the Pulmonary valve, aortic valve, and the right superior vena cava, constitute unique groups of one tissue each, well distinguished from the rest.

The aorta, main pulmonary artery, mitral, and tricuspid valves constitute a cluster of four tissue types. Finally, there is a group of ten tissues derived from the myocardium. A more detailed analysis and discussion of this data set is presented by Niedermeier. As well as being used with discrete analytical data, such as the trace metal concentrations discussed above, principal components analysis has been extensively employed on digitized spectral profiles. A simple example will illustrate the basis of these applications. Infrared spectra of 21 samples of acrylic, PVC, styrene, and nylon polymers, as thin films, were recorded in the range 4000-600 cm^{-1}. Each spectrum was normalized on the most intense absorption band to remove film thickness effects, and reduced to 216 discrete values by signal averaging.

The resulting 21 × 216 data matrix was subject to principal components analysis. It is evident from this plot that these three components are sufficient to provide effective clustering of the samples with clear separation between the groups and types of polymer. The first component, *PC*1, forms an axis which would allow the partitioning between acrylic polymer and other samples. *PC*2 provides for two partitions; both the nylon and PVC polymers are separated from the styrene and acrylic polymers. *PC*3 allows the separation between styrenes and others. It can be seen from these 'spectra' that where a partition between sample types if formed, the majority of absorption bands in the corresponding spectra receive strong positive or negative weighting. *PC*2 produces two partitions.

The bands in nylon spectra receive positive weightings and bands in PVC spectra. The power of principal components analysis is in providing a mathematical transformation of our analytical data to a form with reduced dimensionality. From the results, the similarity and difference between objects and samples can often be better assessed and this makes the technique of prime importance in chemometrics. Having introduced the methodology and basics here, future chapters will consider the use of the technique as a data preprocessing tool.

Factor analysis

The extraction of the eigenvectors from a symmetric data matrix forms the basis and starting point of many multivariate chemometric procedures. The way in which the data are preprocessed and scaled, and how the resulting vectors are treated, has produced a wide range of related and similar techniques. By far the most common is principal components analysis. As we have seen, PCA provides n eigenvectors derived from a $n \times n$ dispersion matrix of variances and covariances, or correlations. If the data are standardized prior to eigenvector analysis, then the variance-covariance matrix becomes the correlation matrix [see Equation (25) in Chapter 1, with $s_1 = s_2$]. Another technique, strongly related to PCA, is factor analysis.

Factor analysis is the name given to eigen analysis of a data matrix with the intended aim of reducing the data set of n variables to a specified number, p, of fewer linear combination variables, or *factors*, with which to describe the data. Thus, p is selected to be less than n and, hopefully, the new data matrix will be more amenable to interpretation.

The final interpretation of the meaning and significance of these new factors lies with the user and the context of the problem. A full description and derivation of the many factor analysis methods reported in the analytical literature is beyond the scope of this book. We will limit ourselves here to the general and underlying features associated with the technique.

A more detailed account is provided by, for example, Hopke and others. The principal steps in performing a factor analysis are,

— preprocessing of the raw data matrix,

— computing the symmetric matrix of covariances or correlations, *i.e.* the *dispersion matrix,*

— extracting the eigenvalues and eigenvectors,

— selecting the appropriate number of factors with which to describe the data, and

— rotating these factors to provide a meaningful interpretation of the factors.

Table 6

Normalized MS data for cyclohexane and hexane mixtures

	% Cyclohexane				
	90	*80*	*50*	*20*	*10*
m/z	*A*	B	C	D	*E*
27	13.79	19.05	20.80	28.30	24.55
29	12.93	15.87	26.40	44.04	38.18
39	17.24	17.46	20.00	20.02	18.18
40	4.31	4.76	4.00	3.00	3.64
41	55.17	63.49	14.00	91.09	80.00
42	29.31	29.37	36.80	47.05	41.82
43	21.55	26.19	49.60	74.07	71.82
44	1.72	1.59	1.60	3.00	1.82
54	5.17	4.76	4.00	3.00	1.82
55	31.90	34.13	28.00	24.02	10.00
56	100.00	100.00	100.00	100.00	73.36
57	19.83	25.40	58.40	96.10	100.00
69	29.31	26.98	21.60	16.02	9.09
83	5.17	4.76	4.00	4.00	3.64
84	70.69	68.25	58.40	36.04	18.18
85	6.90	6.35	4.80	5.00	2.73
86	3.45	4.76	12.80	24.02	22.73
Mean	25.20	29.66	30.92	36.33	30.86

Steps (a) to (c) are as for principal components analysis.

However, as the final aim is usually to interpret the results of the analysis in terms of chemical or spectroscopic properties, the method adopted at each step should be selected with care and forethought.

A simple example will serve to illustrate the principles of factor analysis and the application of some of the options available at each stage. Table 7 provides the digitized mass spectra of live cyclohexane/hexane mixtures, each recorded at 17 m/z values and normalized to the most intense, parent ion. Presented with these data, and in a 'real' situation not knowing the composition of the mixtures, our first task is to determine how many discrete components contribute to these spectra, *i.e.* how many components are in the mixtures. We can then attempt to identify the nature or source of each extracted component. These are the aims of factor analysis.

Before we can compute the eigenvectors associated with our data matrix, we need to select appropriate, if any, preprocessing methods for the data, and the form of the dispersion matrix. Specifically, we can choose to generate a covariance matrix or a correlation matrix from the data. Each of these could be derived from the original, origin-centred data or from transformed, mean-centred data. In addition, we should bear in mind the aim of the analysis and decide whether the variables for numerical analysis are the m/z values or the composition of the sample mixtures themselves.

Thus we have eight options in forming the transformed, symmetric matrix for extracting eigenvectors. We can form a 5×5 covariance, or correlation, matrix on the origin- or mean-centred compositional values. Alternatively, a 17×17 covariance, or correlation, matrix can be formed from origin- or mean-centred m/z values. Each of these transformations can be expressed in matrix form as a transform of the data matrix X to a new matrix

Table 7

Results of principal components analysis on the logarithms of the trace metals concentration data

	PC1	*PC2*	*PC3*	*PC4*	*PC5*	*PC6*	*PC7*	*PC8*	*PC9*	*PC10*	*PC11*	*PC12*	*PC13*
(a) *Eigenvalues*													
Variance	7.49	3.47	0.99	0.38	0.23	0.15	0.09	0.08	0.05	0.02	0.01	0.000	0.001
% Variance	57.7	26.7	7.7	2.9	1.8	1.2	0.7	0.6	0.4	0.1	0.1	0.0	0.0
Cumulative % contribution	57.7	84.4	92.1	95.0	96.8	98.0	98.7	99.4	99.8	999.9	100	100	100
(b) Eigenvectors													
Log Cu	–0.17	0.47	0.08	0.08	0.07	0.16	–0.07	0.17	0.35	0.47	–0.43	–0.22	0.35
Log Mn	0.20	0.39	–0.05	0.57	–0.30	0.12	0.14	0.27	–0.16	–0.54	–0.17	0.01	0.13
Log Mo	0.63	0.49	–0.04	0.33	0.26	–0.52	0.36	–0.09	0.03	–0.30	0.20	0.02	0.26
Log Zn	0.10	0.01	0.95	0.10	0.12	–0.11	–0.11	0.10	–0.08	–0.03	0.08	–0.05	–0.06
Log Cr	0.33	0.04	–0.19	–0.03	0.74	0.26	–0.30	0.20	–0.23	–0.08	–0.06	–0.21	0.01
Log Ni	0.29	0.27	–0.05	–0.24	–0.30	–0.26	–0.50	–0.26	–0.45	0.28	–0.06	–0.02	–0.08
Log Cs	0.36	–0.04	–0.07	0.15	–0.20	0.02	–0.05	–0.12	0.35	0.11	0.58	–0.55	0.10
Log Ba	0.35	–0.14	–0.03	0.17	0.04	–0.05	–0.16	0.08	0.19	0.19	0.14	0.68	0.48

Log Sr	0.34	−0.11	−0.01	0.33	0.27	−0.31	0.24	−0.50	0.19	0.10	−0.32	0.04	−0.36
Log Cd	0.33	0.19	0.17	−0.36	−0.07	0.59	0.41	−0.38	−0.17	0.05	−0.02	0.07	0.16
Log Al	0.35	−0.03	−0.05	0.06	−0.18	−0.11	0.44	0.63	−0.21	0.38	−0.14	−0.09	−0.11
Log Sn	−0.09	0.51	0.01	0.14	0.08	0.26	0.38	0.05	0.08	0.22	0.42	0.34	−0.53
Log Pb	0.34	0.07	0.04	−0.41	−0.15	0.06	−0.22	0.26	0.55	−0.31	−0.26	0.07	−0.29

Y followed by calculating the appropriate dispersion matrix, C (the variance-covariance, or correlation matrix). The relevant equations are

$$Y = XA + B \tag{33}$$

and

$$C = Y^T.Y/(n - 1) \tag{34}$$

The nature of C depends on the definition of A and B. A is a scaling diagonal matrix; only the diagonal elements need be defined. B is a centring matrix in which all elements in any one column are identical. For covariance about the origin,

$$a_{jj} = 1 \text{ and } b_{ij} = 0 \tag{35}$$

For covariance about the mean,

$$a_{jj} = 1 \text{ and } b_{ij} = -\tilde{x}_j \tag{36}$$

For correlation about the origin,

$$a_{jj} = \left(\frac{1}{n}\sum_{i=1}^{n} x_{ij}\right)^{-1/2}$$

$$b_{ij} = 0 \tag{37}$$

For correlation about the mean,

$$a_{jj} = \left(\frac{1}{n-1}\sum_{i=1}^{n}(x_{ij} - \tilde{x}_j)^2\right)^{-1/2}$$

$$b_{ij} = \tilde{x}_j .a_{jj} \tag{38}$$

where $\tilde{x}_j$ is the mean value of column j from the data matrix.

Mean-centring is a common pre-processing transformation as it provides data which are symmetric about a zero mean. It is recommended as a preprocessing step in many applications. This is not necessary here with our mass spectra, however, as the intensity scale has a meaningful zero. As the analytical data are all in the same units and cover a similar range of magnitude, standardization is not required either and the variance-covariance matrix will be used as the dispersion matrix.

Table 8

The variance-covariance matrix for the MS data and the eigen values and eigen vectors extracted from this

	Covariance matrix				
	A	*B*	*C*	*D*	*E*
A	726.62				
B	726.04	734.27			
C	683.14	713.48	808.63		
D	594.23	655.34	890.97	1157.49	
E	421.65	485.71	754.65	1065.58	1025.79

	Eigenvalues				
Factor	1	2	3	4	5
Eigenvalue	3744.08	703.56	2.84	1.25	1.07
Cumulative % contribution	84.08	99.88	99.95	99.98	100.00

	Eigenvectors				
	F(I)	*F(II)*	*F(III)*	*F(IV)*	*F(V)*
A	0.368	0.557	–0.424	0.607	–0.075
B	0.389	0.486	0.401	–0.462	–0.488
C	0.461	0.121	–0.193	–0.434	0.740
D	0.533	–0.359	0.605	–0.446	0.146
E	0.464	–0.557	–0.505	–0.176	–0.434

The final decision to be made is to whether to operate on the m/z values or the samples (actually the mixture compositions) as the analytical variables. It is a stated aim of our factor analysis to determine some physical meaning of the derived factors. We do not wish simply to perform a mathematical transformation to reduce the dimensionality of the data, as would be the case with principal components analysis. We will proceed, therefore, with an eigenvector analysis of the 5×5 covariance matrix obtained from zero-centred object data.

This is referred to as *Q-mode* factor analysis and in complementary to the scheme illustrated previously with principal components analysis. In the earlier example the dispersion matrix was formed between the measured trace metal variables, and the technique is sometimes referred to as *R-mode* analysis. For the current MS data, processing by *R-mode* analysis would involve the data being scaled along each m/z column and information about relative peak sizes in any single spectrum would be destroyed.

In Q-mode analysis, any scaling is performed within a spectrum and the mass fragmentation pattern for each sample is preserved. The variance-covariance matrix of the mass spectra data is presented in Table 8. In factor analysis we assume that any relationships between our samples from within the original data set can be represented by p mutually uncorrelated underlying factors. The value of p is usually selected to be much less than the number of original variables. These p underlying factors, or new variables, are referred to as *common factors* and may be amenable to physical interpretation.

The remaining variance not accounted for by the p factors will be contained in a *unique factor* and may be attributable, for example, to noise in the system. The first requirement is to determine the appropriate value of p, the number of factors necessary to describe the original data adequately. If p cannot be specified then the partition of total variance between common and unique factors cannot be determined. For our simple example with the mass spectra data it appears obvious that $p = 2$, *i.e.* there are two common factors which we may interpret as being due to two components in the mixtures.

The first two factors account for more than 99% of the total variance. The choice is not always so clear, however, and in the chemometrics literature a number of more objective functions have been described to select appropriate values of p. The eigenvectors in Table 8 have been normalized, i.e. each vector has unit length, *viz.*,

$$(0.368)^2 + (0.389)^2 + (0.461)^2 + (0.533)^2 + (0.464)^2 = 1 \quad (39)$$

To perform factor analysis, the eigenvectors should be converted so that each vector length represents the magnitude of the eigenvalue. This conversion is achieved by multiplying each element in the normalized eigenvector matrix by the square root of the corresponding eigenvalue. From Table 8, the variance associated with the first factor is its eigenvalue, 3744.08, and the first eigenvector is converted to the first factor by multiplying by $\sqrt{(3744.08)}$, *viz.*

$$\text{Factor 1} = \begin{pmatrix} 0.368 & \sqrt{3744.08} \\ 0.389 & \sqrt{3744.08} \\ 0.461 & \sqrt{3744.08} \\ 4.533 & \sqrt{3744.08} \\ 0.464 & \sqrt{3744.08} \end{pmatrix} = \begin{pmatrix} 22.52 \\ 23.82 \\ 28.24 \\ 32.64 \\ 29.40 \end{pmatrix} \quad (40)$$

The elements in each of the factors are the factor loadings, and the complete factor loading matrix for our MS data is given in Table 9. This conversion has not changed the orientation of the factor axes from the original eigenvectors but has simply changed their absolute magnitude. The lengths of each vector are now equal to the square root of the eigenvalues, *i.e.* the factors represent the standard deviations.

Table 9

The factor loading matrix from a Q-mode analysis of the MS data

	F(I)	F(II)	(FIII)	F(IV)	F(V)
A	22.52	14.78	–0.71	0.68	–0.08
B	23.82	12.88	0.68	–0.52	–0.51
C	28.24	3.20	–0.32	–0.48	0.77
D	32.64	–9.51	1.02	0.50	0.15
E	28.40	–14.78	–0.85	–0.20	–0.45

From Table 8, the first factor accounts for 3744.08/4452.80 = 84% of the variance in the data. Of this, $22.52^2/3744.08$ = 13.5% is derived from object or sample A, 15.2% from B, 21.3% from C, 28.5% from D, and 21.5% from E, The total variance associated with object A is accounted for by the five factors. Taking the square of each element in the factor matrix (remember, these are standard deviations) and summing for each object provides the amount of variance contributed by each object.

For sample A,

$$22.52^2 + 14.78^2 + (-0.71)^2 + 0.68^2 + (-0.08)^2 = 726.6 \quad (41)$$

and for the other samples,

$$\begin{aligned} &B,\ 23.82^2 + 12.88^2 + 0.68^2 + 0.52^2 + 0.51^2 = 734.3 \\ &C,\ 28.24^2 + 3.20^2 + 0.32^2 + 0.48^2 + 0.77^2 = 808.6 \\ &D,\ 32.64^2 + 9.51^2 + 1.02^2 + 0.50^2 + 0.15^2 = 1157.5 \\ &E,\ 28.40^2 + 14.78^2 + 0.85^2 + 0.20^2 + 0.45^2 = 1025.8 \quad (42) \end{aligned}$$

These values are identical to the diagonal elements of the variance-covariance matrix from the original data, Table 8, and represent the variance of each object. With all five factors, the total variance is accounted for. If we use fewer factors to explain the data, and this is after all the point of performing a factor analysis, then these totals will be less than 100%. Using just the first two factors, for example, then

$$\text{A, } 22.52^2 + 14.78^2 = 725.6,\ 725.6/726.6 = 0.999$$

$$\text{B, } 23.82^2 + 12.88^2 = 733.3,\ 733.3/734.3 = 0.999$$

$$\text{C, } 28.24^2 + 3.20^2 = 807.7,\ 807.7/808.6 = 0.999$$

$$\text{D, } 32.64^2 + 9.51^2 = 1155.8,\ 1155.8/1157.5 = 0.998$$

$$\text{E, } 28.40^2 + 14.78^2 = 1025.0,\ 1025.0/1025.8 = 0.999 \quad (43)$$

The final values listed in Equation 43 represent the fraction of each object's variance explained by the two factors. They are referred to as the *communality values*, denoted h^2, and they depend on the number of factors used. As the number of factors retained increases, then the communalities tend to unity.

The remaining $(1 - h^2)$ fraction of the variance for each sample is considered as being associated with its unique variance and is attributable to noise. Returning to our mass spectra, having calculated the eigenvalues, eigenvectors, and factor loadings, we must decide how many factors need be retained in our model. In the absence of noise in the measurements, the eigenvalues above the number necessary to describe the data are zero. In practice, of course, noise will always be present.

However, as we can see with our mass spectra data a large relative decrease in the magnitude of the eigenvalues occurs after two values, so we can assume here that $p = 2$. Hopke provides an account of several objective functions to assess the correct number of factors.

Having reduced the dimensionality of the data by electing to retain two factors, we can proceed with our analysis and attempt to interpret them. Examination of the columns of loadings for the first two factors in the factor matrix, Table 9, shows that some values are negative.

The physical significance of these loadings or coefficients is not immediately apparent. The location of the orthogonal vectors in the two-factor space has been constrained by the three remaining but unused factors. If these three factors are not to be used then we can rotate the first two factors in the sample space and possibly find a better position for them; a position which will provide for a more meaningful interpretation of the data.

Table 10

The rotated factor loading matrix, retaining only the first two factors and using varimax

	F(I)	F(II)
A	7.16	25.97
B	9.39	25.40
C	19.10	21.04
D	30.80	14.40
E	31.09	7.64

Of the several factor rotation schemes routinely used in factor analysis, that referred to as the *varimax* technique is most commonly used. Varimax rotation moves each factor axis to a new, but still orthogonal, position so that the loading projections are near either the origin or the extremities of these new axes.' The rotation is rigid, to retain orthogonality between factors, and is undertaken using an iterative algorithm.

Using the varimax rotation method, the rotated factor

loadings for the first two factors from the mass spectra data are given in Table 10 and are plotted. The relative position of the objects to each other has remained unchanged, but all loadings are now positive. In fact, all loadings are present in the first quadrant of the diagram and in an order we can recognize as corresponding to the mixtures compositional analysis.

Table 11

Normalized mass spectral data for cyclohexane and hexane

m/z	*Cyclohexane*	*Hexane*
1	2	3
27	13.3	22.9
28	15.5	16.4
29	9.6	41.8
39	18.5	13.1
40	5.2	3.3
41	52.6	72.1
42	25.9	38.5
43	16.3	70.5
44	1.5	2.5
54	5.9	0.8
55	34.1	7.4
56	100.0	55.7
57	8.9	100.0
69	28.1	1.6
83	5.9	0.8
84	79.3	0.8
85	6.7	0.8
86	0.7	22.9

Sample A is predominantly cyclohexane (90%) and E hexane (90%). If the mass spectra of the two pure components were present in, or added to, the original data matrix, then the loadings associated with these samples would align themselves closely with the pure factors. Such, in fact, is the case. Table 11 provides the normalized mass spectra of cyclohexane and hexane, and Table 12 gives the varimax rotated factor loadings for the now 7 × 7 variance-covariance matrix from the data now containing the mixtures and the pure components.

As expected the single-components spectra are closely aligned with the axes of the derived and rotated factors. Varimax rotation is a commonly used and widely available factor rotation technique, but other methods have been proposed for interpreting factors from analytical chemistry data. We could rotate the axes in order that they align directly with factors from expected components. These

Table 12

The rotated factor loadings for the complete MS data set, including the two pure components, cyclohexane (XI) and hexane (X2)

	F(I)	F(II)
A	3.23	28.05
B	6.45	26.15
C	8.71	25.63
D	18.51	21.57
E	30.69	15.36
X1	30.85	8.50
X2	31.12	2.45

axes, referred to as test vectors, would be physically significant in terms of interpretation and the rotation procedure is referred to as *target transformation*. Target transformation factor analysis has proved to be a valuable technique in chemometrics.

The number of components in mixture spectra can be

identified and the rotated factor loadings in terms of test data relating to standard, known spectra, can be interpreted. In this chapter we have been able to discuss only some of the more common and basic methods of feature selection and extraction. This area is a major subject of active research in chemometrics.

Chapter 7

Regression Analysis

The computational procedures discussed in this chapter are concerned with describing quantitative relationships between two or more variables. In particular we are interested in studying how measured *independent* or response variables vary as a function a single so-called *dependent* variable. The class of techniques studied is referred to as *regression analysis*. The principal aim in undertaking regression analysis is to develop a suitable mathematical model for descriptive or predictive purposes.

The model can be used to confirm some idea or theory regarding the relationship between variables or it can be used to predict some general, continuous response function from discrete and possibly relatively few measurements. The single most common application of regression analysis in analytical laboratories is undoubtedly curve-fitting and the construction of calibration lines from data obtained from instrumental methods of analysis. Such graphs, for example absorbance or emission intensity as a function of sample concentration, are commonly assumed to be linear, although non-linear functions can also be used.

The fitting of some 'best' straight line to analytical data provides us with the opportunity to examine the fundamental principles of regression analysis and the criteria for measuring '*goodness of fit*'. Not all relationships can be adequately described using the simple linear model, however, and more complex functions, such as quadratic and higher-order polynomial equations, may be required to fit the experimental data.

Finally, more than one variable may be measured. For example, multiwavelength calibration procedures are finding increasing applications in analytical spectrometry and multivariate regression analysis forms the basis for many chemometric methods reported in the literature.

Linear regression

It frequently occurs in analytical spectrometry that some characteristic, y, of a sample is to be determined as a function of some other quantity, x, and it is necessary to determine the relationship or function between x and y, which may be expressed as $y = f(x)$. An example would be the calibration of an atomic absorption spectrometer for a specific element prior to the determination of the concentration of that element in a series of samples. A series of n absorbance measurements is made, y_i, one for each of a suitable range of known concentration, x_i.

The n pairs of measurements (x_i, y_i) can be plotted as a scatter diagram to provide a visual representation of the relationship between x and y. In the determination of chromium and nickel in machine oil by atomic absorption spectrometry the calibration data presented in Table 1 were obtained. These experimental data are shown graphically in Figure 1. At low concentrations of analyte and working at low absorbance values, a linear relationship is to be expected between absorbance and concentration, as predicted by Beer's Law.

Visual inspection of Figure 1(a) for the chromium data confirms the correctness of this linear function and, in this case, it is a simple matter to draw by hand a satisfactory straight line through the data and use the plot for subsequent analyses. The equation of the line can be estimated directly from this plot. In this case there is little apparent experimental uncertainty. In many cases, however, the situation is not so clear-cut.

Figure 1 (b) illustrates the scatter plot of the nickel data. It is not possible here to draw a straight line passing through all points even though a linear relationship between absorbance and concentration is still considered valid. The deviations in the absorbance data from expected, ideal values can be assumed to be due to experimental errors and uncertainties in the individual measurements and not due to some underlying error in the theoretical relationship.

Table 1

Absorbance data measured from standard solutions of chromium and nickel by AAS (a). Calculation of the best-fit, least-squares line for the nickel data, (b)

(a)

Chromium concn. ($mg\ kg^{-1}$):	0	1	2	3	4	5	(x)
Absorbance:	0.01	0.11	0.21	0.29	0.38	0.52	(y)
Nickel concn. ($mg\ kg^{-1}$):	0	1	2	3	4	5	(x)
Absorbance:	0.02	0.12	0.14	0.32	0.38	0.49	(y)

(b)

For Nickel: $\bar{x} = 2.50$ and $\bar{y} = 0.245$

							Sum
$(x_i - \bar{x})$:	−2.50	−1.50	−0.50	0.50	1.50	2.50	
$(y_i - \bar{y})$:	−0.225	−0.125	−0.105	0.075	0.135	0.245	
$(x_i - \bar{x})(y_i - \bar{y})$:	0.562	0.187	0.052	0.037	0.202	0.621	1.655
$(x_i - \bar{x})^2$:	6.25	2.25	0.25	0.25	2.25	0.25	17.50

$$b = 1.655/17.50 = 0.095$$

$$a = 0.0075$$

If multiple measurements of absorbance were made for each standard concentration, then a normal distribution for the absorbance values would be expected. These values would be centred on some mean absorbance value y_i.

The task for an analyst is to determine the 'best' straight line regressed through the means of the experimental data. The data set comprises pairs of measurements of an independent variable x (concentration) and a dependent variable y (absorbance) and it is required to fit the data using a linear model with the well known form,

$$y_i = a + bx_i \qquad (1)$$

where a and b are constant coefficients characteristic of the regression line, representing the intercept of the line with the y-axis and the gradient of the line respectively. The values of y represent the estimated, model values of absorbance derived from this linear model.

The generally accepted requirement for deriving the best straight line between x and y is that the discrepancy between the measured data and the fitted line is minimized. The most popular technique employed to minimize this error between model and recorded data is the *least-squares* method. For each measured value, the deviation between the derived model value and the measured data is given by $y_i - y_i$.

The total error between the model and observed data is the sum of these individual errors. Each error value is squared to make all values positive and prevent negative and positive errors from cancelling. Thus the total error, E, is given by,

$$\text{error, } \varepsilon = \sum_{i=1}^{n}(y_i - y_i)^2 \qquad (2)$$

The total error is the sum of the squared deviations. For some model defined by coefficients *a* and *b*, this error will be a minimum and this minimum point can be determined using partial differential calculus.

From Equations (1) and (2) we can substitute our model equation into the definition of error,

$$\varepsilon = \sum_{i=1}^{n} (a + bx_i - y_i)^2 \qquad (3)$$

The values of the coefficients *a* and *b* are our statistically independent unknowns to be determined. By differentiating with respect to *a* and *b* respectively, then at the minimum,

$$\frac{\delta\varepsilon}{\delta a} = \sum_{i=1}^{n} 2(a + bx_i - y_i)^2 = 0$$

$$\frac{\delta\varepsilon}{\delta b} = \sum_{i=1}^{n} 2x_i(a + bx_i - y_i)^2 = 0 \qquad (4)$$

where *a* and *b* are least squares estimates of the intercept, *a*, and slope, *b*.

Expanding and rearranging Equations (4) provides the two simultaneous equations,

$$na + b\Sigma x_i = \Sigma y_i \qquad (5)$$

$$a\Sigma x_i + b\Sigma x_i^2 = S(y_i x_i)$$

from which the following expressions can be derived,

$$a = y - b\overline{x} \qquad (6)$$

and

$$b = \frac{\Sigma(x_i - \bar{x})(y_i - \bar{y})}{S(x_i - \bar{x})^2} \tag{7}$$

where $\bar{x}$ and $\bar{y}$ represent the mean values of x and y.

For the experimental data for Ni, calculation of a and b is trivial (a = 0.0075 and b = 0.095) and the fitted line passes through the central point given by $\bar{x}$, $\bar{y}$. Once values for a and b are derived, it is possible to deduce the concentration of subsequently analysed samples by recording their absorbances and substituting the values in Equation (1). It should be noted, however, that because the model is derived for concentration data in the range defined by x_i it is important that subsequent predictions are also based on measurements in this range. The model should be used for interpolation only and not extrapolation.

Errors and Goodness of Fit

It is often the case in chemical analysis that the independent variable, standard solution concentrations in the above example, is said to be *fixed*. The values of concentration for the calibration solutions can be expected to have been chosen by the analyst and the values to be accurately known.

The errors associated with x, therefore, are negligible compared with the uncertainty in y due to fluctuations and noise in the instrumental measurement. To use Equations (6) and (7) in order to determine the characteristics of the fitted line, and employ this information for prediction, it is necessary to estimate the uncertainty in the calculated values for the slope, b, and intercept, a. Each of the absorbance values, y_i, has been used in the determination of a and b and each has contributed its own uncertainty or error to the final result.

Estimates of error in the fitted line and estimates of confidence intervals may be made if three assumptions are valid,

(a) the absorbance values are from parent populations normally distributed about the mean absorbance value,

(b) the variance associated with absorbance is independent of absorbance, *i.e.* the data are *homoscedastic*, and,

(c) the sample absorbance means lie on a straight line.

These conditions are illustrated in Figure 2 which illustrates a theoretical regression line of such data on an independent variable.

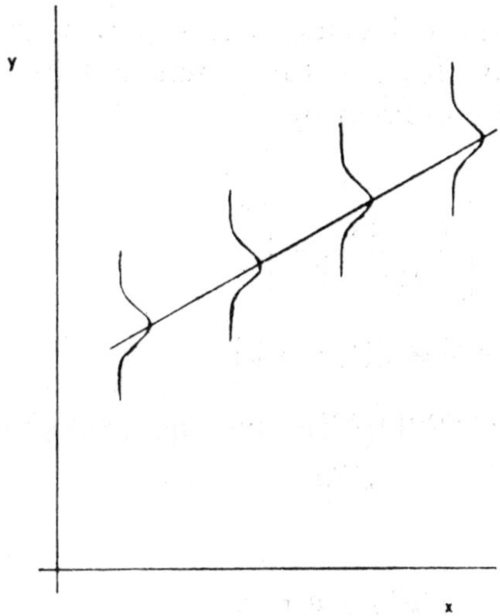

Fig. 1. A regression line thrpugh mean values of homoscedastic data

The deviation or residual for each of the absorbance values in the nickel data is given by $y_i - y_{i'}$, *i.e.* the observed values minus the calculated or predicted values according to the linear model. The sum of the squares of these deviations, Table 2, is the residual sum of squares, and is denoted as SS_D. The least squares estimate of the line can be shown to provide the best possible fit and no other line can be fitted that will produce a smaller sum of squares.

$$SS_D = \varepsilon = \Sigma(y_i - y_i)^2 = 0.00599 \tag{8}$$

The variance associated with these deviations will be given by this sum of squares divided by the number of degrees of freedom,

$$\sigma_D^2 = SS_D/(n-2) = S(y_i - y_i)^2/(n-2) \tag{9}$$

The denominator, $n - 2$, is the residual degrees of freedom derived from the sample size, n, minus the number of parameters estimated for the line, a and b.

The standard deviations or errors of the estimated intercept and slope values, denoted by σ_a, and σ_b respectively, are defined by

$$\sigma_D\left[\frac{1}{n}\frac{\Sigma x_i^2}{\Sigma(x_i - \tilde{x})^2}\right]^{0.5} \tag{10}$$

$$s_b = sD/[S(x_i - \tilde{x})^2]^{0.5}$$

from which the confidence intervals, *CI*, can be obtained,

$$\boldsymbol{CI}(a) = a \pm t\sigma_a$$

and

$$\mathbf{CI}(b) = b \pm t\sigma_b \tag{11}$$

where t is the value of the two-tailed t-distribution with $(n - 2)$ degrees of freedom. Table 2 gives the results for $CI(a)$ and $CI(b)$ using 95% confidence intervals for the nickel absorbance data.

How well the estimated straight line fits the experimental data can be assessed by determining the *coefficient of determination* and the correlation coefficient.

Table 2
Errors and goodness of fit calculations associated with the linear regression model for nickel AAS data from Table 1

Nickel concn. (mg kg - 1):	0	1	2	3	4	5
Absorbance (measured):	0.02	0.12	0.14	0.32	0.38	0.49
Absorbancc (estimated):	0.007	0,102	0.197	0.292	0.387	0.482

$SS_D = 0.00599$

$s_D = 0.0015$	$s_a = 0.028$	$s_b = 0.0093$
CI(a) = 0.0075 +/−0.078		CI(b) = 0.095 + /−0.026
$SS_T = 0.177$	$SS_R = 0.171$	$r^2 = 0.966$

The total variation associated with the y values, SS_T, is given by the sum of the squared deviations of the observed y values from the mean y value,

$$SS_T = \Sigma(y_i - \bar{y})^2 \tag{12}$$

This total variation comprises two components, that due to the residual or deviation sum of squares, SS_D, and that from the sum of squares due to regression, SS_R:

$$SS_T = SS_D + SS_R \tag{13}$$

SS_D is a measure of the failure of the regressed line to fit the data points, and SS_R provides a measure of the variation in the regression line about the mean values. The ratio of SS_R to SS_T indicates how well the model straight line fits the experimental data. It is referred to as the coefficient of determination and its value varies between zero and one.

From Equation (13), if $SS_D = 0$ (the fitted line passes through each datum point) the total variation in y is explained by the regression line and $SS_T = SS_R$ and the ratio is one. On the other hand, if the regressed line fails completely to fit the data, SS_R is zero, the total error is dominated by the residuals, *i.e.* $SS_T \sim SS_D$, then the ratio is zero and no linear relationship is present in the data.

The coefficient of determination is denoted by r^2,

$$r^2 = SS_R / SS_T \tag{14}$$

and r^2 is the square of the correlation coefficient, r.

From our data of measured absorbance *vs.* nickel concentration, $r^2 = 0.966$, indicating a good fit between the linear model and the experimental model. As discussed in Chapter 1, however, care must be taken in relying too much on high values of r^2 or r as indicators of linear trends.

The data should be plotted and examined visually. In quantitative spectroscopic analysis an important parameter is the estimate of the confidence interval of a concentration value of an unknown sample, x_u, derived from a measured instrument response. This is discussed in detail by Miller and can be obtained from the standard deviation associated with x_u,

$$\sigma_{x(u)} = \frac{\sigma_D}{b}\left[\frac{1}{m} + \frac{1}{n} + \frac{(y_u - \bar{y})^2}{b^2 \Sigma (x_i - \tilde{x})^2}\right] \tag{15}$$

where y_u is the mean absorbance of the unknown sample from m measurements. Thus, from a sample having a mean measured absorbance of 0.25 (from five observations),

$$\sigma_{x(u)} = 0.248 \tag{16}$$

and the 95% confidence limits of x_u are

$$CI(x_u) = 2.55 \pm 0.69 \tag{17}$$

Regression through the origin

Before leaving linear regression, a special case often encountered in laboratory calibrations should be considered. A calibration is often performed using not only standard samples containing known amounts of the analyte but also a blank sample containing no analyte.

The measured response for this blank sample may be subtracted from the response values for each standard sample and the fitted line assumed, and forced, to pass through the origin of the graph. Under such conditions the estimated regression line, Equation (1), reduces to

$$y_i = bx_i$$

and

$$\varepsilon = \Sigma(bx_i - y_i)^2 \tag{18}$$

The resulting equation for b, following partial differentiation, is

$$b = \Sigma(x_i y_i)/\Sigma x_i^2 \tag{19}$$

The option to use this model is often available in statistical computer packages, and for manual calculations the arithmetic is reduced compared with the full linear regression discussed above.

A caveat should be made, however, since forcing the line through the origin assumes that the measured blank value is free from experimental error and that it represents accurately the true, mean blank value. For the nickel data from Table 1, using Equation (19) b = 0 0.0094, and the sum of squares of the deviations, SS_D, is 0.00614. This value is greater than the computed value of SS_D for the model using data not corrected for the blank, indicating the poorer performance of the model of Equation (18).

Polynomial Regression

Although the linear model is the model most commonly

encountered in analytical science, not all relationships between a pair of variables can be adequately described by linear regression. A calibration curve does not have to approximate a straight line to be of practical value. The use of higher-order equations to model the association between dependent and independent variables may be more appropriate.

The most popular function to model non-linear data and include curvature in the graph is to fit a power-series polynomial of the form

$$y = a + bx + cx^2 + dx^3 + \ldots \tag{20}$$

where, as before, y is the dependent variable, x is the independent variable to be regressed on y, and a, b, c, d, *etc.* are the coefficients associated with each power. The method of least squares was employed in the previous section to fit the best straight line to analytical data and a similar procedure can be adopted to estimate the best polynomial line. To illustrate the technique, the least squares fit for a quadratic cuve will be developed. This can be readily extended to higher power functions.

The quadratic function is given by

$$y = a + bx + cx^2 \tag{21}$$

and the following simultaneous equations can be derived:

$$\begin{aligned} a\Sigma 1 + b\Sigma x + c\Sigma x^2 &= \Sigma y \\ a\Sigma x + b\Sigma x^2 + c\Sigma x^3 &= \Sigma yx \\ a\Sigma x^2 + b\Sigma x^3 + c\Sigma x^4 &= \Sigma yx^2 \end{aligned} \tag{22}$$

and in matrix notation,

$$\begin{bmatrix} n & \Sigma x & \Sigma x^2 \\ \Sigma x & \Sigma x^2 & \Sigma x^3 \\ \Sigma x^2 & \Sigma x^3 & \Sigma x^4 \end{bmatrix} \begin{bmatrix} a \\ b \\ c \end{bmatrix} = \begin{bmatrix} \Sigma y \\ \Sigma yx \\ \Sigma yx^2 \end{bmatrix} \tag{23}$$

which can be solved for coefficients *a*, *b*, and *c*.

The extension of the technique to higher order polynomials, *e.g.* cubic, quartic, *etc.*, is straightforward. Consider the general *m*'th degree polynomial

$$y = a + bx + cx^2 + \ldots + zx^m \tag{24}$$

This expands to $(m + 1)$ simultaneous equations from which $(m + 1)$ coefficients are to be determined. The terms on the right-hand side of the matrix equation will range from Σy_i to $\Sigma(x_i^m . y_i)$ and on the left-hand side from $\Sigma 1$ to $S x_i^{2m}$.

A serious problem encountered with the application of polynomial curve-fitting is the fundamental decision as to which degree of polynomial is best. Visual inspection of the experimental data may indicate that a straight line is not appropriate. It may not be immediately apparent, unless theory dictates otherwise, whether say, a quadratic or cubic equation should be employed to model the data. As the number of terms in the polynomial is increased, the correlation between the experimental data and the fitted curve will also increase.

In the limit, when the number of terms is one less than the number of the data points the correlation will be unity, *i.e.* the curve will pass through every point. Such a polynomial, however, may have no physical significance. In practice, statistical tests, based on the use of the *F*-ratio, can be employed to examine the significance of terms added to a polynomial and to indicate whether observed increases in the correlation coefficient are statistically significant.

Table 3 shows results of recorded fluorescence emission intensity as a function of concentration of quinine sulphate in acidic solutions. These data are plotted in Figure 3 with regression lines calculated from least squares estimated lines for a linear model, a quadratic model and a cubic model. The correlation for each fitted model with the experimental data is also given. It is obvious by visual inspection that the straight line represents a poor estimate of the association between the data despite the apparently high value of the correlation coefficient.

The observed lack of fit may be due to random errors in the measured dependent variable or due to the incorrect use of a linear model. The latter is the more likely cause of error in the present case. This is confirmed by examining the differences between the model values and the actual results, Figure 2 With the linear model, the residuals exhibit a distinct pattern as a function of concentration. They are not randomly distributed as would be the case if a more appropriate model was employed, *e.g.* the quadratic function.

The linear model predicts the relationship between fluorescence intensity, *I*, and analyte concentration, *x*, to be of the form,

$$I_i = a + bx_i + \varepsilon_i \tag{25}$$

Table 3
Measured fluorescence emission intensity as a function of quinine concentration

Quinine concn. (mg kg⁻¹):	0	5	10	15	20	25
Fluorescence intensity: (arb. units)	10	180	300	390	460	520

where ε is a random error, assumed to be normally distributed, with a variance, σ^2, independent of the value of I. If these assumptions are valid and Equation (25) is a true model of the experimental data then the variance Of E will be equal to the variance about the regression line.

If the model is incorrect, then the variance around the regression will exceed the variance of ε. These variances can be estimated using ANOVA and the *F*-ratio calculated to compare the variances and test the significance of the model.

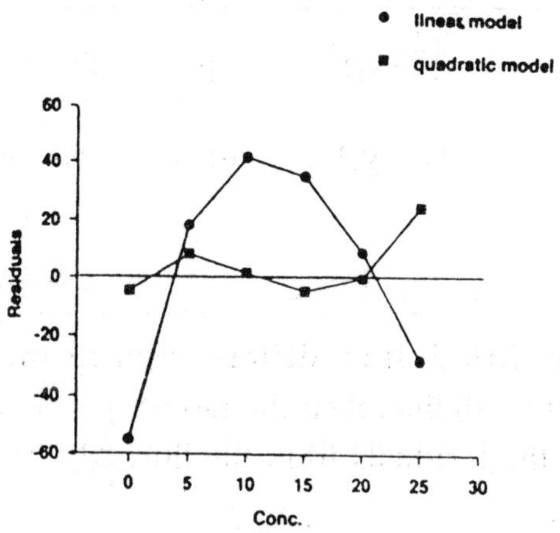

Fig. 2. Residuals (y, -y) as a function of concentration (x) for best fit linear and quadratic models.

The form of the ANOVA table for multiple regression is shown in Table 4. The completed table for the linear model fitted to the fluorescence data is given in Table 5. This analysis of variance serves to test whether a regression line is helpful in predicting the values of intensity from concentration data. For the linear model we wish to test whether the line of slope *b* adds a significant contribution to the zero-order model. The null hypothesis being tested is,

$$H_0: b = 0 \tag{26}$$

i.e. the mean concentration value is as accurate in predicting emission intensity as the linear regression line.

Table 4
ANOVA tablefor multiple regression

Source of variation	*Sum of Squares (SS)*	*Degrees of freedom (df)*	*Mean Squares (MS)*	*F-ratio*
Regression	$(\bar{y} - y_i)^2$	p	SS_{reg}/p	MS_{reg}/MS_{res}
Residuals (error)	$(y_i - y_i)^2$	n–p–1	$SS_{res}/(n-p-1)$	
Total	$(y_i - \bar{y})^2$	n–1	$SS_{tot}/(n-1)$	

When the fitted line differs significantly from a horizontal ($b = 0$) line, then the term $\Sigma(\bar{I} - I_i)^2$ will be large relative to the residuals from the line, $\Sigma(I_i - I_i)^2$.

Table 5
ANOVA table for the linear regression model applied to the fluorescence data, emission intensity as a function of concentration

Source of variation	*Sum of Squares*	*df*	*Mean Squares*	*F-ratio*
Regression	163 206	1	163 206	74.8
Residuals	8728	4	2182	
Total	171934	5	34 388	

$I = 65.24 + 19.31x$

$r^2 = 0.949$

As expected, this in fact is the case for the linear model, $F_{1,4} = 74.8$, compared with $F_{1,4} = 7.71$ from tables for a 5% level of significance. So the null hypothesis is rejected, the linear regression model is significant, and the degree to which the regression 2 equation fits the data can be evaluated from the coefficient of determination, r^2 given by Equation (14).

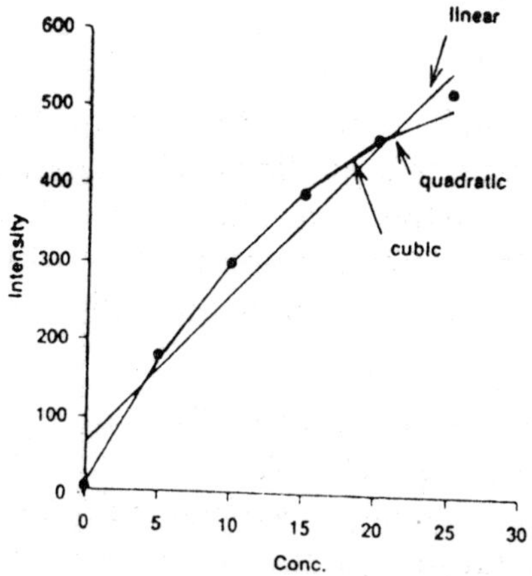

Fig. 3. Orthogonal linear, quadratic and cubic ,model for the fluorescence intensity data from table 3

Table 6
AMOVA table for the quadratic regression model of fluorescence intensity as a function of concentration

Source of variation	Sun of Squares	*df*	Mean Squares	F-ratio
Regression	171 807	2	85 903	2038
Residuals	126	3	42	
Total	171 934	5	34 387	

$$I = 14.64 + 34.49x - 0.61x^2$$

$$r^2 = 0.999$$

A similar ANOVA table can be completed for the quadratic model, Table 6. Does the addition of a quadratic term contribute significantly to the first-order, linear model? The equation tested is now

$$I_i = a + bx_i + cx_i^2 + \varepsilon_i \quad (27)$$

and the null hypothesis is

$$H_0: b = c = 0 \quad (28)$$

Once again the high value of the F-ratio indicates the model is significant as a predictor. This analysis can now be taken a step further since the Sum of the squares associated with the regression line can be attributed to two components, the linear function and the quadratic function.

This analysis is accomplished by the decomposition of the sum of squares, Table 7. The total sum of squares values for the regression can be obtained from Table 6 and that due to the linear component, x, from Table 5. The difference is attributed to the quadratic term. The F-value indicates the high significance of each term.

Table 7
Sum of Squares decomposition for the quadratic model

Source of variation	*Sun of Squares*	*df*	*Mean Squares*	*F-ratio*
x	163 206	1	163 206	3873
x^2	8601	1	8601	204
Total	171807	2	85903	

The exercise can be repeated for the fitted cubic model, and the ANOVA table and sums of squares decomposition are shown in Tables 8 and 9 respectively. In this case, the F-statistic for the cubic term ($F = 5.8$) is not significant at the 5% level. The cubic term is not required and we can conclude that the quadratic model is sufficient to describe the analytical data accurately, a result which agrees with visual inspection of the line, Figure 3(b).

In summary the three models tested are

$$I = 65.24 + 19.31x$$
$$I = 14.64 + 34.49x - 0.61x^2 \qquad (29)$$
$$I = 11.03 + 38.80x - 0.97x^2 + 0.0096x^3$$

Table 8
ANOVA table for the linear regression model applied to the fluorescence data, emission intensity as a function of concentration

Source of variation	*Sun of Squares*	*df*	*Mean Squares*	*F-ratio*
Regression	171 901	3	57 300	3522
Residuals	32	2	16	
Total	171 933	5	34 387	

$I = 11.03 + 37.8x$ û $0.97x^2 + 0.0096x^3$

$r^2 = 0.999$

Table 9
Sum of Squares decomposition for the cubic model

Source of variation	*Sun of Squares*	*df*	*Mean Squares*	*F-ratio*
x	163 206	1	163 206	10 031
x^2	8601	1	8601	529
x^3	94	1	94	5.8
Total	171 901	2	57 300	

The relative effectiveness and importance of the variables can be estimated from the relative magnitudes of the regression coefficients. This cannot be done directly on these coefficients, however, as their magnitudes are dependent on the magnitudes of the variables themselves. In Equation (29), for example, the coefficient for the cubic term is small compared with those for the linear and quadratic terms, but the cubic term itself may be very large. Instead, the *standardized regression coefficients*, B_i, are employed. These are determined by

$$B_k = b_k\sigma k/\sigma_y \tag{30}$$

where σ_k is the standard deviation of the variable x_k and α_y is the standard deviation of the dependent variable, y.

For the cubic model,

$$\begin{aligned} B_1 &= b\sigma_x/\sigma_y = 37.8\ (9.35/185.4) = 1.91 \\ B_2 &= c\sigma_x 2/\sigma_y = -0.97\ (243.6/185\text{-}4) = 1.27 \\ B_3 &= d\sigma 3/\sigma_y = 0.0096\ (6143.5/185.4) = 0.32 \end{aligned} \tag{31}$$

As expected, the relative significance of the standard regression coefficient B_3 is considerably less than those of the standardized linear and quadratic coefficients, B_1 and B_2.

Orthogonal polynomials

The fluorescence emission data were modelled using linear, quadratic, and cubic equations and the quadratic form was determined as providing the most appropriate model. Despite this, on moving to the higher, cubic, polynomial the coefficient of the cubic term is not zero and the values for the regression coefficients are considerably different from those obtained for the quadratic equation.

In general, the least squares polynomial fitting procedure will yield values for the coefficients which are dependent on the degree of the polynomial model. This is one of the reasons why the use of polynomial curve fitting often contributes little to understanding the causal relationship between independent and dependent variables, despite the technique providing a useful curve fitting procedure.

With the general polynomial equation discussed above, the value of the first coefficient, a, represents the intercept of the line with the y-axis. The b coefficient is the slope of the line at this point, and subsequent coefficients are the values of higher orders of curvature. A more physically significant model might be achieved by modelling the experimental data with a special polynomial equation; a model in which the coefficients are not dependent on the specific order of equation used. One such series of equations having this property of independence of coefficients is that referred to as *orthogonal polynomials*.

Bevington presents the general orthogonal polynomial between variables y and x in the form

$$y = a + b(x - \beta) + c(x - \gamma_1)(x - \gamma_2) + d(x - \delta_1)(x - \delta_2)(x - \delta_3) + \ldots \quad (32)$$

As usual, the least squares procedure is employed to determine the values of the regression coefficients a, b, c, d, *etc.*, giving the minimum deviation between the observed data and the model.

Also, we impose the criterion that subsequent addition of higher-order terms to the polynomial will not change the value of the coefficients of lower-order terms. This extra constraint is used to evaluate the parameters β, γ_1, γ_2, δ_1, *etc.* The coefficient a represents the average y value, b the average slope, c the average curvature, *etc.*

The computation of orthogonal polynomials is laborious but the arithmetic can be greatly simplified if the values of the independent variable, x, are equally spaced and the dependent variable is homoscedastic. In this case,

$$\beta = \tilde{x}$$

$$\gamma = \beta \pm \Delta\left[\frac{n^2 - 1}{12}\right]^{0.5} \tag{33}$$

$$\delta = \beta,\ \beta \pm \Delta\left[\frac{3n^2 - 7}{20}\right]^{0.5}$$

where

$$D = x_{i+1} - x_i. \tag{34}$$

and

$$a = \bar{y}$$

$$b = \frac{\Sigma y_i(x_i - \beta)}{\Sigma(x_i - \beta)^2}$$

$$c = \frac{\Sigma[y_i(x_i - \gamma_1)(x_i - \gamma_2)]}{\Sigma[(x_i - \gamma_1)(x_i - \gamma_2)]^2} \tag{35}$$

$$d = \frac{\Sigma[y_i(x_i - \delta_1)(x_i - \delta_2)(x_i - \delta_3)]}{\Sigma[(x_i - \delta_1)(x_i - \delta_2)(x_i - \delta_3)]^2}$$

Orthogonal polynomials are particularly useful when the order of the equation is not known beforehand. The problem of finding the lowest-order poly-nomial to represent the data adequately can be achieved by first fitting a straight line, then a quadratic curve, then a cubic, and so on. At each stage it is only necessary to determine one additional parameter and apply the *F*-test to estimate the significance of each additional term.

For the fluorescence emission data,

$$\beta = 12.5$$
$$\gamma_1 = 21.04,\ \gamma_2 = 3.96 \tag{36}$$
$$\delta_1 = 12.5,\ \delta_2 = 23.74,\ \delta_3 = 1.26$$

and, from Equations (34),

$$a = 306.7$$
$$b = 19.31$$
$$c = -0.608 \tag{37}$$
$$d = 0.0089$$

Thus the orthogonal linear equation is given by

$$I_i = 306.7 + 19.31\,(x_i - 12.5)$$

the quadratic by

$$I_i = 306.7 + 19.31\,(x_i - 12.5) - 0.608(x_i - 21.04)(x_i - 3.96)$$

and the cubic model by

$$I_i = 306.7 + 19.31(x_i - 12.5) - 0.608(x_i - 21.04)(x_i - 3.96) + 0.0089(x_i - 12.5)(x_i - 23.74)(x_i - 1.26) \tag{38}$$

These equations are illustrated graphically in Figure 5. As before, an ANOVA table can be constructed for each model and the significance of each term estimated by sums of squares decomposition and comparison of standard regression coefficients.

Multivariate regression

The discussion of regression analysis and its applications has been limited to modelling the association between a dependent variable and a single independent variable. Chemometrics is more often concerned with multivariate measures. Thus it is necessary to extend our account of regression to include cases in which several or many independent variables contribute to the measured response. It is important to realize at the outset that the term independent variables as used here does not imply statistical independence, as the x variables may be highly correlated.

In the simplest example, the dependent response variable, y, may be a function of two such independent variables, x_1 and x_2.

$$y = a + b_1x1 + b_2x_2 \tag{39}$$

Again a is the intercept on the ordinate y-axis, and b_1 and b_2 are the *partial regression coefficients*. These coefficients denote the rate of change of the mean of y as a function of x_1, with x_2 constant, and the rate of change of y as a function of x_2 with x_1 constant. Multivariate regression analysis plays an important role in modern process control analysis, particularly for quantitative UV-visible absorption spectrometry and near-IR reflectance analysis. It is common practice with these techniques to monitor absorbance, or reflectance, at several wavelengths and relate these individual measures to the concentration of some analyte.

The results from a simple two-wavelength experiment serve to illustrate the details of multivariate regression and its application to multivariate calibration procedures. For quantitative analysis, measurements at a single wavelength, *e.g.* λ_{14}, would be adequate if no interfering species are present. In the presence of other absorbing species, however, more measurements are needed. In Table 10 are presented the concentrations and measured absorbance values at λ_{14} of seven standard solutions containing known amounts of tryptophan along with three samples which we will assume contain unknown amounts of tryptophan.

All solutions have unknown concentrations of a

second absorbing species present, in this case the amino acid tyrosine. Regression equation were known in advance. Either some theoretical considerations determine the variables or, as in many spectroscopic examples, visual inspection of the data provides an intuitive feel for the greater relevance of some variables compared with others. In such cases, serious problems associated with the selection of appropriate variables may not arise.

The situation is not so simple where no sound theory exists and variable selection is not obvious. Then some formal procedure for choosing which variables to include in a regression analysis is important and the task may be far from trivial. The problems and procedures for selecting variables for regression analysis can be illustrated by considering the use of near-IR spectrometry for quantitative analysis.

Despite its widespread use in manufacturing and process industries, the underlying theory regarding specific spectral transitions associated with the absorption of radiation in the near-IR region has been little studied. Unlike the fundamental transitions observed in the mid-IR region, giving rise to discrete absorption bands, near-IR spectra are often characterized by overtones and combination bands and the observed spectra are typically complex and, to a large extent, lacking in readily identifiable features. It rarely arises, therefore, that absorption at a specific wavelength can be attributed to a single chemical entity or species.

For quantitative analysis a range of measurements, each at different wavelengths, must be recorded in order to attempt to correct for spectral interference. In the limit, of course, the whole spectrum can be employed as a list or vector of variates. The dependent variable, y, can then be represented by a linear model of the form

$$y = a + \Sigma b_i x_i + \varepsilon_i \tag{42}$$

where y is the concentration of some analyte, x_i is the measured response (absorbance or reflectance) at i specific wavelengths, and a and b are the coefficients or weights associated with each variate.

Table 10

UV absorbance data recorded at seven wavelengths, $A_9 \ldots A_{27}$, of 14 solutions containing known amounts of tryptophan. The spectra of two test solutions containing 11 and 25 mg kg^{-1} tryptophan respectively are also included

	Tr (mg kg^{-1})	A_9	A_{12}	A_{15}	A_{18}	A_{21}	A_{24}	A_{27}
	2	0.632	0.292	0.318	0.436	0.296	0.069	0.079
	4	0.558	0.275	0.418	0.468	0.258	0.116	0.072
	6	0.565	0.300	0.392	0.501	0.279	0.040	0.052
	8	0.549	0.332	0.502	0.509	0.224	0.055	0.018
	10	0.570	0.351	0.449	0.480	0.222	0.056	0.025
	12	0.273	0.309	0.427	0.324	0.156	0.056	0.080
	14	0.276	0.378	0.420	0.265	0.163	0.019	0.006
	16	0.469	0.444	0.550	0.456	0.181	0.063	0.053
	18	0.504	0.551	0.585	0.524	0.172	0.110	0.078
	20	0.554	0.566	0.654	0.513	0.168	0.070	0.083
	22	0.501	0.553	0.667	0.521	0.143	0.103	0.035
	24	0.464	0.636	0.691	0.525	0.122	0.077	0.100
	26	0.743	0.743	0.901	0.785	0.313	0.088	0.072
	28	0.754	0.793	0.939	0.773	0.261	0.024	0.095
Mean	15	0.529	0.466	0.565	0.506	0.204	0.068	0.061
s	8.367	0.139	0.174	0.188	0.139	0.072	0.030	0.030
X1	11	0.254	0.324	0.337	0.337	0.110	0.035	0.034
X2	25	0.497	0.656	0.771	0.513	0.150	0.053	0.083

Table 11

Absorbance values of tryptophan standard solutions recorded at two wavelengths, A_{14} and A_{21}. Three 'unknown' test solutions, X_1, X_2, and X_3, are included with their true tryptophan concentration shown in parenthesis

Tryptophan concn. (mg kg⁻¹)	*Absorbance A_{14}*	*Absorbance A_{21}*
0	0.356	0.0390
5	0.3068	0.2110
10	0.3980	0.1860
15	0.3860	0.0450
20	0.6020	0.1580
25	0.6680	0.1070
29	0.8470	0.2010
X1 (7)	0.3440	0.2010
X2 (14)	0.3670	0.0500
X3 (27)	0.0810	0.2110

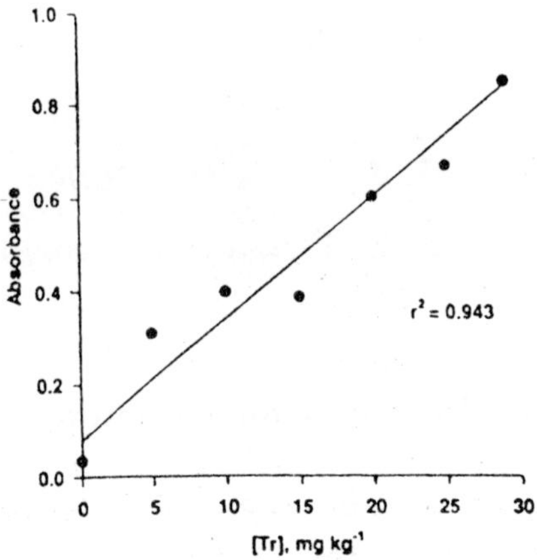

Fig. 4: The least square linear model of absorbance (A_{14}) vs. concentration of trypophan, data from table 10.

The effect of this interferent is to addnoise and distort the univariate calibration graph, as shown in Figure 4. The best-fit linear regression line is also shown, as derived from

$$\text{Concentration tryptophan, } Tr = -2.00 + 38.51\,A_{14} \tag{40}$$

where A_i is the absorbance at λ_i.

Despite the apparently high r^2 value for this model ($r^2 = 0.943$), its predictive ability is poor as can be demonstrated with the three test samples:

Actual:	7	14	27	mg kg^{-1}
Predicted:	10.26	11.14	28.20	mg kg^{-1}

If a second term, say the absorbance at λ_{21}, is added to the model equation, the predictive ability is improved considerably. Thus by including A_{21}, the least-squares model is

$$Tr = -0.00067 + 43.68A_{14} - 39.78A_{21} \tag{41}$$

with the test samples,

Actual:	7	14	27	mg kg^{-1}
Predicted:	7.03	14.04	26.99	mg kg^{-1}

This model as given by Equation (41) could be usefully employed for the quantitative determination of tryptophan in the presence of tyrosine.

Of course, the reason for the improvement in the calibration model when the second term is included is that A_{21} serves to compensate for the absorbance due to the tyrosine since λ_{21} is in the spectral region of a tyrosine absorption band with little interference from tryptophan, Figure 6. In general, the selection of variables for multivariate regression analysis may not be so obvious.

For a complete spectrum, extending from say 1200 to 2000 nm, i may take on values of several hundreds and the solution of the possible hundreds of simultaneous equations necessary to determine the full range of the coefficients in order to predict y from the analytical data is computationally demanding.

Table 12

Correlation matrix between tryptophan concentration and absorbance at seven wavelengths for the 14 standard solutions from Table 11

	Tr	A_9	A_{12}	A_{15}	A_{18}	A_{21}	A_{24}	A_{27}
Tr	1							
A_9	0.225	1						
A_{12}	0.955	0.474	1					
A_{15}	0.919	0.554	0.969	1				
A_{18}	0.589	0.877	0.765	0.832	1			
A_{21}	−0.228	0.830	0.020	0.135	0.615	1		
A_{24}	0.015	0.250	0.083	0.108	0.220	0.207	1	
A_{27}	0.393	0.376	0.510	0.474	0.456	0.271	0.298	1

In preparing such a multivariate calibration model, therefore, it would be reasonable to address two key points. Firstly, which of the variates contribute most significantly to the prediction model and which variates can be left out without reducing the effectiveness of the model? If most of the calibration information can be demonstrated to reside in only a few measurements then the computational effort is reduced considerably. Secondly, is there any penalty, other than increased data processing time, in having more variates in the set of equations than strictly necessary? After all, with the data processing power now available with even the most modest personal computer, why not include all measurements in the calibration? As an easily managed example of multivariate data analysis we shall consider the spectral data presented in Table 11.

These data represent the recorded absorbance of 14 standard solutions containing known amounts of tryptophan, measured at seven wavelengths, in the UV region under noisy conditions and in the presence of other absorbing species. Two test spectra, *X*1 and *X*2, are also included. No single wavelength measure exhibits an obvious linear trend with analyte concentration and a univariate calibration is unlikely to prove successful. The matrix of correlation coefficients between the variables, dependent and independent, given in Table 12.

The independent variable most highly correlated with tryptophan concentration is the measured absorbance at λ_{12}, A_{12}, *i.e.*

$$Tr = a + b_1 A_{12} \qquad (43)$$

and by least-squares modelling,

$$Tr = -6.31 + 45.74A_{12} \qquad (44)$$

and for our two test samples, of concentrations 11 and 25 p.p.m., *X*1 = 8.51 mg kg^{-1}and *X*2 = 23.69 mg kg^{-1}.

Despite the apparent high correlation between tryptophan concentration and A_{12}, the univariate model is a poor predictor, particularly at low concentrations. In order to improve the performance of the calibration model other information from the spectral data could be included.

The absorbance at $\lambda\lambda_{21}$, for example, is negatively correlated with tryptophan concentration and may serve to compensate for the interfering species present. Including A_{21} gives the bivariate model defined by

$$Tr = a + b_1A_{12} + b_2A_{21} \tag{45}$$

By ordinary least squares regression, Equation (45) can be solved to provide

$$Tr = -0.51 + 45.75A_{12} - 28.43A_{21} \tag{46}$$

with a coefficient of determination, r^2, of 0.970. The model *vs.* actual data and the residuals plot. *X*1 and *X*2 are evaluated as 11.19 and 25.24 mg kg^{-1} respectively.

Although the bivariate model performs considerably better than the univariate model, as evidenced by the smaller residuals, the calibration might be improved further by including more spectral data. The question arises as to which data to include.

In the limit of course, all data will be used and the model takes the form

$$Tr = a + b_1A_9 + b_2A_{12} + b_3A_{15} + \ldots + b_7A_{27} \tag{47}$$

To determine by least-squares the value of each coefficient requires we use eight simultaneous equations. In matrix notation the normal equations can be expressed as,

$$Tr = A.b \tag{48}$$

where

$$A = \begin{bmatrix} \Sigma 1 & \Sigma A_9 & & \Sigma A_{27} \\ \Sigma A_9 & \Sigma A_9 & \ldots & \Sigma A_9 A_{27} \\ \Sigma A_{12} & \Sigma A_9^2 & & \Sigma A_{12} A_{27} \\ | & \Sigma A_{12} A_9 & & \\ \Sigma A_{27} & & & \Sigma A_{27}^2 \end{bmatrix}$$

$$b^{T} = [a\ b_1\ b_2\ b_3\ b_4\ b_5\ b_6\ b_7]$$

$$Tr^{T} = [\Sigma Tr\ \Sigma A_9Tr\ \Sigma A_{12}Tr\ \Sigma A_{15}Tr\ \Sigma A_{18}Tr\ \Sigma A_{21}Tr\ \Sigma A_{24}Tr\ \Sigma A_{27}Tr]$$

(49)

Calculating the individual elements of matrix A and computing its inverse in order to solve Equation (48) for b can give rise to computational errors, and it is common practice to modify the calculation to achieve greater accuracy.

If the original data matrix is converted into the correlation matrix, then each variable is expressed in the standard normal form with zero mean and unit standard deviation.

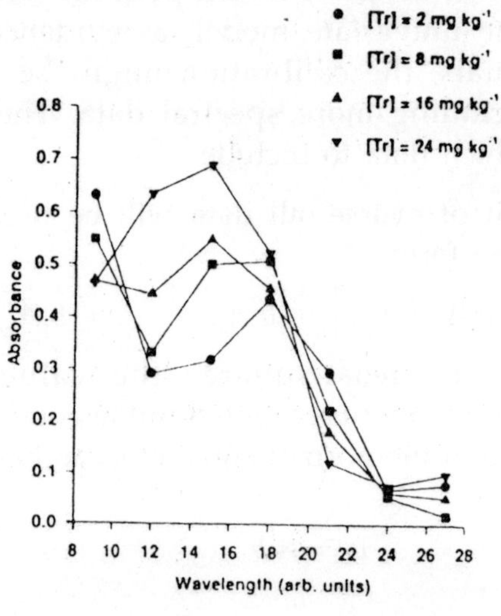

Fig. 5: Some of the spectra from table 11

The intercept coefficient using these standardized variables will now be zero and the required value can be calculated later. The regression equation in matrix form is then

$$R.B = r \tag{50}$$

where R is the matrix of correlation coefficients between the independent variables, r is the vector of correlations between the dependen variable and each independent variable, and B is the vector of standard regression coefficients we wish to determine.The individual elements of R and r are available from Table 12 and we may calculate B by rearranging Equation (50):

$$B = \mathbf{R}_x^{-1}.r_y \tag{51}$$

and,

$$B^T = [-0.28\ 0.709\ 0.419\ -0.006\ -0.052\ 0.006\ -0.044]$$

To be used in a predictive equation these coefficients must be 'unstandardized', and, from Equation (30),

$$b_i = B_i \sigma_y / \sigma_i$$

Hence

$$b^T = [-16.83\ 34.08\ 18.67\ -0.36\ -6.08\ 1.71\ -12.38] \tag{52}$$

The constant intercept term is obtained from Equation (47),

$$a = y - b_1 \bar{x}_1 - b_2 \bar{x}_2 - b_3 \bar{x}_3 - b_4 . \bar{x}_4 - b_5 \bar{x}_5 - b_6 \bar{x}_6 - b_7 \bar{x}_7$$

$$= -0.465 \tag{53}$$

Predicted regression results compared with known tryptophan concentration values. The calculated concentrations for X1 and X2 are 11.44 and 25.89 p.p.m. respectively. Although the predicted concentrations for our two test samples are inferior to the results obtained with the bivariate model, the full. Unfortunately, including all seven terms in the model has also added random noise to the system; A_{24} and A_{27} are measured at long wavelengths where negligible absorption would be expected from any component in the samples.

In addition, where several hundred wavelengths may be monitored with a high degree of colinearity between the data, it is necessary and worthwhile using an appropriate subset of the independent variables.

For predictive purposes it is often possible to do at least as well with a carefully chosen subset as with the total set of independent variables. As the number of independent variables increases the number of subsets of all possible combinations of variables increases dramatically and a formal procedure must be implemented to select the most appropriate variables to include in the regression model.

A very direct procedure for testing the significance of each variable involves fitting all possible subsets of the variates in the equation and evaluating the best response. However, this is rarely possible. With p variables the total number of equations to be examined is 2^p, if we include the equation containing all variates and that containing none.

Even with only eight variables, the number of equations is 256, and to examine a complete spectrum containing many hundreds of measures the technique is neither feasible nor practical. In some cases there may exist a strong practical or theoretical justification for including certain variables in the regression equation. In general, however, there is no preconceived assessment of the relative importance of some or all of the independent variables.

One method, mentioned briefly previously, is to examine the relative magnitudes of the standard regression coefficients. For our experimental data, from B^T [Equation (51)], this would indicate that A_9, A_{12}, and A_{15} are the most important. More sophisticated strategies are employed in computer software packages. For cases where there are a large number of significant variates, three basic procedures are in common use.

These methods are referred to as the *forward selection procedure*, the *backward selection procedure*, and the *stepwise method*. The forward selection technique starts with an empty equation, possibly containing a constant term only, with no independent variables. As the procedure progresses, variates are added to the test equation one at a time.

The first variable included is that which has the highest correlation with the dependent variable y. The second variable added to the equation is the one with the highest correlation with *y*, after *y* has been adjusted for the effect of the first variable, *i.e.* the variable with the highest correlation with the residuals from the first step.

This method is equivalent to selecting the second variable so as to maximize the partial correlation with *y* after removing the linear effect of the first chosen variable. The procedure proceeds in this manner until no further variate has a significant effect on the fitted equation. From Table 12, the absorbance at λ_{12} exhibits the highest correlation with tryptophan concentration and this is the first variable added to the equation, Equation (43). To choose the second variable, we could select A_{15} as this has the second highest absolute correlation with *Tr* but this may not be the best choice. Some other variable combined with A_{12} may give a higher multiple correlation than A_{15} and A_{12}. Multiple correlation represents the simple correlation between known values of the dependent variable and equivalent points or values as derived from the regression equation.

Partial correlation, on the other hand, is the simple correlation between the residuals from the regression line or planes on the variable whose effects are removed. For our UV absorbance data we wish to remove the linear effect of A_{12} regressed on *Tr* so that we can subsequently assess the correlations of the other variables.

From Equation (44), for the univariate model using A_{12},

$$Tr = -6.31 + 45.74A_{12}$$

and regressing A_{12} on to each of the remaining independent variables gives

$$\begin{aligned} A_9 &= 0.32 + 0.40A_{12} \\ A_{15} &= 0.06 + 1.07A_{12} \\ A_{18} &= 0.21 + 0.60A_{12} \\ A_{21} &= 0.19 + 0.08A_{12} \\ A_{24} &= 0.06 + 0.01\ A_{12} \\ A_{27} &= 0.02 + 0.08A_{12} \end{aligned} \tag{54}$$

The matrix of residuals ($Tr - Tr$, $A_9 - A_{15} - A_{15}$, *etc.*) is given in Table 13, and the corresponding correlation matrix between these residuals in Table 14. From Table 14 the variable having the largest absolute correlation with Tr residuals is A_9. Therefore we select this as the second variable to be added to the regression model.

Hence, at step 2,

$$Tr = -0.60 + 52.10\ A_{12} - 16.58A_9 \tag{55}$$

Forward regression proceeds to step 3 using the same technique. The variables A_9 and A_{12} are regressed on to each of the variables not in the equation and the unused variable with the highest partial correlation coefficient is selected as the next to use.

Table 13
Matrix of residuals for each variable after removiing the linear model using A_{12}

$Tr - Tr$	$A_9 - A_9$	$A_{15} - A_{15}$	$A_{18} - A_{18}$	$A_{21} - A_{21}$	$A_{24} - A_{24}$	$A_{27} - A_{27}$
–5.330	0.205	– 0.054	0.051	0.083	0.005	0.036
–2.557	0.138	0.067	0.093	0.046	0.052	0.030
–1.694	0.135	0.011	0.111	0.065	–0.024	0.008

–1.149	0.106	0.087	0.100	0.007	–0.010	–0.029
–0.013	0.120	0.013	0.059	0.004	–0.009	–0.023
3.897	–0.161	0.036	–0.071	–0.059	–0.008	0.035
2.759	–0.185	–0.044	–0.172	–0.157	–0.046	–0.044
1.757	–0.019	0.015	–0.020	–0.044	–0.003	–0.002
–1.109	–0.026	–0.065	–0.017	–0.062	0.042	0.014
0.208	0.018	–0.012	–0.037	–0.067	0.002	0.018
2.800	–0.030	0.015	–0.021	–0.091	0.035	–0.029
1.025	–0.100	–0.049	–0.067	–0.119	0.008	0.029
–1.842	0.136	0.046	0.129	–0.064	0.018	–0.007
–2.116	0.127	0.031	0.087	0.008	–0.047	0.012

If we continue in this way then all variables will eventually be added and no effective subset will have been generated, so a stopping rule is employed. The most commonly used *stopping rule* in commercial programs is based on the *F*-test of the hypothesis that the partial correlation coefficient of the variable to be entered in the equation is equal to zero. No more variables are added to the equation when the F-value is less than some specified cut-off value, referred to as the *minimum F-to-enter value*.

Table 14

Matrix of correlatinos between the residuals from Table 13

	Tr – Tr	A_9–A_9	A_{15} – A_{15}	A_{18}– A_{18}	A_{21}– A_{21}	A_{24}– A_{24}	A_{27}– A_{27}
Tr–Tr	1						
A_9–A_9	–0.88	1					
A_{15}–A_{15}	0.08	0.34	1				
A_{18}–A_{18}	–0.73	0.91	0.57	1			
A_{21}–A_{21}	–0.81	0.92	0.42	0.91	1		
A_{24}–A_{24}	–0.15	0.12	0.01	0.16	0.11	1	
A_{27}–A_{27}	–0.35	0.15	–0.18	0.11	0.29	0.29	1

A completed forward regression analysis of the UV absorbance data is presented in Table 15. Using a cut-off *F*-value of 4.60 ($F_{1,14}$ at 95% confidence limit), three variables are included in the final equation:

$$Tr = -0.77 + 33.92A_{12} - 19.47A_9 + 18.05A_{15} \tag{56}$$

Calculated values for *X*1 and *X*2 are 11.30 and 25.72 mg kg^{-1} respectively.

Table 15

Forward regression analysis of the data from Table 11. After three steps no remaining variable has a F-to-enter value exceeding the declared minimum of 4.60, and the procedure stops

Step 1: Variable entered:	A_{12}					
Dependent variable	Tr					
Variables in equation	Constant			A_{12}		
Coefficient	–6.31			45.74		
Variable not in equation	A_9	A_{15}	A_{18}	A_{21}	A_{24}	A_{27}
Partial correlation coefficient	–0.88	–0.10	–0.74	–0.83	–0.22	–0.36
F-to-enter	43.20	0.14	16.19	29.87	0.64	1.90
Step 2: Variable entered:	A_9					
Variables in equation	Constant	A_{12}		A_9		
Coefficient	–0.60	52.10		–16.58		
Variable not in equation	A_{15}	A_{18}	A_{21}	A_{24}	A_{24}	A_{27}
Partial correlation coefficient	–0.65	0.25	–0.10	–0.01	–0.43	
F-to-enter	8.84	0.87	0.12	0.03	2.66	
Step 3: Variable entered:	A_{15}					
Variables in equation	Constant	A_{12}	A_9		A_{15}	
Coefficient	–0.77	33.92	–19.47		18.05	
Variable not in equation	A_{18}	A_{21}	A_{24}		A_{27}	
Partial correlation coefficient	–0.07	–0.30	–0.03		–0.40	
F-to-enter	0.06	1.10	0.01		2.11	

An alternative method is described by backward elimination. This technique starts with a full equation containing every measured variate and successively deletes one variable at each step. The variables are dropped from the equation on the basis of testing the significance of the regression coefficients, i.e. for each variable is the coefficient zero? The F-statistic is referred to as the computed F-io-remove. The procedure is terminated when all variables remaining in the model are considered significant.

Table 16 illustrates a worked example using the tryptophan data. Initially, with all variables in the model, A_{18} has the smallest computed *F*-to-remove value and this variable is removed from the model and eliminated at the first step. The procedure proceeds by computing a new regression equation with the remaining six variables and again examining the calculated *F*-to-remove values for the next candidate for elimination.

This process continues until no variable can be removed since all *F*-to-remove values are greater than some specified maximum value. This is the stopping rule; *F*-to-remove = 4 was employed here. It so happens in this example that the results of performing backward elimination regression are identical with those obtained from the forward regression analysis. This may not be the case in general. In its favour, forward regression generally involves a smaller amount of computation than backward elimination, particularly when many variables are involved in the analysis.

However, should it occur that two or more variables combine together to be a good predictor compared with single variables, then backward elimination will often lead to a better equation. Finally, stepwise regression, a modified version of the forward selection technique, is often available with commercial programs. As with forward selection, the procedure increases the number of variables in the equation at each step but at each stage the possibility of deleting a previously included variable is considered.

Thus, a variable entered at an earlier stage of selection may be deleted at subsequent, later stages. It is important to bear in mind that none of these subset multiple linear regression techniques are guaranteed or even expected to produce the best possible regression equation. The user of commercial software products is encouraged to experiment.

Principal components regression

It is often the case with multiple regression analysis involving large numbers of independent variables that there exists extensive colinearity or correlation between these variables. Colinearity adds redundancy to the regression model since more variables may be included in the model than is necessary for adequate predictive performance.

Of the methods available to the analytical chemist for regression analysis with protection against the problems induced by correlation between variables, principal components regression, PCR, is the most common employed.

Our findings can summarised as follows:

(a) Select the smallest number of variables possible. Including unnecessary variables in our model Will introduce bias in the estimation of the regression coefficients and reduce the Precision of the predicted values.

(b) Use the maximum information contained in the independent variables. Although some of the variables are likely to be redundant, potentially important variables should not be discounted solely in order to reduce the size of the problem.

(c) Choose independent variables that are not, highly correlated with each other. Colinearity can cause numerical instability in estimating regression coefficients.

Although subset selection along with multiple linear regression provides a means of reducing the number of variables studied, the method does not address the problems associated with colinearity. To achieve this, the regression coefficients should be orthogonal. The technique of generating orthogonal linear combinations of variables in order to extract maximum information from a data set was encountered previously in eigen analysis and the calculation of principal components. As an example consider the variables A_{12}, A_{15}, and A_{18} from the UV absorbance data of Table 11. These three variables are highly correlated between each other as can be seen from Table 12. This intercorrelation can also be observed in the scatter plot of these variables. By principal components analysis two new variables can be defined containing over 99% of the original variance of the three original variables.

The first principal component alone accounts for over 90% of the total variance and a plot of *Tr* against PCI. The use and application of principal components in regression analysis has been extensively reported in the chemometrics literature. We can calculate the principal components from our data set, so providing us with a set of new, orthogonal variables. Each of these principal components will be a linear combination of, and contain information from, all the original variables.

The PCR technique described here follows the methodology described by Martens and Naes and is applied to the data from Table 11. The original data are preprocessed by mean-centring. The variance-covariance dispersion matrix is then computed and from this square, symmetric matrix we calculate the normalized eigenvalues and eigenvectors. From each eigenvector, the principal component scores are determined, and by conventional regression analysis the calibration model is developed.

The stepwise procedure is illustrated in Table 17 and we will now follow the steps involved. The general linear regression equation is given by

$$y = a + X.b \tag{57}$$

where b is the vector of estimates of the regression coefficients to be determined. This vector b can be written as the product of the eigenvectors and the y-loadings,

$$b = P.q \tag{58}$$

where P is the matrix of eigen vectors, or loadings. Each column of P is an eigenvector for each factor included in the regression model. Elements of the P matrix are p_{jk} (j = 1 . . . m, the number of original variables, and k = 1 . . . K, the number of factors or principal components used in the model).

The vector q represents the y-loadings which can be determined by regression of y on T, the matrix of scores, t_k for each principal component. Martens and Naes derive q from

$$q = D.T^T.y \tag{59}$$

where D is a diagonal matrix, with each diagonal element equal to $1/\tau_k$ (τ_k = the eigenvalue of factor k). Working through our example in Table 17 will serve to illustrate the technique in operation. The mean-centred transformed data ($x_i - \bar{x}$ and $y_i - \bar{y}$) is presented as the matrix X_0 and vector y_0.

The eigenvalues of X_0 are provided in Table 18 and

it is evident that the data can be adequately described by two or three principal components. The eigenvector corresponding to the first principal component is p_1,

$$p_1^T = [-0.334 -0.555 -0.614 -0.442 -0.076 -0.01 -0.045] \quad (60)$$

and the greatest weights are given to A_9, A_{12}, A_{15}, and A_{18}.

The vector of scores, t_{11}, is obtained from,

$$t_1 = X_0 . P_1$$

With only one principal component in the model, $T = t_1$ and $D = 1/\tau_1 = 0.879$; thus,

$$q_1 = 0.879 t_1 y_0 = -23.405 \quad (61)$$

and the estimated regression coefficients for the one-factor model, from Equation (58), are

$$b = p_1 . q_1 \quad (62)$$

with a constant a given by

$$a = y - x^T . b \quad (63)$$

Therefore,

$$Tr(\text{single factor}) = -8.99 + 7.82A_9 + 12.99A_{12} + 14.37A_{15} + 10.34A_{18} + 11.78A_{21} + 0.24A_{24} + 1.06A_{27} \quad (64)$$

The algorithm proceeds by subtracting the effect of the first factor from X_0 and y_0, yielding the residual matrix X_1 and vector y_1. The process is repeated with the second scores determined from the second eigenvector and a two factor model developed.

$$Tr(\text{two factor}) = 0.54 - 13.96A_9 + 25.40A_{12} + 24.09A_{15} + 0.35A_{18} - 13.29A_{21} - 0.52A_{24} + 0.83A_{27} \quad (65)$$

and if a further factor is included,

$$Tr(\text{three factor}) = -0.571 - 12.95A_9 + 26.86A_{12} + 22.83A_{15} - 0.49A_{18} - 13.84A_{21} - 0.20A_{24} + 1.56A_{27} \quad (66)$$

with predicted *vs.* actual data.

Table 18

Eigenvalues of the mean-centred original data (Table 11). Over 97% of the original variance can be accounted for in the first two principal components

Eigenvalue	*Percentage contribution*	*Cumulative percentage contribution*
1.138	79.08	79.08
0.263	18.28	97.36
0.017	1.18	98.54
0.014	0.97	99.51
0.003	0.21	99.72
0.002	0.14	99.86
0.002	0.14	100.00

For the one, two, and three factor models the sums of the squares of the *y* residuals are 337, 11.6, and 11.6 respectively and the predicted concentrations for the test samples X_1 and X_2 are,

	X_1 *(11 mg kg⁻¹)*	X_2 *(25 mg kg⁻¹)*
One factor	5.78	20.18
Two factors	10.93	25.98
Three factors	10.90	26.00

Thus, as anticipated from visual examination of the eigenvalues, two factors are sufficient to describe the

Table 19

Backward regression analysis of the data from Table 11. After four steps, three variables remain in the regression equation; their F-to-remove values exceed the declared maximum value of 4.0

			Step 0: All variables entered					
Dependent variable	Tr							
Variables in equation	*Constant*	A_9	A_{12}	A_{15}	A_{18}	A_{21}	A_{24}	A_{27}
Coefficient	–0.465	–16.83	34.08	18.67	–0.36	–6.08	1.71	–12.38
F-*to-Remove*		5.96	12.43	5.03	0.001	0.08	0.04	0.78
			Step 1: Remove A_{18}					
Variables in equation	*Constant*	A_9	A_{12}	A_{15}	A_{21}	A_{24}	A_{27}	
Coefficient	–0.62	–16.45	34.85	17.12	–4.83	2.09	–13.25	
F-*to-Remove*		6.92	16.54	6.32	0.17	0.04	1.01	
			Step 2: Remove A_{24}					
Variables in equation	*Constant*	A_9	A_{12}	A_{15}	A_{21}	A_{24}		
Coefficient	–0.53	–16.14	34.50	17.28	–5.32	–12.35		
F-*to-Remove*		7.83	18.67	7.23	0.23	1.09		
			Step 3: Remove A_{21}					
Variables in equation	*Constant*	A_9	A_{12}	A_{15}	A_{27}			
Coefficient	–0.62	–18.69	36.67	16.37	–14.88			
F-*to-Remove*		73.03	33.29	7.64	2.12			

calibration and the regression model. In employing principal components as our regression factors we have succeeded in fully utilizing all the measured variables and developed new, uncorrelated variables.

In selecting which eigenvectors to use, the first employed is that corresponding to the largest eigenvalue, the second that corresponding to the next largest eigenvalue, and so on. This strategy assumes that the major eigenvectors correspond to phenomena in the X data matrix of relevance in modelling the dependent variable y.

Although this is generally accepted as being the case for most analytical applications, another data compression method can be employed if variables having high variance but little relevance to y are thought to be present.

Partial least squares regression

The calibration model referred to a partial least squares regression (PLSR) is a relatively modern technique, developed and popularized in analytical science by Wold. The method differs from PCR by including the dependent variable in the data compression and decomposition operations, *i.e.* both y and x data are actively used in the data analysis.

This action serves to minimize the potential effects of x variables having large variances but which are irrelevant to the calibration model. The simultaneous use of X and y information makes the method more complex than PCR as two loading vectors are required to provide orthogonality of the factors. The method illustrated here employs the orthogonalized PLSR algorithm developed by Wold and extensively discussed by Martens and Naes.

As with PCR, the dependent and independent variables are mean centred to give data matrix X_0 and vector y_0. Then for each factor, $k = 1 \ldots K$, to be included in the regression model, the following steps are performed.

(a) The loading weight vector w_k is calculated by maximizing the covariance between the linear combination of X_{k-1} and y_{k-1} given that $w_k^T.w_k = 1$.

(b) The factor scores, t, are estimated by projecting X_{k-1} on w_k.

(c) The loading vector P_k is determined by regressing X_{k-1} on t_k and similarly q_k by regressing y_{k-1} on t_k.

(d) From $(X_{k-1} - t_k.p_k^T)$ and $(y_{k-1} - t_k.\ q_k^T)$ new matrices X_k and y_k are formed.

The optimum number of factors to include in the model is found by observation and usual validation statistics. For our tryptophan UV absorbance data these steps provide the results shown in Table 19.

The loading weight vector, w_1, is calculated from

$$w_1 = c.X_0.y_0 \quad (67)$$

where the scaling factor c is given by

$$C = (y_0^T.X_0.X_0^T.y_0)^{0.5} \quad (68)$$

$$= 0.036$$

The factor scores and loadings are estimated by

$$t_1 = X_0.w_1$$

$$p_1 = (X_0^T.\ t_1)/(t_1^T.\ t_1)$$

$$q_1 = (y_0^T.\ t_1)/(t_1^T.\ t_1) \quad (69)$$

The matrix and vector of residuals are finally computed,

$$X_1 = X_0 - t_1.p_1^T \quad (70)$$

and

$$y_1 = y_0 - t_1 \cdot q_1^T \tag{71}$$

The regression coefficients can be calculated by

$$b = W(P^T.W)^{-1}\, q \tag{72}$$

and

$$a = y - X^T.b \tag{73}$$

where W is the matrix of loading weights, each column is a weight vector, and P the matrix of loadings.

With the single factor in the model the regression equation is,

$$Tr(\text{one factor}) = -8.73 + 3.01A_9 + 17.13A_{12} + 17.85A_{15} + 8.64A_{18} - 1.83A_{21} + 0.05A_{24} + 1.03A_{27} \tag{74}$$

The procedure is repeated with a second factor included and,

$$Tr(\text{two factors}) = -0.53 - 13.90A_9 + 25.64A_{12} + 23.89A_{15} + 0.30A_{18} - 13.27A_{21} - 0.62A_{24} + 0.59A_{27} \tag{75}$$

and with three factors,

$$Tr(\text{three factors}) = -0.31 - 12.55A_9 + 31.03A_{12} + 19.41A_{15} - 0.74A_{18} - 12.78A_{21} - 2.82A_{24} - 4.92A_{27} \tag{76}$$

The sums of squares of the residuals for the one, two, and three-factor models are 201, 11.53, and 10.64 respectively and the estimated tryptophan concentrations from the test solutions are

	X_1 (11 mg kg^{-1})	X_2 (25 mg kg^{-1})
One factor	6.35	22.01

Two factors	10.93	25.98
Three factors	11.18	25.92

As with PCR, a regression model built from two orthogonal new variables serves to provide good predictive ability. Regression analysis is probably the most popular technique in statistics and data analysis, and commercial software packages will usually provide for multiple linear regression with residuals analysis and variables subset selection.

Unsupervised Analysis

The organization in the Periodic Table, for example, allows us to study group chemistry with deviations from general behaviour for any element to be recorded as required. In a similar manner, much organic chemistry can be catalogued in terms of the chemistry of generic functional groups. In infrared spectroscopy, the concept of correlation between spectra and molecular structures is exploited to provide the basis for spectral interpretation; in general each functional group exhibits well defined regions of absorption.

Consider the data shown in Table 1, obtained from an analysis of a serie's of alloys. This is only a relatively small data set but it may not be immediately apparent that these samples can be organized into well defined groups defining the type or class of alloy according to their composition.

The data from Table I are expressed diagrammatically in Figure 1. Although we may guess that there are two similar groups based on the Ni, Cr, and Mn content, the picture suffers from the presence of extraneous data. The situation would be more complex still if more objects were analysed or more variables were measured. As modern analytical techniques are able to generate large quantities of qualitative and quantitative data, it is necessary to seek and apply formal methods which can serve to highlight similarities and differences between samples.

Table 1

Concentration, expressed as mg kg^{-1}, of trace metals in six alloy

	Ni	Cr	Mn	V	Co
A	6.1	1.1	1.2	5.2	4.0
B	1.6	3.8	4.1	4.0	3.9
C	1.2	3.1	2.9	3.6	6.4
D	5.1	1.5	1.6	4.2	3.2
E	4.8	1.8	1.2	3.7	3.0
F	2.1	3.4	4.4	4.3	4.1

The general problem is one of *classification* and the contents of this chapter are concerned with addressing the following, broadly stated task. Given a number of objects or samples, each described by a set of measured values, we are to derive a formal mathematical scheme for grouping the objects into classes such that objects within a class are similar, and different from those in other classes.

The number of classes and the class characteristics are not known *a priori* but are to be determined from the analysis. It is the last statement in the challenge facing us that distinguishes the techniques studied here from supervised pattern recognition schemes to be examined. In supervised pattern recognition, a training set is identified with which the parent class or group of each sample is known, and this information is used to develop a suitable discriminant function with which new, unclassified samples can be examined and assigned to one of the parent classes.

In the case of *unsupervised pattern recognition, often referred to as cluster analysis or numerical taxonomy*, no class knowledge is available and no assumptions need be made regarding the class to which a sample may belong. Cluster analysis is a powerful investigative tool, which can aid in determining and identifying underlying patterns and structure in apparently meaningless tables of data. Its use in analytical science is widespread and increasing. Some of the varied areas of its application are model fitting and hypothesis testing, data exploration, and data reduction.

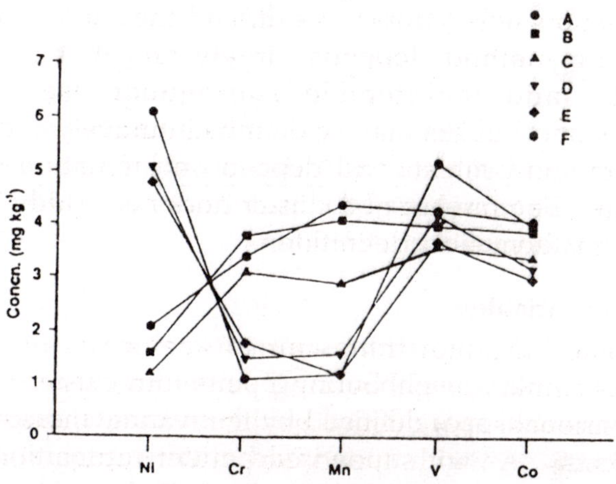

Fig. 1. The trace metal data from Table 1 plotted to illustrate the presence of two groups

The general scheme, or algorithm, followed in order to perform unsupervised pattern recognition and undertake cluster analysis, proceeds in the following manner. The data set comprising the original, or suitably processed, analytical data characterizing our samples is first converted into some corresponding set of similarity, or dissimilarity, measures between each sample.

The subsequent aim is to ensure that similar objects

are clustered together with minimal separation between objects in a class or cluster, whilst maximizing the separation between different clusters. It is the concept of similarity between objects that provides the richness and variety of the wide range of techniques available for cluster analysis. To appreciate this concept, it is worth considering what may constitute a cluster.

Two variate measures on a set of 50 samples are represented in a simple scatter plot. It is evident from visual inspection that there are many ways of dividing the patter space and producing clusters or groups of objects. There is no single 'correct' result, and the success of any clustering method depends largely on what is being sought, and the intended subsequent use of the information. Clusters may be defined intuitively and their structure and contents will depend on the nature of the problem. The presence of a cluster does not readily admit precise mathematical definition.

Choice of variable

All clustering algorithms aim to achieve is to group together similar, neighbouring points into clusters in the n-dimensional space defined by the n-variate measures on the objects. As with supervised pattern recognition, and other chemometric techniques, the selection of variables and their pre-processing can greatly influence the outcome.

It is worth repeating that cluster analysis is an exploratory, investigative technique and a data set should be examined using several different methods in order to obtain a more complete picture of the information contained in the data. The initial choice of the measurements made and used to describe each object constitute the frame of reference within which the clusters are to be established. This choice will reflect an analyst's judgement of relevance for the purpose of classification, based usually on prior experience. In most cases the number of variables is determined empirically and often tends to exceed the minimum required to achieve successful classification. Although this situation may guarantee satisfactory classification, the use of an excessive number of variables can severely effect computation time and a method's efficiency. Applying some preprocessing transformation to the data is often worthwhile. Standardization of the raw data can be undertaken, and is particularly valuable when different types of variable are measured.

But it should be borne in mind that standardization can have the effect of reducing or eliminating the very differences between objects which -are required for classification. Another technique worth considering is to perform a principal components analysis on the original data, to produce a set of new, statistically independent variables. Cluster analysis can then be performed on the first few principal components describing the majority of the samples' variance. Finally, having performed a cluster analysis, statistical tests can be employed to assess the contribution of each variable to the clustering process. Variables found to contribute little may be omitted and the cluster analysis repeated

Similarity measures

Similarity or *association coefficients* have long been associated with cluster analysis, and it is perhaps not surprising that the most commonly used is the correlation coefficient. Other similarity measures are rarely employed. Most are poorly defined and not amenable to mathematical analysis, and none have received much attention in the analytical literature. Table 2(a) provides the full symmetric matrix of these coefficients of similarity for the alloy data from Table 1. With such a small data set, a cluster analysis can be performed manually to illustrate the stages involved in the process.

The first step is to find the mutually largest correlation in the matrix to form centres for the clusters. The highest correlation in each column of Table 2(a) is shown in boldface type. Objects A and D form mutual highly correlated pairs, as do objects B and C. Note that although object E is most highly correlated with D, they are not considered as forming a pair as D most resembles A rather than E. Similarly, object F is not paired with B, as B is more similar to C.

Table 2

The matrix of correlations between objects from Table 1, (a). Samples A and D, B and C form new objects and a new correlation matrix can be calculated, (b). Sample E then joins AD and F joins BC to provide the final step and apparent correlation matrix, (c)

(a)	*A*	*B*	*C*	*D*	*E*	*F*
A	1	–0.62	–0.39	0.99	0.97	–0.44
B	–0.62	1	0.95	–0.68	–0.74	0.94
C	–0.39	0.95	1	–0.48	–0.51	0.89
D	0.99	–0.68	–0.48	1	0.98	–0.51
E	0.97	–0.74	–0.51	0.98	1	–0.61
F	–0.44	0.94	0.89	–0.51	–0.61	1

(b)	*AD*	*BC*	*E*	*F*
AD	1	–0.54	0.97	–0.47
BC	–0.54	1	–0.62	0.91
E	0.97	–0.62	1	–0.61
F	–0.47	0.91	–0.61	1

(c)	*ADE*	*BCF*
ADE	1	–0.56
BCF	–0.56	

The resemblance between the mutual pairs is indicated in

the diagram shown in Figure 3, which links A to D and B to C by a horizontal line drawn from the vertical axis at points representing their respective correlation coefficients. At the next stage, objects A and D, and B and C, are considered to comprise new, distinct objects with associative properties and are similar to the other objects according to their average individual values.

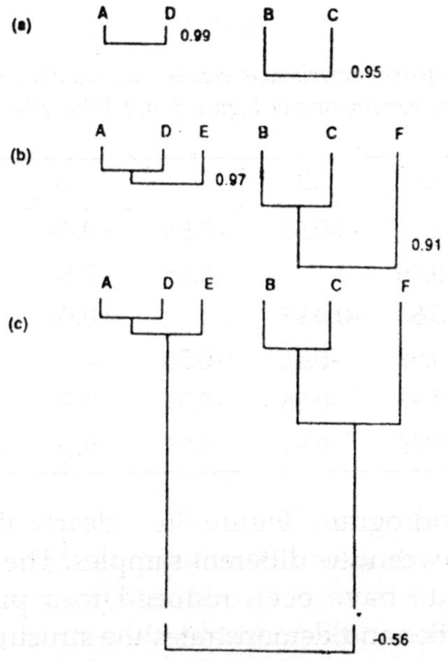

Fig. 2. The stages of hierarchical clustering shown graphically as dendrograms

Table 2(b) shows the newly calculated correlation matrix. Clusters AD and BC have a correlation coefficient calculated from the sum of the correlations of A to B, D to B, A to C, and D to C, divided by four. The correlation between AD and E is the average of the original A to E and D to E correlations. The clustering procedure is now repeated, and object E joins cluster AD and object F joins BC, Figure 3(b). The process is continued until all clusters are joined and the final similarity matrix is produced as in Table 2(c) with the resultant diagram, a *dendrogram*, shown in Figure 3(c). That two groups, ADE and BCF, may be present in the original data is demonstrated. From this extremely simple example, the basic steps involved in cluster analysis and the value of the technique in classification are evident.

Table 3

The matrix of apparent correlations between the six alloy samples, derived from the dendrogram of Figure 3 and Table 2(b) and (c)

(a)	A	B	C	D	E	F
A	1	–0.56	–0.56	0.99	0.97	–0.56
B	–0.56	1	0.95	–0.56	–0.56	0.91
C	–0.56	–0.0.95	1	–0.56	–0.56	0.91
D	0.99	–0.56	–0.56	1	0.97	–0.56
E	0.97	–0.56	–0.56	0.97	1	–0.56
F	–0.56	0.91	0.91	–0.56	–0.56	1

The final dendrogram, Figure 3(c), clearly illustrates the similarity between the different samples. The original raw tabulated data have been reduced to a pictorial form which simplifies and demonstrates the structure within the data. It is pertinent to ask, however, what information has been lost in producing the diagram and to what extent does the graph accurately represent our original data.

From the dendrogram and Table 2(b) the apparent correlation between sample B and sample F is 0.9 1, rather than the true value of 0.94 from the calculated similarity matrix. This error arose owing to the averaging process in treating the BC pair as a single entity, and the degree of distortion increases as successive levels of clusters are averaged together. Table 3 is the matrix of apparent correlations between objects as obtained from the dendrogram. These apparent correlations are sometimes referred to as *cophenetic values*, and if these are plotted against actual correlations. A numerical measure of the similarity between the values can be calculated by computing the linear correlation between the two sets. If there is no distortion, then the plot would form a straight line and the correlation would be 1. In our example this correlation, $r = 0.99$.

Distance measures

The correlation coefficient is too limiting in its definition to be of value in many applications of cluster analysis. It is a measure only of colinearity between variates and takes no account of non-linear relationships or the absolute magnitude of variates.

Instead, distance measures which can be defined mathematically are more commonly encountered in cluster analysis. Of course, it is always possible at the end of a clustering process to substitute distance with reverse similarity; the greater the distance between objects the less their similarity. An object is characterized by a set of measures, and it may be represented as a point in multidimensional space defined by the axes, each of which corresponds to a variate.

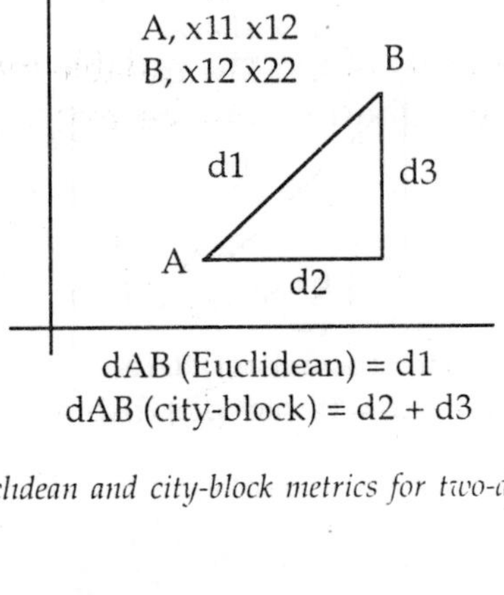

Fig. 3. The Euclidean and city-block metrics for two-dimensional data

A data matrix X defines measures of two variables on two objects A and B. Object A is characterized by the pattern vector, a = x_{11}, x_{12}, and B by the pattern vector, b = x_{21}, x_{22}. Using a distance measure, objects or points closest together are assigned to the same cluster. Numerous distance metrics have been proposed and applied in the scientific literature.

For a function to be useful as a distance metric between objects then the following basic rules apply (for objects A and B):

(a) $d_{AB} > 0$, the distance between all pairs of measurements for objects A and B must be non-negative,

(b) $d_{AB} = d_{BA}$, the distance measure is symmetrical and can only be zero when A = B.

(c) $d_{AC} + d_{BC} > d_{AB}$, the distance is commutative for all pairs of points. This statement corresponds to the familiar triangular inequality of Euclidean geometry.

The most commonly referenced distance metric is the Euclidean distance, defined by

$$d_{AB} = \left[\sum_j (x_{1_j} - x_{2_j})^2 \right]^{1/2} \tag{1}$$

where $x_{i,j}$ is the value of the j'th variable measured on the i'th object. This equation can be expressed in vector notation as

$$d_{AB} = \left[\sum_j (a_j - a_j)^2 \right]^{1/2} \tag{2}$$

or

$$d_{AB} = [(a - b)^T.(a - b)]^{1/2} \tag{3}$$

In general, most distance metrics conform to the general Minkowski equation,

$$d_{AB} = \left[\sum_j (x_{1_j} - x_{2_j})^m \right]^{1/m} \tag{4}$$

When $m = 1$, Equation (4) defines the city-block metric, and if $m = 2$ then the Euclidean distance is defined. These measures on two dimensional data.

If the variables have been measured in different units, then it may be necessary to scale the data to make the values comparable. An equivalent procedure is to compute a weighted Euclidean distance,

$$d_{AB} = \left[w_j \sum_j (a_j - b_j)^2 \right]^{1/2} \tag{5}$$

or

$$d_{AB} = [(a - b)^T.\ W(a - b)]^{1/2} \tag{6}$$

W is a symmetric matrix, and in the most simple case *W* is a diagonal matrix, the diagonal elements of which, w_{ii}, are the weights or coefficients applied to the vectors corresponding to the variables in the data matrix. Weighting variables is largely subjective and may be based on a *priori* knowledge regarding the data, such as measurement error or equivalent variance of variables. If, for example, weights are chosen to be inversely proportional to measurement variance, then variates with greater precision are weighted more heavily. However, such variates may contribute little to an effective clustering process.

One weighted distance measure which does occur frequently in the scientific literature is the *Mahalanobis distance*,

$$d_{AB} = [(a - b)^T . Cov^{-1}(a - b)]^{1/2} \qquad (7)$$

where *Cov* is the full variance-covariance matrix for the original data. The Mahalanobis distance is invariant under any linear transformation of the original variables. If several variables are highly correlated, this type of weighting scheme down-weights their individual contributions. It should be used with care, however. In cluster analysis, use of the Mahalanobis distance may produce even worse results than equating the variance of each variable and may serve only to decrease the clarity of the clusters.

Table 4

Three samples, or objects, characterized by five measures, $x_1 \ldots x_5$.

	x_1	x_2	x_3	x_4	x_5
A	2.1	5.2	3.1	4.1	2.1
B	2.5	4.0	4.0	4.6	3.5
C	5.1	9.2	7.1	7.0	5.0

Before proceeding with a more detailed examination of clustering techniques, we can now compare correlation and distance metrics as suitable measures of similarity for cluster analysis. A simple example serves to illustrate the main points. In Table 4, three objects (A, B, and C) are characterized by five variates. The correlation matrix and Euclidean distance matrix are given in Tables 5 and 6 respectively, and, as before, manual clustering can be undertaken to display the similarity between objects.

Using the correlation coefficient, objects A and C form a mutually highly similar pair and may be joined to form a new object AC, with a correlation to object B formed by

Table 5

The correlations matrix of (a), of data from Table 4 and clustering objects with highest mutual correlation, (b)

(a)	*A*	*B*	*C*
A	1	0.69	0.96
B	0.69	1	0.63
C	0.96	0.63	1

and the first cluster is AC

(b)	*AC*	*B*
AC	1	0.66
B	0.66	1

averaging the A to B, C to B correlations. If the Euclidean distance matrix is used as the measure of similarity, then objects A and B are the most similar as they have the mutually lowest distance separating them. Different results may be obtained using different measures. If the variables x_1, x_2 . . . x_5, represent trace elements in, say, water samples and the measures their individual concentrations, then samples A and B would form a group with the differences possibly due to natural variation between samples or experimental error. Sample C could come from a different source.

The distance metric in this case provides a suitable clustering measure. On the other hand, if x_1, x_2 . . . x_5 denoted, say, wavelengths and the response values a measure of absorption or emission at these wavelengths, then a different explanation may be sought. Then A and C are similar, differing only in scale or concentration, whereas spectrum B has a different profile. Hence, correlation provides a suitable measure of similarity. If, as spectra, the data had been normalized to the most intense response, then A and C would have been closer and the distance metric more meaningful.

Table 6

The Euclidean distance matrix (a) of data from Table 4 and clustering objects with the smallest inter-object distance, (b)

(a)	*A*	*B*	*C*
A	0	2.15	7.60
B	2.15	0	7.17
C	7.60	7.17	0

and the first cluster is AB

(b)	*AB*	*C*
AB	0	7.38
B	7.38	0

The first stage in cluster analysis is to compute the matrix of selected distance measures between objects. As the entire clustering process may depend on the choice of distance it is recommended that results using different functions are compared.

Clustering techniques

By grouping similar objects, clusters are themselves representative of those objects and form a distinct group according to some empirical rule. It is implicit in producing clusters that such a group can be represented further by a *typical element* of the cluster. This single element may be a genuine member of the cluster or a hypothetical point, for example an average of the contents characteristics in multidimensional space.

One common method of identifying a cluster's typical element is to substitute the mean values for the variates describing the objects in the cluster. The between-cluster distance can then be defined as the Euclidean distance, or other metric, between these means. Other measures not using the group means are available. The nearest-neighbour distance defines the distance between two closest members from different groups.

The *furthest-neighbour* distance on the other hand is that between the most remote pair of objects in two groups. A further inter-group Measure is obtained by taking the average of all the inter-element measures between elements in different groups. As well as defining the inter-group separation between clusters, each of these measures provides the basis for a clustering technique, defining the method by which clusters are constructed or divided.

In relatively simple cases, in which only two or three variables are measured for each sample, the data can usually be examined visually and any clustering identified by eye. As the number of variates increases, however, this is rarely possible and many scatter plots, between all possible pairs of variates, would need to be produced in order to identify major clusters, and even then clusters could be missed. To address this problem, many numerical clustering techniques have been developed, and the techniques themselves have been classified. For our purposes the methods considered belong to one of the following types.

— Hierarchical techniques in which the elements or objects are clustered to form new representative objects, with the process being repeated at different levels to produce a tree structure, the dendrogram.

— Methods employing optimization of the partitioning between clusters using some type of iterative algorithm, until some pre-defined minimum change in the groups is produced.

— Fuzzy cluster analysis in which objects are assigned a membership function indicating their degree of belonging to a particular group or set.

In order to demonstrate the calculations and results associated with the different methods. The positions of the points are representative of different shaped clusters, the single point (L), the extended group (B,C,D), the symmetrical group (A,E,F,G), and the asymmetrical cluster (H,I,J,K).

Hierarchical techniques

When employing hierarchical clustering techniques, the original data are separated into a few general classes, each of which is further subdivided into still smaller groups until finally' the individual objects themselves remain Such methods may be agglomerative or divisive. By agglomerative clustering, small groups, starting with individual samples, are fused to produce larger groups as in the examples studied previously. In contrast, divisive clustering starts with a single cluster, containing all samples, which is successively divided into smaller partitions.

Hierarchical techniques are very popular, not least because their application leads to the production of a dendrogram which can provide a two-dimensional pictorial representation of the clustering process and the results. Agglomerative hierarchical clustering is very common and we will proceed with details of its application. Agglomerative methods begin with the computation of a similarity or distance matrix between the objects, and result in a dendrogram illustrating the successive fusion of objects and groups until the stage is reached when all objects are fused into one large set.